A Critical Analysis of Vikram Seth's Poetry and Fiction

A Critical Analysis of Vikram Seth's Poetry and Fiction

Seemita Mohanty

ATLANTIC
PUBLISHERS & DISTRIBUTORS (P) LTD

Published by
ATLANTIC
PUBLISHERS & DISTRIBUTORS (P) LTD
B-2, Vishal Enclave, Opp. Rajouri Garden,
New Delhi-110027
Phones : 25413460, 25429987, 25466842

Sales Office
7/22, Ansari Road, Darya Ganj,
New Delhi-110002
Phones : 23273880, 23275880, 23280451
Fax : 91-11-23285873
web : www.atlanticbooks.com
e-mail : info@atlanticbooks.com

ISBN 978-81-269-0831-8

Printed in India
at Nice Printing Press, Delhi

Dedicated to

My father whose love, support, and encouragement are a part of this book

Acknowledgements

I take this opportunity to express my gratitude to all those writers and critics whose literary collections have offered me food for thought.

My deep sense of gratitude goes to my esteemed teacher Prof. Sarat Chandra Satapathy, Head, Department of English, Utkal University, Bhubaneswar, for his help, advice, support and guidance. His recommendations and suggestions have been invaluable for the successful completion of this book. Special thanks to my parents, particularly my father, for giving me the courage and strength I needed to complete my work. Words alone cannot express the thanks that I owe to them for their love and support. Sincere thanks are also due to other family members and my colleagues and friends who endured this long process with me, always offering me encouragement and support. I am also grateful to my husband and my two daughters who have borne my long absences from home without complaint.

Last but not least, I would like to thank Dr. K.R. Gupta, Chairman, Atlantic Publishers & Distributors (P) Ltd., New Delhi for publishing the book in a very nice form.

Preface

In recent times, the publication of each of Vikram Seth's books has been a literary event and his readers are spread worldwide. There has been an unequivocal acceptance of his versatility. The various books that he has written can only make one wonder and appreciate. For instance, his three novels, *The Golden Gate*, *A Suitable Boy* and *An Equal Music*, set in three different continents, enter the 'ethos and mental climate' of each location with such ease and confidence that it becomes pointless to attempt to put a national label on him. Transcending of boundaries or dismantling a given format is something that Seth does with elegance and precision.

Right from the time Seth started writing, he has defied categorization. That is the reason why documentation of Seth's works does not easily give a cohesive picture; he has been radically changing genre and milieu with nearly every book that he has written. It is to his credit that very often when one opens his books, it is only the name of the author on the cover that lets us know that we are reading a book by an Indian. This is possibly a reflection of the fact that Seth is not unduly concerned about any social and cultural identification or the search for roots—probably because he feels at home in the world. He writes good, understandable English, in a reader-friendly manner, and his work does not seem to address any specific issue or adhere to any particular critical theory. He writes in simple English and writes it remarkably well.

The present book, through a critical analysis and assessment of Seth's poetry and fiction, attempts to restate the fact that Seth is a brilliant writer who deserves to be taken seriously, both by the general reader and the discerning scholar and researcher. The analyses concentrate on both his poems and fiction, while attempting to trace the continuity throughout. An attempt has also been made to briefly place Seth as an Indian writer of

English, in the context of the development of Indian English Literature, particularly in the post-Independence period.

On the whole, Seth in his poetry and fiction puts continuous emphasis on love and relationship, and explores their many dimensions in a shifting, changing and corroding background. At the same time he incorporates together the complementary segments of life as available in the modern world into a meaningful form. His creative insight and creative achievement could be considered as one of the finest in the post-1980 Indian English Literature. Structured into seven chapters, the present book is an analytic exposition of all the major novels of Vikram Seth. Beginning with an introduction to the Indian English Literature, the book in the next two chapters gives first and foremost a comprehensive analysis of Seth's collection of poetry, and comes first in the order because as Seth himself says, he is first a poet, and then a novelist. The chapters attempt to explore the themes that dominate his poetry and subsequently his philosophy of life in general.

Chapter IV gives a detailed critical analysis of *The Golden Gate* (1986), a novel in verse, composed entirely of rhyming tetrameter sonnets. The novel is a satirical romance describing the stories of young professionals in San Francisco through their quests and questions to find, and then deal with love in their own lives as well as in each other's.

Chapter V aims at a social and political study of Vikram Seth's book *A Suitable Boy* (1993), that made history as a publishing phenomenon heralding the change from an economist-poet to a full-time writer, making millions in pounds.

Chapter VI is a critical study of Seth's *An Equal Music* (1999), which like *A Suitable Boy* is centered on an ill-fated love affair. Its focus is on music and passion, draped in European settings.

The concluding chapter is self-contained, presenting all the striking features of Vikram Seth's works in a concise and comprehensible form.

The book ends with a comprehensive bibliographic list that will enable the scholars of Indian English Literature to pursue their study further. The book is ideal for all students, research scholars and teachers of English Literature for whom today writers, like Vikram Seth, are opening new vistas of literature teaching and learning.

SEEMITA MOHANTY

Contents

1 Introduction

Vikram Seth's first novel *The Golden Gate*, in verse, was published in 1986 when he was 34; subsequently he has had two more novels, *A Suitable Boy* and *An Equal Music,* published respectively in 1993 and 1999. His latest work is *Two Lives* (2005) a memoir of the marriage of his great uncle and aunt. *The Golden Gate* secured Sahitya Akademi Award for Seth in 1988, and *A Suitable Boy* the Commonwealth Writer's Prize in 1994. The same period also saw Seth publishing his poetry books. They were *Mappings* (1981), *The Humble Administrator's Garden* (1985), *All You Who Sleep Tonight* (1990), and *Beastly Tales from Here and There* (1992). Again, of these, *The Humble Administrator's Garden* won the Commonwealth Poetry Prize for Asia. In addition, Seth has *Three Chinese Poets* (1992): a collection of translations of Chinese poets, Wang Wei (701–762), Li Bai (701–761) and Du Fu (712–770); a libretto, *Arion and the Dolphin* (1994); and a travel book, *From Heaven Lake, Travels through Sinkiang and Tibet* (1983), which also won the 1983 Thomas Cook Travel Book Award. Thus, as it can be seen, Seth's creative period, considering till now, is spread out in the last two decades of the 20th century, from 1981 till 2005, that includes three novels, four poetry books, one book of translation, one libretto, one travel book and one biography. Though as such it is a good range for a creative writer, yet it is mostly in novel and poetry that Seth has distinguished himself and has been established as a major writer in the Indian English Literature in the recent years.

Indian English Literature has a reasonably long period of growth. It began in early 19th century and has continued ever since, acquiring much newer and much larger dimension after Independence, and particularly in the last two decades of the 20th century it got integrated with the development of Indian

Bhasa languages and came to be considered as one of the major Indian language literatures for all purposes. This is interestingly evidenced from a consideration of Sahitya Akademi Awards given every year to the best selected books in Indian languages.

The Akademi Awards were started to be given from 1955, to Indian languages and literature, and in course of time they have acquired immense prestige as substantial recognition for the languages. English was listed as a major language of India from the beginning, and books in Indian English Literature were given due consideration for the Award every year. But interestingly, in a period of 20 years, from 1955 to 1974, covering from mid-fifties to mid-seventies, only 6 Awards were given, when for example, in Hindi 19 Awards were given, and in Bengali 17, Tamil 16, and even in a much less used language like Sanskrit, 10 (*General Information,* Sahitya Akademi, 2003). This is doubly interesting when one considers that annual English language publications in India top the list of all annual Indian Bhasa publications. By an estimate India publishes on an average about 20,000 titles in a year in English and about 18 Indian languages, of which about 40 to 45 per cent are in English, and it ranks seventh in the world in terms of the number of titles published annually, and third in terms of production of titles in English, next to U.S.A. and U.K. (Ed. P.S. Bhatti 1987). By another estimate (Ed. B.S. Kesavan, 1961), the books received by the National Library in Calcutta, in 1960, in 14 Indian languages, including English, numbered 9,732, of which titles in English were 3,167, the second place being taken by Bengali, 1,022. This amounts to a dichotomy, that whereas English language publications in India constitute a very substantial portion of the total publications, the Sahitya Akademi, or the National Akademi of Letters, thought it fit to accord recognition and honour only to 6 books in Indian English literature in a period of 20 years, the longest ever in that period for any Indian language. Then again out of six books four were strictly literature that is novel, the rest two are non-fiction, and one of the six authors was a non-Indian, Verrier Elwin.

All that shows one thing—the reality aspect of Indian English Literature. Even two decades after Independence it had not acquired much credibility and not sufficiently considered at par with other Indian language literatures. But after mid-seventies the acceptance factor became different which we will take up a little later. In fact the importance of English came to be recognized and got well-established in areas other than strictly literary, that is, in matters of communication and administration as well as in journalistic writing, essays and biography etc., in short, mostly non-fiction prose. The first-ever history of Indian English Literature, entitled *Indian Writing in English*, by K.R. Srinivasa Iyengar, published in 1962, had a daunting job to do. First of all the second and third editions of the book came after a decade each, in 1973 and 1983 respectively, by itself an indication of the slow recognition that Indian English Literature was gaining around, which became different after 1983, when subsequent editions of the book came out more frequently. Secondly, the two points made by Iyengar in the Preface to the 3rd edition of his book (1983) with reference to the condition of Indian English Literature in the sixties and seventies, are pertinent, and bear with the facts we are underlining about. The first point relates to the edition itself, an admission that since the publication of the second edition (1973), "there has been witnessed a burst of activity in Indian Writing in English and something akin to a global proliferation of interest in this new literature." The second point also refers to the same edition where the writer justifies adding a "Postscript Chapter" (about 70 pages) which he thought can also stand on its own "as an assessment of Indian Writing in English during the decade it won general recognition, as a distinctive literature of India."

Thus, as we have pointed out, the condition of Indian English Literature, even after two decades of Independence, was not that stable, and it is only after mid-seventies onwards that it started changing towards better, towards a greater credibility and recognition. Therefore, the first-ever *History of Indian English Literature*, as Iyengar's was, the account and the history of development, was not strictly confined to literature alone. It went over to a discussion other than literature, the factors which sustain the growth of literature no doubt; the socio-cultural, even political factors, but which are not strictly necessary in a history of literature. Iyengar himself admits it—"In a 'course' like this criticism is apt to fuse disconcertingly with biography, and literary history with political and cultural history and I have tried to bear in mind the implications of this intimate intermingling of literature and life" (Iyengar, 1962).

Iyengar's motivations and charting of the courses can also be noted in the second history of Indian English literature, entitled *A History of Indian English Literature* by M.K. Naik published in the year 1982, which though a more compact book, and closer to the strictly literary growth of its subject, yet admits that Indian English Literature is "essentially a significant by-product of the eventful encounter between India and Indian ethos on the one hand, and England, the English language and Western culture on the other" and accordingly spreads out its literary discussions to extra literary areas. Similarly too, William Walsh writing for Longman Literature in English Series, in a book entitled *Indian Literature in English* (1990), a survey of the beginning and growth of Indian English Literature, points out the distinctive need of non-literary references—"The treatment of this book falls into six parts and I have followed a generally chronological pattern while keeping the genre separate from each other. I begin with a rapid personal excursus which touches fleetingly on the several major influences that compose this intricate, enigmatic, civilization, from external inversion to land tenure, from religion to politics, from caste to climate" (Author's Foreword).

This attitude of joining strictly literary references with more or less non-literary ones with reference to Indian English Literature has often motivated the historians of Indian English Literature. Thus a literary history, published as recent as 2003, entitled *An Illustrated History of Indian Literature in English* (Ed. Arvind Krishna Mehrotra) while referring to its subject arrangement, maintains that it is "conceived as a comprehensive and wide-ranging whole" and "takes up not only the canonical poets, novelists, and dramatists of the past two hundred years but also scientists, social reformers, anthropologists, and naturalists who have by broad consensus enriched the body of Indian Writing in English." Additionally, the book also provides such illustrations that have only a frail link with literature, such as, Lord Clive receiving from the Moghul, the Grant of the Duanney; The Old Court House, Calcutta; Pioneer Press, Allahabad; leaves of advertisements appearing in books in England towards the end of the eighteenth century; the first page of Tagore's Bengali *Sahaj Patha*; the Great Trial 1922 of Gandhi; Bombay bazaar sculptor's shop-cum-studio; Cartoon from *The New Yorker*; and Jim Corbett with the Rudraprayag Leopard etc.

Thus, all the above books that deal with the growth and development of Indian English Literature, in a historical perspective, beginning from early 19th century onwards, have followed almost a similar pattern. That is, along with highlighting strictly literary genres, such as, fiction, drama etc., they have also given almost equal credit to non-fiction prose—prose written in English with a purpose, and closely related to socio-cultural as well as socio-political ramifications. Rammohan Roy (1772-1833) has been given pride of place. He is named as the "first of the Indian masters of English prose," and at the same time admitted that he "belongs more to Indian history" than to "mere Indo-Anglian literary history" (Iyengar, 1962, 33). Apart from Rammohan Roy, Iyengar also refers to a number of 19th century stalwarts who had distinctive contributions to the socio-cultural conditions as a whole but not so much to strictly Indian English Literature. They were, to name a few, Kesab Chandra Sen (1838-1884), Dayanand Saraswati (1824-1883), Kashinath Trimbak Telang (1830-1893), Mahadev Govind Ranade (1842-1901), Gopal Krishna Gokhale (1866-1915), Dadabhai Naroji (1825-1917), Pherozshah Mehta (1845-1915) and Vivekananda (1863-1902) etc. Similarly, M.K. Naik refers to Rammohan Roy and his contemporaries in Bengal, Bombay and Madras, such as Krishna Mohan Banerji (1813-1885), Bal Shastri Jambhekar (1812-1846) and Canelley Venkata Boriah (1776-1803) who distinguished themselves more in socio-cultural areas than in Indian English Literature. So too, in

Mehrotra's recent *Illustrated History* the beginning of the account is from Rammohan Roy and his contemporaries.

Even in subsequent discussions, in subsequent charting of the course of the history of Indian English Literature, this enlarged dimension, that is, references to very distinguished people, who were not as such involved in literary productions, but used English for their various purposes, could be seen again and again. Thus in continuation of the references to Rammohan, Vivekananda, Gokhale etc., there are invariable references to the writings of Gandhiji and Nehru as well as to such other persons as Verrier Elwin, Ambedkar, Jim Corbet, Salim Ali and M. Krishnan etc. The point is, in charting the growth of Indian English Literature for the last 200 years, the period in which it has developed in India, the attention has not always been on literature as such, but has attempted to enclose such areas and dimensions, that though apparently peripheral to the main lines of development, yet provide it with a general support and credibility.

A perusal of the main lines of development of Indian English Literature is also interesting. Initially the main lines were one line, that is poetry, and a thin line too. Beginning with Vivian Derozio (1809-1831) of Eurasian descent, in the early 19th century, it moved in a small stream through Toru Dutt (1856-77), to name relatively more well-known names, it came to some substantial growth in the later 19th and early 20th century, in the writings of the poets such as, Manmohan Ghose (1869-1924), Aurobindo Ghose (Sri Aurobindo, 1872-1950), Sarojini Naidu (1879-1949) and Harindranath Chattopadhyaya (1898-1998), Derozio published two volumes of poetry: *Poems* (1827) and *The Fakeer of Jungheera: A Metrical and Other Poems* (1828), both short and long poems, mostly influenced by British romantic poets. A pioneer in the use of Indian "myth and legend, imagery and diction," as M.K. Naik points out, a noteworthy feature of Derozio's poetry is its "burning nationalistic zeal" (23). Differently R.K. Dasgupta speaks of "intensity of feeling" in Derozio's verse, and refers to his 'voice' as of the "new humanity of the new universe that emerged in the early decades of the last century" (Derozio, 1980). In fact, Derozio's poetry integrated these different strains in his poetry—a romantic sensibility at par with the contemporary British romantic poetry, and a nationalistic feeling in consonant with the spirit of nationalism then emerging in India at that time. Some good examples would be "Poetic Haunts" of the former type ("Where the billow's bosom swells / Where the ocean casts its shells / Where the wave its white spray flings / Where the sea-mew flaps its wings,") (*Poems,* 101), and "The Harp of India", of the later type ("Thy music once was sweet—who hears it now? / Why doth the breeze sigh over thee in vain? / Silence hath bound thee with her fatal chain / Neglected, mute, and desolate are thou.") (*Poems,* 1).

Toru Dutt had also two books of poetry, one, a book of translation, *A Sheaf Gleaned in French Fields* (1876), containing the translations of 70 French poets, including Hugo, Gautier (1876), and published posthumously, *Ancient Ballads and Legends of Hindustan* (1882). Like Derozio she made extensive use of Indian myth and legends, and like him too, she had a good narrative skill. At the same time, as the times had changed, it was no longer the early British romantic poetry, as had been the case with Derozio, but the contemporary Victorian romantic poetry that motivated her, and influenced her diction. "Our Casuarina Tree" is a good example. It combines a romantic feeling for nature with a sense of nostalgia and an awareness of the tree as a point of hope and strength—"...and flowers are hung / In crimson clusters all the boughs among / Whereon all day are gathered bird and bee / And oft at no close / Sung darkling from our tree, while man repose" and again, "...beneath the moon / When earth lay tranced in a dreamless swoon / And every time the music rose—before / Mine inner vision rose a form sublime / Thy form, O Tree, as in my happy prime / I saw thee, in my own loved native clime." (Gokak: 1989, 97). Naik speaks of Toru Dutt's "quiet strength", of "deep emotion held under artistic restraint", and an "acute awareness of the abiding values of Indian life" (41). Differently, Rosinka Chaudhury points out that Toru Dutt's awareness of her 'Indianness' is not restricted to Indian historical themes and the reworking of Indian legends—"In her poetry" she says, "we confront for the first time a language that is crafted out of the vicissitudes of an individual life...." (Mehrotra: 2003, 69). Toru Dutt died very young. But her poetry, written about 50 years after Derozio's, can be considered as a step in advance in the development of Indian English Literature.

Manamohan Ghose's early years were spent in England (from 1879 to 1894), where he had his education and training, and which also substantially shaped his sensibility. As he latterly settled down in India (Patna, Calcutta, Dacca, as a teacher), he combined two ethoses in his literary production, one of literary trends of the 1890's of London, and the other of the tumultuous years, as he experienced these in Calcutta, in the first two decades of the 20th century. In fact Manmohan was wedded to two worlds, the West and the East, and his love of English literature, as A. Norman Jeffers pointed out, "had a tolerant Indian inclusiveness...in matters of literary convention: in themes and imagery rooted deep in the past" (Ghose, 1974). Ghose wrote continuously beginning from 1894, but he had only one poetry book—*Love Songs and Elegies* published during his lifetime (1898). His second volume *Songs of Love and Death* was published posthumously in 1926, and latterly, in 1974, his other poems—"Orphic Mysteries", "Songs of Pain", "Passion", and the "Mystery of Death", written between 1918-1923; "Immortal Eve", "Songs of Triumph and Mystery of Beauty", written during 1918-1922; as well as a projected epic, "Perseus—The Gorgon Slayer" (1898-1914), a verse drama, "Nollo and Damayanti" (1916) and a 'lyric epic' "Adam Alarmed in Paradise" (1918), all incomplete.

Manmohan's poetry had two dimensions, one, that took up trends from late Victorian poetry at the end of the 19th century, including such trends as a delight in Hellenic mythology and nineteen century classicism along with an absorption of 'dreamy English countryside'. Of this some good examples are "London" (1894), "Poplar", "Beech", and "Weeping Willow" (1916) and "April" (1923)—"April delicious / Young, sunny maiden / Arch, gusty, capricious / With fresh flowers laden / Thrill as with sweet bird-song / After dry March's drought / Blow from thy rainy mouth (*Selected Poems,* 17). The second is a contemplation of pain, death and beauty, occasioned after his wife's death in 1918—"How did I lose you, sweet / I hardly know / Roughly the storm did beat / Wild winds did blow / I with my loving arm / Folded you safe from harm / Cloaked from the weather" ("The Rider on the White Horse", *Selected Poems*, 41). In a Memorial Lecture, in 1924, after Manmohan's death, Rabindranath Tagore spoke of Manmohan's 'wonderful poetic gifts' and 'power of imagination' and expresses his confidence that Manmohan's poetry will give 'universal delight'. In fact, Manmohan's poetry, in the last decades of the 19th and the early decades of the 20th century, placed Indian English Literature on a firm footing.

In this Manmohan was aided by Aurobindo, his younger brother, who like him spent earlier years in England, and later, like him again, settled in India. But Aurobindo's career was more expansive, he came to be recognized as a great Yogi and seer. Consequently writing for him became functional, which he used as a medium for communicating his thoughts, and emphasis on a literary preoccupation became secondary. But his involvement in poetry was almost a continuous one. He carried out a lot of experiments in metrical narrative poems, and in a remarkable epic poem, entitled *Savitri.* The early poems of Aurobindo, mostly written in the last decade of the 19th century reflected, as it happened in the case of Manmohan, the poetic trends that prevailed in England at that time, a type of soft romantic sensibility, and towards the first decade of the 20th century when he was in service and engaged in political activities, including a year in the prison.

The poems additionally took up a strong mystic awareness as well as a trend towards ancient Indian legends to celebrate love and heroism. An early poem "To a Hero-Worshipper" (1891) is a good indicator of early sensibility—"I by the Indian waters vast / Did glimpse the magic of the past / And on the Oaten-piple I play / Warped echoes of an earlier day", and again, "For me the daisy shines a star / The crocus flames a spire / A horn of golden fire / Narcissus glows a silver star..." (*Collected Poems,* 8). Differently, the poem "Lines to Ireland" (1896) is an expression of the poet's latent desire towards revolution and freedom—"...Therefore, that light was she / In whom races of weaker destiny / Their beauteous image of rebellion saw / Treason could not unnerve violence overawe / A mirror to enslaved nations" (*Collected Poems,* 12). This latent desire for revolution took an almost a rhetorical turn in "Invitation" (1908-09), which the poet wrote from inside the Alipore Jail—"I am the lord of tempest and mountain / I am the Spirit of freedom and pride / Stark must he be and a kinsman to danger / Who shares my kingdom and walks at my side" (*Collected Poems*, 39). But slowly the poet's consciousness was moving towards a spiritual awareness, the early indications of which are seen in "The Sea at Night"—"I see beyond a rough / Glimmering infinity I feel the wash / And hear the sibilation of the waves," or in "Revelation"—"Someone leaping from the rocks / Past me ran with wind-blown locks / Like a startled bright surmise / Visible to mortal eyes," (*Collected Poems,* 46-47), both the poems written before 1908. In 1910 Aurobindo moved to Pondicherry, and to a life completely different from the life he had hitherto lived, and all that he wrote after that was a symbolic reflection of a spiritual entity. This was much more evident in the poems that he wrote, particularly after 1926 (24.11.1926, when the descent of the Power of Consciousness took place), a few good examples would be the poems like "Transformation" ("My breath runs in a subtle rhythmic stream / It fills my members with a might divine / ...My body is God's happy living tool / My spirit a vast sun of deathless light" (*Collected Poems*, 161), and "Bird of Fire" (1933) and "Rose of God" (1934) etc. In fact, this spiritual dimension is a singular contribution of Aurobindo to Indian English poetry, and provided a veritable strength to Indian English Literature in the early part of the 20th century.

But it was Sarojini Naidu's poetry that probably had the greatest say in finding out an identity for Indian English poetry, and Indian English Literature as a whole, in the early part of the 20th century. This became so, because of Sarojini's capacity to write poems in lilting measure, almost like songs along with her habit of using highly embellished images and depicting a romantic India of myth, legend and folklore to which her stature as a considerable public figure in the crucial period of freedom-struggle was added. Most of her poems were written and published between 1896 and 1917, and the important collections were *The Golden Threshold* (1905), *The Bird of Time: Songs of Life, Death and the Spring* (1912) and *The Broken Wing: Songs of Love, Death and Destiny* (1917). A posthumous volume entitled *The Feather of the Dawn*, consisting of poems written in the late 1920s, was published in 1961. Taken together Sarojini's poems do not present much development. There is a "continuity of poetic imagination," says Ranjana Sidhant Ash (Mehrotra: 2003, 131). P.C. Katoky also thinks similarly—'there is not much of a growth of poetic personality' (1969, 54). But Katoky also points out her mastery of diction and style, and her great 'love of life and colour'.

In fact, Sarojini's poems present a unity of purpose, understanding and perception. Her sympathies are with multiple colours of Indian life and many layers of Indian living, and all that is presented with joy and understanding. Her poems provide a sense of familiarity and rootedness, and a feeling that they have grown on their own, without being the product of any external influence. Thus as in "Palanquin-Bearers", the swaying movement of the palanquin, a familiar carriage for carrying the bride in the countryside—"Lightly, lightly, we bear her along / She sways like a flower in the wind of our song / She skims like a bird on the foam of a stream / She floats like a laugh from the lips of dream / Gaily, O gaily we glide and sing / we bear her along like a pearl on a string...." The poem welds together flight of imagination, an appreciation of beauty, and the joyous song of the palanquin-bearers. Similarly, the familiar picture of an Indian evening has a romantically motivated atmosphere of joy and happiness—"Sweet is the shade of coconut glade, and the scent of the mango grove / And sweet are the sands at the full O' the moon with the sound of the voices we love" ("Coromandal Fishers"). Differently, a poem like "Village-Song" shows a singular contact through affection, and sympathy—"Honey, child, honey, child, whither are you going? / Would you cast your jewels all to the breezes blowing? / Would you leave the mother who on golden grain has fed you? / Would you grieve the lover who is riding forth to wed you?" The tone of concern, sorrow and oneness—one with them, who are spoken about, is an important element in Sarojini's poetry, that which has made her poems popular and loved. "Her finest lyrics have a perfect structure and an exquisite finish," says M.K. Naik (68). Iyengar agrees, speaks of her 'unfailing verbal felicity and rhythmical dexterity,' and points out how sensitive she was to 'beauty, the beauty of living things' (Walsh, 225). Sarojini Naidu's creative ability put firm strength to Indian English Literature and as we have said, gave it a firm identity.

Harindranath's poetic career was a long one, and he had many volumes of verse. His first collection of lyrics entitled *The Feast of Youth* was published in 1918, and subsequently some of his more important volumes are *The Coloured Garden* (1919), *Perfume of Earth* (1922), *Collected Plays and Poems* (1927), *The Dark Well* (1939), *Lyrics* (1944) etc. He was a competent metrist, and like his sister, Sarojini, had a good command over rhyme and rhythm, and his themes, though motivated by romantic idealism, touched many areas, such as moods of love, liberal outlook and humanitarian compassion, idealism with Marxian overtones, and reflections on beauty as well as mystic, spiritual awareness, in all that he was, one may say, one with other Indian English poets. But his social, progressive ideas, at par with such ideas current at that time (in 1928, he was invited to Moscow to attend the anniversary celebration of the Revolution, and he was a Communist member in the First Indian Parliament) were distinct contributions to Indian English poetry and to Indian English Literature at that time. In the poem "Inheritance" the poet gives a call to mill-workers to rise against exploitation by the rich and powerful—"Refuse to let audacious walls of stone / Shut out from you the sky which is your throne / Allow no one to chain your limbs to blind / Red tyranny...." But his tone is harsher in "On the Pavement of Calcutta"—"The starving children are crying in the streets / The pallid pregnant women are lying in the streets." Differently, in "The Garden of Isolation" separation in love leads to pain and agony—"Out of my life the coloured lights are gone / Deep dark surrounds me and I cannot see /

Night, sorrowful, immense, without a dawn / Descends on me" and in "Mating" a keen awareness of beauty—"See what a royal tinge of gold is waiting / To wed the high-born scarlet in the skies / Look at the delicate fire of vision mating / With the virgin silence in the poet's eyes" or in "Masterstroke" the realization of a calm, spiritual vision—"All quietly I sat and heard / The myriad voices of the broad / Green fields, and saw a sapphire bird / Pass like a fiery glimpse of God." Harindranath's poems had diverse colours and diverse awareness, and all that went to strengthen Indian English poetry and provide it with meaning and position.

We have noted how Indian English Literature, particularly in one form, that is, poetry, beginning from early 19th century, moved tardily and haltingly, in a limited manner, almost like an appendage of a much larger movement, through the good part of a century, till it came to a fruitful identity towards the end of the 19th century and early 20th, mostly in the 40 years between 1890 and 1930. In fact, the strains of what was achieved by about the end of the third decade continued, across Independence, almost to the end of the sixth decade when new factors and new consciousness emerged in Indian English poetry, as a sequence of the changing modes after Independence, and at par with the changes in the other categories of Indian English Literature, as well as in much larger areas of Indian language or Bhasa Literatures, when new generations of Indian English Literature succeeded in establishing it as an important component of broader Indian literature.

The first indication of the change came in the accord of recognition given by the Sahitya Akademi, India's National Akademi of Letters, by including Indian English Literature in its annual award scheme that began from 1955, as one of the 15 major language literatures of India. But, the first award did not come in 1955, it came five years after, in 1960, and that was in novel. The first award in poetry came in 1981, for Jayant Mahapatra's poetry volume *Relationship*. Subsequently, till the end of the eighties awards for poetry were given to new poets, such as, Nissim Ezekiel, (*Latter-Day Psalms,* 1983), Keki N. Daruwalla (*The Keeper of the Dead,* 1984), Kamala Das

(*Collected Poems*, 1985) and Shiv K. Kumar (*Trapfalls in the Sky*, 1987). These poets as well as a few more constituted the new generation of relatively more important Indian English poets after 1930, that is, after Manmohan, Aurobindo, Sarojini and Harindranath. This new generation of post-Independence Indian English poets flourished mostly in the three decades, from the beginning of the fifties till the end of seventies and provided newer attitudes and sensibility, at par with the contemporary times, in short, much greater substantiality and identity in comparison to the earlier group of the early part of the century.

Though Jayanta Mahapatra was the first post-Independence Indian English poet to receive Sahitya Akademi Award, Nissim Ezekiel was the first poet of this new generation of poets. His first book *A Time to Change and Other Poems* was published in 1952. His subsequent books are *Sixty Poems* (1953), *The Third* (1959), *The Unfinished Man* (1960), *Hymns in Darkness* (1976) and *Latter-Day Psalms* (1982). Jayanta Mahapatra's first book was published in 1971; his books are *Close the Sky, Ten by Ten* (1971), *Swayambara and Other Poems* (1971), *A Father's Hours* (1976), *A Rain of Rites* (1976), *Waiting* (1979), *Relationship* (1980), *The False Start* (1980), *Life Signs* (1983), *Dispossessed Nests* (1986), and *Burdens of Waves and Fruit* (1988). Keki N. Daruwalla's first book was published in (1970); his books are *Under Orion* (1970), *Apparition in April* (1971), *Crossing of Rivers* (1976), *The Keeper of the Dead* (1982) and *Landscapes* (1987). Kamala Das's first book was published in 1965; her books are *Summer in Calcutta* (1965), *The Descendants* (1967), *The Old Playhouse and Other Poems* (1973), and *Collected Poems* (1984). Shiv K. Kumar's first book was published in 1970; his books are *Articulate Silences* (1970), *Cobwebs in the Sun* (1974), *Subterfuges* (1976), *Woodpeckers* (1979) and *Trapfalls in the Sky* (1986). Another considerable poet who could not get Akademi recognition in the eighties due to technical reasons (as he had been settled in U.S.A.) was A.K. Ramanujan. His books are, *The Striders* (1966), *Relations* (1971), *Selected Poems* (1976) and *Second Sight* (1986). And still another poet was Dom Moraes, who got recognition in 1994 and his books are *Poems* (1960), *John Nobody* (1965) and *Poems 1955–65* (1966).

It can be said that post-Independence Indian English poetry emerged almost like a movement, wherein not only the poets we have mentioned above but also many more poets were involved. M.K. Naik in his *History of Indian English Literature* refers to their changed attitudes very succinctly—"In the fifties arose a school of poets who tried to turn their backs on the romantic tradition and write a verse more in tune with the age, its general temper and its literary ethos" (192). R. Parthsarathy in his Introduction to *Ten Twentieth Century Indian Poets* (1976), points out another related aspect—"An important characteristics of Indian verse in English in the mid-twentieth century has been its emergence from the mainstream of English literature and its appearance as part of Indian literature. It has been said that it is Indian in sensibility and content, and English in language. It is rooted in and stems from the Indian environment, and reflects its mores, often ironically" (3). K. Ayyappa Paniker also with reference to these poets, provides a similar view—"The other dimension of Indian poetic tradition is its vital connection with poetry in the Indian languages. Like Indian language poetry, Indian English is also regional in inspiration" (1991, 14).

Bruce King expands the observation and speaks of the larger roots of the 'Movement'—"Their poetry is part of the process of modernization which includes urbanization, industrialization, mobility, independence, social change, increased communication (in the form of films, television, radio, journals and newspapers), national and international transportation networks, mass education and resulting paradox that as an independent national culture emerges it also participates in the international, modern, usually westernized world" (1987, 3). P.K. Jagdeb, in his unpublished thesis, entitled "Post-Independence Indo-Anglian Poetry" (Utkal University, 1997), detailed the three-decades of growth of Indian English poetry. He called the first decade, that is, the fifties as the 'transitional' decade, when the strains of earlier romantic and spiritual poetry continued, and new poetry, independent of romantic or spiritual leanings emerged, particularly in the poems of Nissim Ezekiel and Dom Moraes.

He called sixties as the decade of 'creativity', when the momentum gathered in the fifties in favour of new poetry bore fruit. The earlier two poets continued to be active, and the newer poets who emerged were A.K. Ramanujan, R. Parthasarathi and the outstanding woman-poet Kamala Das.

The seventies, Jagdeb called, as the decade of expansion and consolidation, when the achievement of new poetry was consolidated and so to say, it came of age, and the still newer poets to emerge were K.N. Daruwalla, Shiv K. Kumar and Jayanta Mahapatra etc. Jagdev concludes—"The post-Independence poet was under no obligation to be nationalistic, or overtly spiritual or romantic as his pre-Independence counterpart was. One may note a sense of freedom where the poet freely scrutinizes, criticizes, and exposes the society around him and even his own self. This change in the attitude led him to write what may be called 'poetry of wit', with its concomitants such as irony, sarcasm, paradox and ambiguity etc., which as it appears, they have found handy to express their understanding of the complexity and comprehensiveness of the present-day life" (352). In short, the body of such poetry not only got established but gained respectability as a significant part of the total Indian poetry produced at the time. The large number of poets who wrote in English never thought of it as a foreign language and never used it as such. It came to them almost as naturally as their own mother tongue and assumed a shape and structure distinctly Indian. Secondly, these poets, like the poets in Indian languages, looked at themselves and at the realities and spoke of their creative growth and identity in a distinctly Indian context.

The road from Derozio's to Nissim Ezekiel was full of many vicissitudes. But at the end English got integrated with Indian life, and Indian English Literature became primarily Indian literature, and only secondarily English. As in poetry, so too, similar situation came to develop in Indian English novel. The novel did not have as long a heritage as poetry had, though S.K. Mund who did work on Indian novel in English in the 19th century, testifies that there were some—"Seventeen works have been carefully selected and studied as full-fledged novels..." (Mund: 1997, 162). But for all purposes, and as a serious entity,

Indian English novel came to attain respectability after the nineteen thirties, and in the beginning in the works of Mulk Raj Anand and subsequently in the novels of Raja Rao and R.K. Narayan, the 'major trio', (Naik, 155) whose first novels were published in 1935, 1938 and 1935, respectively.

Mulk Raj Anand (1905-2004) has a number of novels to his credit. Beginning with *Untouchable* (1935), his first novel, he had six more before Independence. They are *Coolie* (1936), *Two Leaves and a Bud* (1937), *The Village* (1939), *Among the Black Waters* (1941), *Sword and the Sickle* (1942) and *The Big Heart* (1945). Early in life Anand was associated with Non-Cooperation Movement. While in Europe, he developed leanings towards the left, and had even joined International Brigade during the Spanish Civil War. Subsequently, he was a convert towards Gandhian ideas. These, as well as his knowledge of Indian peasants and a strong indignation against the obscurantist ways of contemporary Indian social system, all got reflected in his novels and shaped his attitudes. Anand's novels form a fictional chronicle, said Naik, in which his "eclectic humanism and his humanitarian compassion for the underdog remain as persistent themes" (156). The novel *Untouchable* describes an eventful day in the life of Bakha, an introspective young sweeper from the sweeper's colony in a small cantonment town in northern India. During the course of the day, as he goes through the day's humiliating routine, a life of torment and degradation, a range of solutions by way of release are suggested. First, his father's belief of a 'philosophical resignation'; second, a missionary's promise of a life of social equality under conversion; third, Gandhiji's advocacy of social reform where untouchability has to be eradicated; and lastly of mechanized sanitation through a Nehruvian figure and a poet Iqbal Nath Sarashar, of large-scale popularization of the flush-toilet system.

Untouchable, Anand's first book, is most accomplished, compact and unsparing in its realism. In *Coolie* and *Two Leaves and a Bud* emphasis shifts from caste to class, to miserable life in big cities and tea-gardens, appalling social chronicle, and the tragic denial to a simple peasant of the fundamental right to happiness. The subsequent three novels constitute a trilogy, organized around the varied career of Lal Singh, the protagonist, a Punjabi peasant. The trilogy moves across a complex range of geographical and ideological locations, such as between Communism and Gandhism, and between the comforts of home and the progressive modernity of urban India. *The Big Heart,* the last novel, that has the account of one day of Ananta, the protagonist, a street-wise coppersmith, of great generosity of spirit, who single-handedly tries to bring the lessons of modernity and mechanism to his suspicious and unchanging community, and in the process scarifies his life. Anand's post-Independence novels are a shade lower than his earlier ones. Yet they continue as before the writer's interest in ideological difference, and his concern with pitiable, apathetic social conditions. These books include his semi-autobiographical novels, such as *Seven Summers* (1951), *The Private Life of an Indian Prince* (1953), *Morning Face* (1970), that bagged Akademi Award, and *Confessions of a Lover* (1976), as well as an unusual novel for him, *The Old Woman and the Cow* (1960), that focused on the misfortunes and revolutionary transformation of a female protagonist, called Gauri. "Ananad's novels are instrumental in the history of the Indian novel in English," says Leela Gandhi. "These experiments with social realism, and corresponding attention to the surface of life in pre-Independence India, catches within fiction the complex alliances, misalliances, transformations, and failures of Indian National Movement" (Mehrotra: 2003, 178) In short, a good range, wealth of living characters, exposition of stark realism as well as a deeply felt indignation at social wrongs, and strong humanitarian compassion characterize Anand's novels and provide strength to them. Also, Anand's experiments in style, to import the rich dialects of northern India—words, phrase, expletives, turns of expressions and proverbs drawn from his native Punjabi and Hindi—into English, were pioneering in their efforts, and prepared the way for many subsequent writers.

Raja Rao (1908–2003), in comparison to Anand, wrote sparingly. *Kanthapura,* published in 1938, was his first novel. Subsequently he had four more novels, *The Serpent and the Rope* (1960), *The Cat and Shakespeare* (1965), *Comrade*

Kirillov (1976), and *The Chessmaster and His Moves* (1988). His novels did not have the social dimension or strong humanitarian zeal we have noted in Anand's novels, neither had he Anand's range, nor his wealth of characters or his exposition of ruthless realism. But he had similarities too. For example, Anand's merging of European tradition with that of India, took the form of East-West confrontation in Rao, and Anand's emphasis on Gandhism took a substantial form in Rao's novels, particularly in *Kanthapura.* Similarly, like Anand he effected experiments in style and use of language, and put Indian words, phrases, expletives and idioms, in this case from his native Kannada into English. *Kanthapura* is probably the finest evocation of Gandhism in Indian English fiction. It is the account of a small village in the Malabar heights that came under the spell of Gandhism and the consequences thereto. The story is told as the reminiscences of an old woman (old grandmother), who tells the story in a digressive, talkative manner, and in an almost non-stop style of Indian *Purana* or *Harikatha* mixing freely narration, description, reflection, religious discourse and folklore etc.

The Serpent and the Rope, coming in the aftermath of Independence, shifted from a nationalist narrative to a metaphysical fiction, and the location changed from South India to spread across Europe and India. The story narrates the marriage of Ramaswamy, a young Hindu, with Madeleine, a French lady; their subsequent estrangement occasioned by their different conceptions of love, marriage and family; Ramaswamy's meeting with Savitri, an Indian to the core; their love for each other which transcends physical barriers to rise to a higher level, to higher Love, the ultimate union of the soul with God ; and at the end Ramaswamy sets out to meet his Guru who alone can make him fit for the great consummation. *The Serpent and the Rope* was a complex and many-sided novel; a saga of one's quest for self-knowledge and self-fulfillment—"a truly Indian novel with its roots firmly rooted in native tradition" (Naik: 1982, 168). In the preface to *Kanthapura* Rao spoke of a "spirit, that is one's own". *The Serpent and the Rope* manifests that spirit—the spirit of quest, illumination, and final deliverance, and all that in a deeply felt Indian context. Not only philosophical profundity, or rich symbolism but also lyrical beauty, descriptive power and innovative experimentation with form and style go to make *The Serpent and the Rope* a major achievement. The novels that follow do not reach up to that height. *The Cat and Shakespeare* is a delightful comic tab, so also *Comrade Kirillov*, though each has a philosophical frame and motivation, consonant with *The Serpent and the Rope*. So also in *The Chessmaster and his Moves* which was projected as the first part of a planned trilogy. In short, along with Anand's expansiveness in his novels, Raja Rao's novels provided an intensive, meditative insight into life, and both ways Indian English fiction was highly enriched at the nascent stage.

R.K. Narayan, who had studied in Madras and settled in Mysore, had also, like Anand, started writing from early thirties. His first novel *Swami and Friends* was published in 1935 and subsequently he had three more novels, published before Independence. The novels were *The Bachelor of Arts* (1937). *The Dark Room* (1938) and *The English Teacher Part I and II* (1945). Narayan's first novel *Swami and Friends* is about a child growing up through an idyllic childhood, finally coming face to face with the problems of adulthood. The context is an imaginary town Malgudi, a colonial district town with all its available amenities, like post office, bank etc., in a way the symbol of the new urbanizing India, and the novel deals with Swamy's attempts to adjust with the new, emerging set-up, in a way synonymous with Narayan's own attempts to do that. The account has, on the one hand, the freshness of boyhood days and on the other the pangs of growing up and adjustment, a combination of both "sadness and beauty" (Graham Greene).

The second novel, published after two years, continues Narayan's ambivalences vis-à-vis a boy's growing up period and the new-fangled ideas that one gets from an imposed colonial education. Only that the world has become larger, and the conflict is particularly between the Western ideas of love and marriage and the traditional social set-up in which he lives. The third novel, published only a year after, takes up the conflict at a parallel level in the challenge that a woman puts up against the social and familial set-up though at the end the challenge is contained and the set-up is accepted. Narayan's next novel, published about 7 years after, and immediately before Independence, had a different ring where the attention shifted not so much to social factors as to personal ambits of joy and suffering—to a happy family life and the lack of it. The early novels of Narayan give a "tortuous initiation into modernity", says Pankaj Mishra, "the anxieties and bewilderments and disappointments of a generation of Indians expelled from the past into a new world" (Mehrotra: 2003, 199). These attitudes, related to the twin directions of traditionalism and modernity, to social changes and painful adjustment to that, in a way continued in Narayan's post-Independence novels too, but they acquired different dimensions such as greater human interest and moral complexity as a larger openness to experience.

Narayan's post-Independence novels were many, and he continued to write them till nineties. But his best novels were written in the fifties and sixties after which they became mostly repetitive. Such novels were *The Financial Expert* (1952), *Waiting for the Mahatma* (1955), *The Guide* (1958), *The Man-eater of Malgudi* (1962) and *The Vendor of Sweets* (1967). Ralph J. Crane spoke of three aspects in Narayan's fiction—his comedy, his irony, and his creation of the fictional world of Malgudi (Hawkins-Dady: 1996, 509). In fact Narayan's fictional structure incorporated all that together. It had irony and sympathy, a quiet realism and fantasy, and at the same time the dramas of middle-class life were enacted in Malgudi, an imaginary town with living ambience. Narayan's first novel after Independence was *Mr. Sampat, the Printer of Malgudi* (1949). Written immediately after Independence it provided glimpses of Independent India and how the old colonial world was being cracked open and taken over by new, ambitious men. But it also showed how the main protagonist after being pushed around by diverse confused ambitions finally decides only to live for himself—in a way, the realization of one's own self in the melee of diverse social situations.

The Financial Expert is an exposé of social conditions and an individual's attempts to cash on it. The main protagonist, a small-time middleman moves from a humble position to a position of wealth (financial expert) and finally moves back to his old position, but as a chastened man. In the process we have a whole gallery of characters, from greedy landlords, ungrateful children, embittered parents, unhappy wives to exploited villagers etc.—wide-ranging diverse existence, given to deceit and lies, with no hope of liberation or redemption, yet the novelist views them with sympathy and even affection, and that too, in spite of his comic demeanor and ironical exposition. Thus at the end it is not life's banter that dominates, but the individual's trust and faith. This progression is more vividly structured in the next novel *The Guide*. It has a large dimension related to various socio-cultural strands, and from a context of lies, deceit and insincerity the protagonist moves to a point of sincerity which is almost religious in nature. Thus after all turmoil, smallness and noise, the end is one of meditation and faith—"...he stepped into it, shut his eyes, and turned towards the mountain, his lips muttering the prayer. The morning sun was out by now; a great shaft of light illuminated the surroundings. They held him as if he were a baby. Raju opened his eyes, looked about, and said, 'Velan, it's raining in the hills. I can feel it coming up under my feet, up my legs—'. He sagged down" (1990, 247). The technique involves both past and present, objective narration and autobiographical presentation as well as elements of humour and irony, though irony, as M.K. Naik points out, raises many "disturbing questions about human motives and actions" (1982, 163). *The Guide* remains as the best testimony of Narayan's creative power to comprehend the great range of human diversity and openness of experience.

Waiting for the Mahatma has political frame, with references to the anti-colonial struggle, the activities of Gandhiji, the Quit India Movement, and finally the assassination of Gandhiji. The progression of the soul structured in the earlier two novels is also reflected here in a differing pattern, with mass of people with their ambivalences along with motivated, ambitious leadership on the one hand and Gandhiji alone on the other—the uniqueness of his life and ideas along with the high moral standard he symbolized. That is, Narayan's basic approach how best the illusions of existence can be handled and regulated also continues here. Two other novels, written in the sixties, *The Man-eater of Malgudi* and *The Vendor of Sweets* have both comic sides and irony in plenty and describe in detail social equations and adjustments and mostly expose the seaming sides of man—selfishness, hypocrisy and the propensity to destroy oneself with no attempts to get oneself released from the situations. C.D. Narasimhaiah, while speaking of *The Guide* refers to Narayan's use of the "comic mode to prove the highest kind of reality" (1999, 199). In a similar vein William Walsh too, speaks of Narayan's novels as belonging to a difficult genre, the 'serious comedy'. "Success in it", he says, "calls for a sensibility preserved from ambivalence or fracture, an unusual unity in the point of view as well as a social tradition in which the comic and the sad are not sharply marked off one from the other" (79).

As we have pointed out earlier, the Indian English fiction, unlike Indian English poetry, came of its own only after Independence, and the persons responsible to provide it with a firm foundation were three major writers, Anand, Raja Rao and Narayan. But in a way, the time was also ripe for novel-writing because of multiple factors that came up after Independence—social, political and cultural etc., and provided rich fertilizing ground for writing. This happened in all Indian languages, and particularly so in English, as English continued to be the administrative language and the language of communication, and provided maximum publicity and privilege to the writers.

M.K. Naik in his *A History of Indian English Literature* lists about 80 such writers, both men and women, and more than 150 novels, published in a period of about 30 years after Independence. The writers came from all communities and places in India, as well as by many who had migrated abroad, particularly England. These novels gave distinct and substantial shape to Indian English fiction that came to be reckoned as a major body of fiction writing along with fiction in major Indian languages. The Sahitya Akademi Awards also came handy. Beginning from 1961, when R.K. Narayan got the first-ever Akademi Award for his novel *The Guide*, till 1988, when

Vikram Seth got the Award for his verse-novel *The Golden Gate,* there were other writers who got the Award for novel at different times. We give below a select list of novelists, relatively more important than others, whose novels were representative of the general trends of development, and who acquired national eminence on their own merit. The writers were, apart from Anand, Raja Rao and Narayan, Bhabani Bhattacharya, (1906-), Manohar Malgaonkar (1913-), Kamala Markandaya (1924-), Chaman Nahal (1927-), Nayantara Sahgal (1927-), Anita Desai (1937-) and Arun Joshi (1939–1993); and some of their well-known novels were *So Many Hungers* (1947), *He Who Rides a Tiger* (1952), *A Goddess Named Gold* (1960) and *Shadow from Ladakh* (1966, Sahitya Akademi Award, 1967) by Bhabani Bhattacharya; *Distant Drum* (1960), *A Handful of Rice* (1966), *The Coffer Dam* (1969) and *Nowhere Man* (1972) by Kamala Markandaya; *My True Faces* (1973), *Azadi* (1975, Sahitya Akademi Award, 1977) and *Into Another Dawn* (1977) by Chaman Nahal; *A Time to be Happy* (1985), *Storm in Chandigarh* (1969) and *Rich Like Us* (1985, Sahitya Akademi Award, 1986) by Nayantara Sahgal; *Cry, the Peacock* (1963), *Voices in the City* (1965), *Bye, Bye Blackbird* (1971), *Where Shall We Go This Summer* (1975), *Fire on the Mountain* (1977, Sahitya Akademi Award, 1978) and *Clear Light of Day* (1980) by Anita Desai; and *The Foreigner* (1968), *The Strange Case of Billy Biswas* (1971), *The Apprentice* (1974), and *The Last Labyrinth* (1981, Sahitya Akademi Award, 1982) by Arun Joshi.

As we have already noted, the changes that came to Indian life as a whole after Independence provided a powerful impetus to Indian English writing, particularly to fiction-writing in English. A number of general trends and situations were viewed and analyzed and were creatively formulated again and again. Thus, one such trend was references to changing political situations. It began with references to freedom-struggle and coming of Independence (*A Time to be Happy*), and continued through references to the Second World War (*Distant Drum*), Quit India Movement, and Bengal famine (*So Many Hunger!),* the partition and its horrendous details (*Azadi*), the merger of the States (*Princes*), the partition of Punjab into Punjab and Haryana (*Storm in Chandigarh*), the Chinese aggression (*Shadow from Ladakh*), the aftermath of Nehru's death and Naxalite agitation (*A Situation in New Delhi*) and the Emergency (*Rich Like Us*) etc. These changing political factors, first of all, provided important background to different novels, and at the same time, were integrated with the movement of story and characters and with attitudes and motivation. An equally important trend was a general awareness of the extent of socio-cultural change and the individual's adaptability to it. First of all it was an awareness of the clash of culture—native vs. non-native (*The Coffer Dam*), village vs. town, and between one ideology and the other (*The Coffer Dam*, *Shadow from Ladakh*).

Similarly, another common trend has been what may be called East-West encounter, that is, the contact between the Indians and Indian society, culture and traditional ways of Indian thinking and living with that of the West. This was nothing new in India that had been under British colonial rule for about 200 years. But the release from the colonial rule after Independence, brought in new equations to the old contact when it no longer was an affair between the ruler and the ruled, but between two independent nations, having their independent views and habits of living. Hence the 'encounter' assumed different forms. First it was a direct relationship, a contact at the individual level and the mutual consequences. Thus in the novel *Nectar in a Sieve* a couple from a village establish contact with a well-meaning British doctor and social activist; in *Some Inner Fury* a couple of lovers, an English man and an Indian woman could not get the fruition of their love because of freedom movement; and in *Into Another Dawn* an Indian young man marries an American woman. Secondly, it is a contact at the cultural level, that is, the cultural impact of the British culture on traditional Indian life, which in a way can be considered as the conflict between the tradition and the modernity. The examples could be seen in *The Silence of Desire* that shows the clash between the Western-educated rationalism and religious faith; as also in *The Coffer Dam* that provides a comprehensive picture of Indo-British encounter when a British team arrives to build a dam and Indian responses thereto. Thirdly, this encounter is achieved in the exposition of the living conditions of Indian migrants in England. Two good examples were *Bye, Bye Blackbird,* where British characters are better realized than the Indian ones, and *The Nowhere Man* where the companionship between an old Indian widower and an old British divorcee gets a set-back because of the prejudicial anti-immigrant wave of sixties in Britain.

The theme of exploitation, exploiting the society through fraudulent means, and the suffering of the lower middle-class urban poor can be seen in a number of novels. In *So Many Hunger!*, apart from its context in Bengal famine and the situation in early forties, providing some fine examples of social realism, shows many faces of hunger with particular reference to the dismal conditions in Calcutta brothels. Its main theme of exploitation and the consequent suffering to people covers exploitation of all types—political, economic and social. Similarly, in *He Who Rides a Tiger*, the protagonist, a poor blacksmith, seriously punished for a very minor offense (stealing a bunch of bananas), takes it on the society through a system of fraud, exposing by the way how people in general are vulnerable to fraudulent deals and cunning exploitation. In a different dimension, to give another example, *A Handful of Rice* deals with the suffering of urban poor, presented in the living conditions of a married couple, an urban vagabond and the daughter of a poor tailor, where the girl goes through unrelieved suffering. In fact the woman's problems have found place in many novels. First, it is woman's differing role and suffering, as in *Nectar in a Sieve*, where the central figure, a rustic woman who had a hard peasant life, was forced by adverse economic conditions to migrate to the city with her husband, where her suffering instead of abetting, intensifies, and they both are fleeced white by unscrupulous and unsympathetic persons. So too, in *A Handful of Rice,* already referred to, the unmitigated suffering of the couple tends to make the woman the greater victim—"He gripped her wrist, and the single thin glass bangle she wore broke. His blood, hers scarlet, spurted and seeped between them, but he did not let her go, and the fan was still in her hand. 'You're lying.' He shook her wrist until the fan dropped, 'who gave it to you—one of your admirers?" Her mouth was working, but she did not reply. Her breath came in short, high, frightened gasps, 'you bitch', he said...." (219). There are other aspects of woman too, away from suffering and distress, a desire to establish one's femininity and identity—a modern woman's search for sexual freedom and self-realization. Two good examples were *A Time to be Happy* and *Storm in Chandigarh*. Both the novels had political context and in both the women carried a bold, strong voice.

Corruption of power, and corrosion of values in public life, particularly after Independence have been taken up as points of discussion in many novels, a good example of which was the novel *Rich Like Us* that shows how the position of both civil servants and people at large have been compromised after Independence, of which the Emergency only provides a background. But a serious mindset that troubled many of the sensitive novelists of the period and got formulated in their novels in the relationships of the characters was a lack of communication at the mental level and the resultant break-down of familial and social ties. One can call it a psychological attitude of 'aloneness' with its attendant psychological complexities. This is evidenced in many novels, more particularly in the novels of Anita Desai. Thus, for example, to speak briefly, in her novel *Cry, the Peacock*, the protagonist, a young woman, obsessed with a sense of death and astrological prediction, fails to have any effective communication with her husband whom she kills at the end. Similarly in her novel *Voices in the City*, with a Calcutta setting, a brother and two sisters, try to rebel against middle-class life, longing for creativity and self-expression, but end up in tragic situations with one sister committing suicide. An interesting example is Desai's award-winning novel *Fire on the Mountain*, where two souls confront each other, socially, one by nature (the girl) and the other by necessity. But their togetherness was only an apparent relationship; no effective communication could be possible between them. In a broader term it was a matter of alienation—alienated from one's own self, from one's own society, and from humanity at large, a mindset which was not especially Indian, but came to stay globally as an attitude towards life, particularly in the modern conditions of living and afflicted all sensitive souls. The novels of Arun Joshi, more than other novels, show this attitude more prominently. In *The Foreigner*, the protagonist, born of an Indian father and English mother, in Kenya, without a family and a country of his own, is a person alienated from humanity. Similarly, in *The Strange Case of Billy Biswas,* the protagonist renounces a social position and status, joins a primitive tribe and remains alienated from the society he best understood and of which he was a part. In *The Apprentice* the protagonist, a clerk involved in corruption and 'Mammonism' of post-Independence India, gets alienated from his own self and remains vacillating between the choices of good and bad. In each case the novelist has tried to find out a solution biding to some type of transformation and togetherness, but the emphasis remains on alienation as a basic motif—an important motif too in Indian English novel, and more generally in Indian English Literature, in the post-Independence decades in India.

The development of Indian English novel after Independence has been phenomenal. No doubt an awareness of England and English language and literature remained in the subconscious, as all these writers were English-educated, mostly belonged to the upper echelons of the society, and many of them had close contact with England at a functional level. Yet they remained true to Indian culture, Indian heritage and tradition, and to sprawling segments of Indian life, and what they portrayed in their novels was basically the account of many changes, socially, politically, and in human matters, that came over India after Independence. These writers laid a foundation of a new literature in English, particularly in novel, separate from Indian language-literatures, but generally akin to it as a new branch of development, on which, still newer, but more substantial and more truly Indian literature, after 1980, and writers like Salman Rushdie (*Midnight's Children*, Booker Prize, 1981), Vikram Seth (the first among the new writers to get the Sahitya Akademi recognition in 1988), Amitav Ghosh (Akademi Award, 1989,

The Shadow Lines), Shashi Deshpande (Akademi Award, 1990, *That Long Silence*), I. Allan Sealy (Akademi Award, 1991, *The Trotter-Nama*), Sunetra Gupta (Akademi Award, 1996, *Memories of Rain*), Kiran Nagarkar (Akademi Award, 2000, *Cuckold*), Amit Chaudhuri (Akademi Award, 2002, *A New World*), Upamanyu Chatterjee (Akademi Award, 2004, *English August*) and Arundhati Roy (Booker Prize, 1997, *The God of Small Things*) flourished.

The nourishment they got was from many sources, including the world of Indian-living that had got settled by that time, and had enveloped the mindset of all Indian writers, but in no less measure in their attitudes of self-realization and independence from all external influences, in their desire to strike on their own and grow on their own, not only in terms of motivations and points of view, but also in form. What the novelists demonstrated, say Shyamala A. Narayan and Jon Mee, "was a command of the dominant forms of the English-novel, and the right of Indian novelists to be taken seriously in terms of the criteria of Western novel-writing" (Mehrotra: 2003, 231).

WORKS CITED

Bhatti, P.S., ed. *Indian Publishing, Then and Now*. New Delhi: S. Chand & Company, 1987.

Derozio, Henry Louis Vivian. *Poems*. Calcutta: Oxford University Press, 1980.

Ghose, Manmohan. *Selected Poems*. New Delhi: Sahitya Akademi, 1974.

Gokak, V.K., selected & ed. *The Golden Treasury of Indo-Anglian Poetry*. New Delhi: Sahitya Akademi, 1989.

Hawkins-Dady, Mark, ed. *Readers Guide to Literature in English*. London: F.D. Publishers, 1996.

Iyengar, K.R. Srinivasa. *Indian Writing in English*, Revised & Updated Edition. New Delhi: Sterling Publishers Private Ltd., 1990.

Jagadev, Prafulla Kumar. "Post-Independence Indo-Anglian Poetry: Themes and Structure." Diss. Utkal University, 1997.

Katoky, P.C. "A Study of Sri Aurobindo and Four Others," *Indo-English Poetry*, Guwahati: Guwahati University, 1969.

Kesavan, B.S., ed. *India's National Library*. Calcutta: National Library 1961.

King, Bruce. *Modern Indian Poetry in English*, New Delhi: Oxford University Press, 2001.

Markandaya, Kamala. *A Handful of Rice*. Delhi: Hind Pocket Books (P.) Ltd., 1966.

Mehrotra, Arvind Krishna, ed. *An Illustrated History of Indian Literature in English*. New Delhi: Permanent Black, 2003.

Mund, Subhendu Kumar. *The Indian Novel in English: Its Birth and Development*. Delhi: Prachi Prakashan, 1997.

Naik, M.K. *A History of Indian English Literature*. New Delhi: Sahitya Akademi, 1982.

Naik, M.K. and Shayamala A. Narayan. *Indian English Literature, 1980–2000: A Critical Survey*. Delhi: Pencraft International, 2004.

Narasimahiah, C.D. "Essays on Indian English Literature." *The Swan and the Eagle*. 3rd Edition, Revised & Enlarged, New Delhi: Vision Books, 1999.

Narayan, R.K. *The Guide*. Mysore: Indian Thought Publications, 1990.

Paniker, K. Ayyappa. *Modern Indian Poetry in English*, New Delhi: Sahitya Akademi, 1991.

Parthasarathy, R. *Ten Twentieth Century Indian Poets*. Delhi: Oxford University Press, 1976.

Sri Aurobindo. *Collected Poems*. Pondicherry: Sri Aurobindo Ashram, 1972.

Walsh, William. *Indian Literature in English*. London: Longman, 1990.

2 Poems 1981-1994

Vikram Seth's first poetry-collection titled *Mappings* was published in 1981. Subsequently he had three more poetry-collections titled *The Humble Administrator's Garden* (1985), *All You Who Sleep Tonight (1990) and Beastly Tales from Here and There (1992)*. Besides, he had a bunch of Chinese poems, translated from *Three Chinese Poets*, all belonging to 8th century A.D.—Wang Wei (701–762), Li Bai (701–761) and Du Fu (712–770), and a Libretto, entitled *Arion and the Dolphin* (1994). But his "longest work in verse" (Seth, 1995: xiv) which he called *The Golden Gate* (1986) and which was set in the 1980s in the area around the San Francisco Bay, was as he himself pointed out, "in essence a novel" (Seth, 1995: xiv). Thus, Seth has 6 poetry books, including a book of translations and a libretto, and all these were published in a comprehensive collection in 1995 by Viking, entitled *The Poems 1981–1994*.

In his Introduction to *The Poems 1981–1994*, Seth posed three questions to himself, related to poetry. The questions were, first, "How did I begin to write it?" Secondly, "Why do I write so much of it in rhyme and metre?" And thirdly, "Do I see myself as an Indian or American or Commonwealth writer—and as a poet or a novelist?" He himself answered them. To the first question he pointed out that he started writing poems in earnest when he was unhappily in "love" as a university student. At the same time he maintained that the poems were "exaggeratedly sentimental", and memorable only for their "banality". To the second question he confessed that he wrote most of his poems in "free verse". That's because he said, he read a great deal of the free verse of other poets, as of Whitman or Lawrence, and when lines came to his mind when he needed poetry, either "to delight or remind or suggest or console", was almost invariably in metre and often in "rhyme". Concurrently he pointed out it was difficult to explain the "emotional power" of such poetry, and said that "since verse 'in form' is what I usually find myself reading or recalling, it is what I almost always find myself writing." To the third question he answered that such imaginative categories were fascinating but in the final analysis irrelevant. He saw himself as an Indian, and primarily as a poet, and pointed out that the wish to write about anything is such a "rare" and "mysterious" feeling that it is pointless to preempt or constrain it by notions of "subject or geography or genre". Elsewhere, in a poem "From a Traveller" (*The Poems*) while commenting on the style of writing of a friendly letter the poet refers to a "balanced power":

> ....It is very fine—
> Latinate and resonant, the words precisely hefted.
> As for craft, rhyme and metre are well
> But this has more, a balanced power. (94)

Seth's views on his own poetic craft are illuminating. An examination of his poems to that effect would be relevant and fruitful.

MAPPINGS

The poems collected in *Mappings,* the poet points out in a brief Foreword, were written when he was in his twenties, and was a student in England and latterly in California. Though the poet was appreciative of his poems, which he rather humorously called "the first fruits of my self-determined genius", yet he found it difficult to get a publisher initially and published it by himself, and peddled it among his friends and relatives. Afterwards, after about 10 years, when the book was considered for a reprint by Penguin India he was not enthusiastic. He called his poem as his "juvenilia" and considered them as "embarrassingly callow". He only agreed when a friend told him that she much preferred his "voice" in *Mappings* to that of his later book of poems. Despite whatever the poet thought of his poems, they were neither sentimental nor callow. They had, as his friend correctly pointed out, a distinct voice and attitude—a voice tender and youthful, and a fine sensitiveness to items of life around. At the same time his concern for craft was both flexible and balanced. As a first book *Mappings* showed good deal of promise and power.

Mappings has a total of 23 poems, of which two are translations. The rest 21 poems have a good mix. For example, there are references to places, such as "Panipat", "Departure Lounge", "Grand Canyon", "Home Thought from the Bay", "From Mount Tamalpais", "Aubade" and "Quakina Bridge" etc., references to seasons and nature, such as "A Winter Word", "Rain", "The Yellow Cricket", "At Evening", "Moonless Night", "Moths", "Tomatoes" etc.... In addition there are poems occasioned by particular contexts, such as "Sea and Desert", "Rakhee", "From the Memoirs of Babur, First Moghul Emperor of Hindustan", "Party for the Retirement of the Oldest-serving British Museum Reading Room Book Attendant", "The Walker", "The Tale of Melon City" and "Divali" etc., addressing individuals, such as "To a Fellow Traveller", "To Manijeh", etc., and such other poems that are reflective in nature and have grown out of a study of time and relationship such as "Switching Off", "Sonnet", "Time-Zones", "After Three Years", "The Sultan's Turret", "The Balcony", "Close of Play", "Six Octets", "Distressed Homonyms", "Progress Report", "Mappings", etc.... Though these are apparent divisions yet what dominate most of the poems of *Mappings* is a reflective spirit and the poet's desire to understand and identify human relationship. In fact, a probe into human relationship is an important trend in the poems. Occasionally it is parental, but in most cases it is a relationship touching on the contact between two persons verging on love. Allied to this are such sentiments as desire for attachment and adjustment, and operation of such feelings as pleasure and bliss on the one hand, and bitterness and emptiness on the other. Strong sensitivity to nature and nature's beauty, understanding through time and change across time, references to routine things of life and attachment to life, sense of distance and nearness, personal and impersonal assessment of relationship, a knowing sense of pain hidden by levity, changing mindset linked by different places, incapacity to fight time and counter death, awareness of final extinction and how that can be avoided, a strong social awareness about misery and how people are deprived, and about life, and about hope and uncertainty—these are various strands that provide the poetic structure. On the whole one can say that the poems of *Mappings* show a young, sensitive soul ranging from love to nature and mutability, in a mindset of both levity and seriousness and in a frame flippant and ruminative. An examination of some select poems will bear out these details.

The first poem "Panipat" shows the poet's concern for two worlds, the one here, at present, his own, and the other in the past, the foreign, and the poet's attempt at adjustment with both. The first world is detailed with aunts "gossiping" in the courtyard, parrots "cackling" in the neem trees, sitting place near a wall covered up to make a "septic tank", besides other such objects as "pandits", "panir", "paan", "koyal singing", and "Family, music, faces / Food, land, everything". The second world has birds too but different ones—nightingale, wren, black bird, and the trees are also different from neem—beeches, elms. The adjustment takes place at two levels. First, as a transition, in the mental state, through music—"I sit with my flute near the place...", "I glide from stop to stop", "...Its mournful meditative / Mood moves into a tune"...and the music takes the poet away from the local time and place,

> Leading me God knows where—
>   Into a universe
> Beyond—beyond Panipat! (3)

The poet's reference to music is strongly reminiscent of Wordsworth's reference to music in "The Solitary Reaper" where the song is sung also with a "melancholy strain," and as in here, so too in Wordsworth, the music provides transport to a different realm of joy and happiness. The second level is concerned with sense-perception-taste of eating a slice of mango which leads to an awareness of both familiar and foreign ("Well-known and alien"). In fact the poem's perception is a unified one, from routine familiar details ("My aunts sit in the courtyard / Gossiping, shelling peas."), through "mournful meditative mood" and in a context of trees and birds to a semi-mystical, romantic expansion of mind.

The second poem, "Sea and Desert" also deals with mental expansiveness, a romantic state of feeling, a state of calm and peace, in contact with nature's beauty and through recollection of tender relationship. From the beginning the nature and the loved being are together—"The moon, the Pacific, and you beside me," and again—"I have been watching you / Your face lit in the full moon, restless, still." The result is an awareness of happiness—"it is the cause / Of so much of my peace" and a continuing sense of happiness —"...will recur / Again and again for one with sea and moon." Nature's calm mingles with a contemplation of human beauty ("Your face with its / Clean lines and tousled hair is beautiful") leads to peace of mind ("Of so much of my peace") and an unbelievable happiness ("How do I merit such happiness ?"), almost reminiscent, as in the earlier case, of Wordsworth's sonnet "It is a Beauteous Evening" where the poet speaks of a "beauteous evening, calm and free" and where the "broad sun" sinks down "in its tranquility".

The sense of relationship developed in "Sea and Desert" is further developed in "Departure Lounge", one of the finest poems of *Mappings*. This is parental relationship, that is, the relationship between the father and son. Again, as in the earlier poem, here too, we have both the sense of nearness and distance, and two different times are involved—the present and the past, one through available realistic details, and the other through memory. The present context is Boston Airport,

> Among the lobsters and pushcarts
> At Boston Airport we
> Walk up and down, father and son... (7)

And again the same,

> Your arm around my shoulder, we
> Stroll through the lounge. The hand
> Arcs round the clock; flight 43
> Is called;... (12)

The past that comes through the memory, has also specificities. First, how is the father's condition when he escaped from the house,

> Orphaned at two, you ran away
> From Baoji at fifteen.
> The tin shack, the Mussourie store,
> Hunger, the freezing rain... (10)

Secondly, the father's dream of a habitation,

> Your paradigm
> For paradise—greenery
> And a small river; Delhi politics; (11)

This is one aspect. The other aspect is more important. It is a change in attitude, the change that comes through time and with greater realization. First, it is a matter of resistance, the son's distance from his father—

> My act to you had one intent,
> To thwart you. I recall
> The fear, hate, the contempt I felt
> At that. (8)

Next, the change that comes through time,

> Or that those clear-edged scenes
> Of boyhood are less focused now;
> Since I no longer hate,
> 'The self they made me' I can free
> The myths that bore the freight
> Of self-dislike, self-pity and despair? (9)

Finally, it is the realization of the bond that exists between the two—a deep intimacy, and the capacity to accept the relationship with an adult understanding,

> Well, I was blind; but it was dark
> And both of us have moved
> Into a clearer sunlight. I, now
> Certain that I was loved... (10)

and,

> We meet on neutral ground: next time
> May be at home. I should

Tell you as you walk through the door
I'll miss you.... (12)

The poem is both a personal testament of the changes in relationship, as well as an impersonal assessment of it. On the one hand it shows a deeply troubled spirit that slowly comes to grip with an increasing realization of the factors of relationship. On the other, the poem records human predicament against which the value of parental relationship is assessed and judged—

...To live with happiness,
In what is an unfinished state
Till we die. You possess
What was not there then when I was boy,
This uninvasive joy? (12)

"To a Fellow-Traveller" also deals with relationship. The basis is in a short duration contact, about 7 hours, in the air, in a flight. The poet refers to this with a touch of humour, at his own cost,

I had always hoped, somehow, sometime, somewhere
I'd meet someone like you, I also deemed
Such visions built on vodka and on air. (18)

but also at the same time tries to give it an element of seriousness, of a ruminative and reflective nature, of a relationship realized on more serious consideration almost of an inexorable type that exists among the created things of the Universe,

...I remember you with love
Richer than I believed seven swift hours
Could ever wake; perhaps some semblance of
The love that moves the sun and other stars. (19)

Yet the poet is skeptical of the relationship and its continuity, and whatever might have been its intensity, for a short while he is wary of it,

...I don't care where or when,
I have your number but am somewhat chary
Of using it. Will you call me? And then
The two of us could meet. You know I'm wary
Of ruffling the calm waters of your mind.... (19)

The poem moves at two levels—the past, seen vividly in the context of surrounding realities and with reference to nature, and the present, where past provides a dimension and is relieved. Thus the past realities—

> The pilot is obtuse, the plane is late,
> The flight attendants flighty, and the sheer
> Monotony of a sedentary state
> Maintained for seven hours...
> as also references to nature—
> ...but the snow—
> Fluffed cloud-terrain heavy with evening light,
> ...and the darkening flare
> Of the chased sunset merging with the night? (18)

and again—

> The short shard of rainbow
> Above the clouds, the layered sky above.... (19)

Also the realities of the present are mixed up with that of the past—

> ...dip my Pepperidge Farm
> Cookie into my tea and think of you
> And how you laughed and held me by the arm
> On Shattuck when I left. (17)

"To a Fellow-Traveller" is a mix of different states of mind, and of different moods, of excitement and relaxation, of a desire to hold to something as permanent but which fleets about, of a belief that probably something has been achieved but one is uncertain, of a tone which is both detached and intense and an approach which has wit, humour and logic—one the whole a serious, and not too serious assessment of relationship and companionship, a matter of love and not of love.

The relationship is seen from a different angle in "Rakhi"—the relationship between the brother and sister, and the occasion is the social custom of the sister tying the knot of affection on the wrist of the brother ('Rakhi') on the Rakhi Purnima day. First of all, it is a bond which survives distance, time and individual:

It was a contract of trust
With more than you. I know
I left my home too many
Years ago. (20)

But secondly, there is also admission of change—change through separation and time, change in attitude,

Your rakhi came,
Showing how things have changed...

and again,

...and your brother
Too will be strange when next
We meet each other. (20)

It is also a change in perception and understanding. That is while the continuity of the social system is admitted, almost like a routine observed once a year and hence assumes a routine acquiescence at an apparent, external level, the change is more integral at the mental level. Hence the approach is hesitant, yes and no, a feeling of distance as well as of intimacy and relationship to that extent is complicated—

How we must both have changed;
Only the custom stays,
Educing from the past
The undying days. (21)

Relationship, particularly references to love-relationship in a covert way, can be seen as a guiding theme in many of the poems of Seth. For example, in "To Manijeh" it is connected with memory and is seen with a veneer of fun, almost like tongue in the check manner:

O Scorpio Cat
When you have gone
My eyes will turn
To lumps of stone. (27)

and,

But worst, some random
Woman's clear laugh

Will nearly cut
My liver in half. (28)

In "The Walkers" it is joined with a suggestive awareness of nature. First, with a "brace of startled ravens" who "suddenly rose in joint / defensive chorus for their living-space," and then,

The walkers laughed companionably; then one
who filled the other's heart with clear delight
said, pointing up at Snowdon, 'Look, the sun
has not yet thawed the snow; no, there, that white—' (29)

In "Aubade" feelings of love are also mixed up with nature—nature forming as background to realize love, a situation reminiscent of the beginning of Fitzgerald's *Omar Khayyam*:

Wake up! The smudge of dawn
Low on the hills has shot
The bay with light. Don't miss
These minutes....
I grant I want to see
Your face against the dawn
Wake up, therefore, for me. (33)

Omar Khayyam also provides the title and the background in "The Sultan's Turret," where love is joined with nature (dawn) and sleep; and the close physical intimacy of two persons;

Dawnlight; I wake; and wait for you, uneasy
With early dreams....
But I'm content, wombed in the quilt with you
To let the car-hums, chirrups, ticks and tocks
And your soft breathing holds me.... (35)

In "The Yellow Cricket" love is associated with trust, the context being the contemplation about a cricket, its colour, its flight etc., and nature providing background to the changing emotions of love. First, the sudden realization of love that has all along been there, but has been thought of as missed, like the sudden realization of the cricket's bright colour—

...bright
Gold flame, unthought of
Now revealed—

Like love that has
Lain long concealed. (34)

Secondly, the cricket's assurance of solid ground as against its fear of losing it is compared with love's trust with its fear:

How he now squats
As drab as dust
Love, let it not
Be fear but trust. (34)

Nature also provides background to love in "At Evening," but the contemplation is not towards assurance but towards loneliness. Thus at the beginning it is an uncertain mood:

Let me now sleep, let me not think, let me
Not ache with inconsistent tenderness

Then it is an awareness of nature getting dark and blind:

Now only movement marks the birds from the pines;
Now it is dark; the blinded stars appear;

And then to one's own feelings of being left alone, where one cannot even see or hear:

I am alone; you cannot read these lines...
Who are with me and cannot hear my voice
And take my hand and abrogate the choice. (36)

The uncertain mood of a lover continues in "The Balcony" too. Initially it is like patting one's own back that dejection in love is not the end of all things. One can survive.

If I have bent so far and not snapped, it
cannot destroy me now. This thing will pass
as it has passed before.

As nature survives, and everything else in life survives:

This room is the same. The grass
in post-drought green, the violet hills, this light
of early evening are the same. (39)

Thus, as the poet surveys the activities of a pair of lovers below on the car-park, he thinks of his own love and himself, the uncertain mood moves towards an assurance that in spite of reverses, both, that is, he himself and his love, do continue and remain the same:

...My eyes jaywalk the road and go
to where you live, jog, laugh, love, talk—and
I am suddenly glad that I've survived this love
and that it too survives. (39)

But one can also argue about love, and try to reason out of an uncertain or restless mood, and try to reach a state of composure. In "Progress Report," it is a report how love has progress, a change in time, and an admission that it can be different, towards a calm of mind out of frayed emotions—"My need has frayed with time." The context is nature's calm ("I can walk across the flood / Of gold silk popples on the straw-gold hills / Under a deep Californian sky that expels / All truant clouds" and "Watch squads of cattle graze / By the radio-telescope) and playful activity of animals" ("By a small bush covered gully I blundered on / Five golden fox-cubs playing in the sun") also suggestive of nature's calm and peace. Yet the mood is hesitant, it is more of assertion than of conviction, the attitude is as if it can be argued about and hence the conclusion has a touch of humour as well as irony- "But that I only mention by the way." The attitude is given to clearer argumentation in "Distressful Homonyms". The beginning is almost like an academic point—"Since for me now you have no warmth to spare / I sense I must adopt a sane and spare / Philosophy to ease a restless state." The same argumentative vein continues even when the poet thinks how love-emotions need to the composed:

...love, like the rest
Of our emotions, sometimes needs a rest.
Happiness, too, no doubt. (58)

The hesitant and uncertain mood as related to love-relationship continues in spite of emotions or arguments for or against.

In fact, the poet gives the theme of relationship a greater elaboration in the poem "Six Octets", a grouping of 6 short poems, where relationship has been viewed in the context of mixed feeling—feelings of companionship, pleasure and bliss along with such other feelings as bitterness, failure and emptiness. The poem begins with an appreciation of a woman's beauty, both physical and mental: "Lovelier / Still is that gold-shot hair, that mouth, those eyes," and "That blend of gentle whim and forcefulness," and hence the request for companionship: "May I request a glass." Thus initially it is a desire to establish relationship, slowly the desire develops towards friendship: "Hands held in friendship, hands caressed in love," and it gets linked with the joy in nature seen in the flight of birds: "While above / the patio red winged blackbirds swirl in flight." But it moves further, to a sense of happiness and bliss:

> Even this instant coffee tastes delicious
> It's drunk with pleasure and I'm drunk with bliss. (55)

At the same time there are other trends, first, a hesitant awareness of failure: "You don't love me at all? O God. O shit" and secondly, a sense of bitterness at one's incapacity to sustain oneself in balance: "Why is it true my ample self-affection / Will not suffice to buoy me in rejection?" Slowly the relationship thins and the sense of failure deepens:

> ...we talk only
> Of us, only of us, and what went wrong
> Curious, I suppose to note how our rich strong
> Companionship has thinned to this lament. (56)

The end is one of a sense of emptiness, relationship coming to a diminishing end:

> I've spoiled your mood. I'm sorry. Yes, I will
> Keep clear of you...
> ....but I know
> Too well that these diminishing chords of light
> Will be resolved to soundlessness and night. (57)

But in the last poem (poem 6) the emotional involvement related to relationship is distanced and what we note is an attempt at assessment, to understand the structure of relationship, which is not unitary, but a complex one. Thus it is both, love and bitterness, sweet and wild, and is both accepted and rejected:

> If bitterness there is, still there was love.
> What you and I have shared reminds me of

These plums that we will separately eat
For all their sourness, they are wild and sweet. (57)

The theme of relationship provides one of the basic motivations in Seth's poetry and in *Mappings* it is one of the most important aspects of total poetic strucıure, and one can note its many strands, both overt and covert. Another important dimension can be noted in many references to nature, both as an independent unit as well as linked with other aspects—as a whole, expression of a keen sensitiveness to nature and nature's beauty, almost reminiscent of 19th century English Romantic poetry, particularly of Wordsworth. Such references in *Mappings* are often marked with preciseness and concentration, and go to illustrate the main thrust of the poems. In "Sea and Desert", for example, nature is connected with the poet's contemplation of his lady:

...I have been watching you,
Your face lit in the full moon, restless, still,
As out beyond the strip of foam near the crags
Below, the moon lights up a calm yet shifting
Track on the ocean. (5)

In a "Winter World" nature is connected with personal distress: "Most cold, cold / Is this night; / ... Frost burn upon / My every bone." In "Sonnet" too, nature is linked with the 'lady':

As the slow moon coldly slopes down the sky
The pines hum to themselves and you to yourself
...and the long nights
When outside the whole world is threatening silence,
The pine is swaying in a senseless dream,
Your hand within my hand.... (15)

"Grand Canyon" provides a simple description of nature, unconnected with anything else, but connected with a place, that is, Grand Canyon. Thus this is how it is described:

Swift dawn across the falling wall below;
...and the powdered snow
Of yesterday caught in the juniper limb
Leaning wind-warped over the sheer South Rim. (16)

A similar description we also get in the poem "Rain":

> The rain drips quietly down
> The windowpane
> Through nightfall, midnight, on
> To sublit dawn. (24)

Even in the poem "After Three Years" where the reference is to a sense of decay and a changing mindset with which nature is linked, nature is seen in its own brilliance and with a quick, startling expansion:

> ...Yet at the lawn's cropped edge
> Orange azaleas flame; beyond the hedge
> The sunset reddens steeply towards North Wales. (31)

Also in "From Mount Tamalpais" where the conclusion is towards an illusory uncertainty, nature is seen in its own right, in birds' activities:

> The brown-winged hawks
> Hover and glide
> Below the rock
> While from its shade
> I watch them crest
> Over ridge and hill. (32)

And in "Aubade" we have noted how dawn is described, as in *Omar Khayyam*, precise and pointed:

> ...The smudge of dawn
> Low on the hills has shot
> The bay with light. (33)

In "Point Reyes," though the suggestion is towards realizing hope through uncertainty, yet nature is described in simple, impartial form:

> ...Through the clouds a strand
> Of light rifts down to a silvered zone of sea
> The buffeted gulls circle it uncertainly. (60)

In the poet's accounts of nature, the poem "Bagatelles" shows an interesting variation. It is a group of five short poems, and the poems differently view man's incapacity related to his mental, physical and social aspects, always with a touch of pungent irony, the purpose being to underline, how we do not understand our incapacity and gloat over it. The fifth section in 8 lines is about the sea, simply titled as, "Mere Invocation". The sea is addressed and described in epithets and words that remind us of earlier authors, such as, Homer, Shakespeare and Yeats. In each case the account has two layers, one, an overt description, and the other, a covert ironical attitude—a shy laugh against such descriptions. Thus reminding Homer: "O luminous, dark and serpent-haunted sea," reminding Shakespeare: "Incarnadined and multitudinous sea," and reminding Yeats "O dolphin-torn, O gong-tormented sea," and in frivolous terms: "O snotgreen sea, O scrotumtightening sea." The conclusion is one of irony, not at the cost of the sea, but at the cost of people who describe the sea thus: How weary of description must thou be (48).

A different preoccupation of the poet, seen again and again in the poems of *Mappings,* is a concern for self, We have already noted that in many poems. A good example is the title-poem "Mappings". There are brief references to the poem's location ("I breathe the chilled gold of late afternoon") and to nature as well ("Mallards manoeuvre through / The weedclogged crack. The hills state into blue"). But what dominates the poem is a contemplation on self—its composition, identity, development etc. The composition is wide ranging:

....As I scan
My mappings of these selves—despondent, witty
Calm and uncalm, lost in self-doubt or pity...
The courtier, soldier, scholar—I check the pieces. (62)

The identity is specific and pointed, and the list goes from the youngster to the grown-up:

That was a younger self. I want to touch
His shoulder, make him smile...

and,

....what remains when we
No longer animate the geography
O self and sense; the unassuageable urge
For ecstasy and knowledge; parting; age. (62)

The conclusion is also specific, though the reference is to development, to a developing self, yet in essence it is a continuity, where all the things combine together, "inhere in a seamless me":

> ...my wake,
> The wine, my breathing, the recovering stars,
> Venus, bright as a plane, Jupiter, Mars,
> My pulse, my vagrant selves, my poetry,
> Seem here to inhere in a seamless me. (63)

The search for self in *Mappings* is both a search and a realization. The self is poetic- self, as well as other aspects of self that have nothing much to do with poetry. What is anatomized and established is a total identity—an identity given to "poetry" as well as to other "vagrant selves", and in time and across time, in place and away from place,—a poem remarkable for its self revelation.

The search for one's own self, to identify its structure, motivations, desires and rootedness, can also be seen in two other poems, "A Morning Walk" and "Divali", which also show an additional trend towards social awareness. In the poem "A Morning Walk", the occasion is a morning walk in California where the poet stays and the immediate take-off point is the sight of a spider that rests in its web in an avocado tree, a small piece of nature:

> A web hung from the avocado tree;
> The spider rested in the dew and sun
> And looked about the grove contentedly
> Awaiting visitors. (71)

Initially the poet feels disgusted at the spider being an outsider (foreigner) on the scene, and as he wishes it to be away ("Foreigner, hence!"), his contemplation moves from a Californian spider to Indian spiders ("Our spiders") that are "thin", "spindly", "starved" and "seem perpetually anxious about dinner", and to the sudden realization that he too, is like a foreigner ("...Betrayed the web of jocularity / I had spun round me here") and also like a spider,

I draw my easy non-consumptive breath
Think life sweet, spin rhymes, eat my daily fly... (73)

an affluent being walking through 'affluent' trees (..."I wander / Among these affluent trees and stop and ponder").

In fact the poem's structure is based on two contrasting elements. One is the reality of the place he stays, a condition of affluence, and the other speculative, also a reality, of a condition of misery in his own place, away in India. The first situation is all good ("all things good").

Foods, shelter, health, are mine, interests; loves;
The time to walk through avocado groves

But the second is not so, its misery hits:

To wander through the streets of Calcutta is
To force the whole world's misery on the heart
Children on broken stumps, staring with eyes
White and opaque, begging with hardened art. (72)

The result is a re-examination of oneself, of one's predilection and complacency, and the contrasting situations are viewed with an attitude of irony:

Living abroad, I have lost sight of home,
Locked in my web I have grown happily blind
And blindly happy, and few images come
To jar fine strands of my peace of mind. (72)

Thus, it may be said, the poem "A Morning Walk" is an astute analysis of the poet's own self, and a disturbing one too, and the conditions of living in which the self inheres, in the context of social inequality and discrimination.

A similar social awareness linked with a ruminative analysis of the self, along with one's awareness of one's rootlessness could be seen also in the poem "Divali". Here the location, in contrast shifts from California to Punjab in India, and the contemplation is made from the vantage ground of "home", and in the context of a familiar festival, Divali, the festival of light and family-companionship.

...These walls, this sky
Splintered with wakes of light

These mud-lamps beaded round
The ears this festive night
These streets these voices...

The occasion of the festival, the poet points out, provides great peace of mind,

...Tonight
Below the fire-crossed sky
Of the Festival of Light
Give your soul leave to feel
What distilled peace it can. (70)

At the same time there is justifiable pride in one's own land, expressed through sensitive response to aspects of nature—a portrait of calm, relaxed companionable nature, at par with the joyful atmosphere provided by the Festival of Light:

...the winter wheat—
The flowers of Har-ki-Doon—
The Sal forests—the hills
Inflamed with rhododendron—
The first smell of the rains
On the baked earth—the peaks
Snow-drowned in permanence—
The single mountain lakes. (69)

But this is one direction—the direction in contemplating on one's own home and homeland and the feelings of joy and happiness they promote. The other direction is one of loss, unhappiness and uncertainty and of detractory forces and unwholesome changes. It first begins in a probe into history, how generations ago the poet's "father's family" lived; how also generations ago, somewhat closer in time, the family adjusted with the new dispensation, particularly the British; and how the foreign culture undermined the home culture:

And Kalidas, Sankaracharaya,
Panini, Bhaskar, Kabir,
Surdas sank, and we welcomed
The reign of Shakespeare. (67)

Secondly, the changed system threw up a "happy breed of Babus", who impervious of their own culture, indulged in slavish imitation of the Western, and the poet maintaining himself as one of the "breed":

And as I twist along
Those grooves from image to image
Violet, elm-tree, swan
Pork-pie, gable, scrimmage... (67)

he finds himself nowhere at home:

I know that the whole world
Means exile for our breed
Who are not home at home
And are abroad abroad. (68)

But an awareness of "home" remains strong with the poet, an equally strong social sense—a picture of great debility and misery—a sense that sprouted from the surrounding:

He died last week. My boys
Are starving. Daily we dig
The ground for sweet potatoes

Or,

Who will take care of me
When I am old? No one
Is left (68)

The poet calls it "the cyclic shadow-play / under the sinister sun," almost ironically at his own cost. Yet the poet continues to accept it as home, almost as a matter of strength:

This may as well be my home.
Because no other nation
Moves me thus? (69)

Thus, in spite of sense of "exile" and rootlessness, in spite of the awareness that one is the product of a diverse culture, the trend continues towards acceptance and adjustment, and towards an implied joy:

And when an alap of Marwa
Swims on slow flute-notes over
The neighbours' roofs at sunset
Wordlessly like a lover
It holds me—. (70)

Seth's contemplation on joy and happiness, on life and problems of life, on distress, loneliness and uncertainty as well as on a studied assessment of existence has taken a singular turn in the poem "Close of Play." Apparently the poem is about life and death, or more correctly, how death ends all, and hence the suggestiveness of the title. But death here is not a limited death, limited by time and place. It is a totality, the total extinction of life on earth, the occasion being nuclear explosion, the result of man's foolhardy ambition to acquire ultimate power to subdue each other. The poem "Close of Play" has fearful connotations, and has equally unnerving motivations—a poem with a singular strain in the total oeuvre of Seth's poetry, it may be noted. Though the poem has different layers of perception, one overlapping the other, yet the final perception is one of great fear, of total extinction of life, when earth will "rejoin" its fellow-planets:

> In common lifelessness, circling around
> Their mother-star in deepening entropy.

In fact the first and most important perception is towards a total extinction from which nothing escapes:

> We are the last generations. Surdas, Bach,
> Rembrandt, Du Fu, all life, love, work and worth
> Will end in the particular rain....
> ....life's sap
> May permeate a crippled grass, but we,
> 'The roof and crown of things', if such we are,
> Will be defunct. (41)

and again,

> The apple-blossomed earth will nurse its dead
> Or tortured and denatured crust, and our strain,
> For all its promise, power and prayer, will die. (43)

It is a fearsome situation, almost like one's own destiny, the poet points out, and man is largely responsible for his own undoing:

> ...Too late we perceive
> Our playthings, grown autonomous, knowledge and use,
> This practical, that ideal good at last

Rear doomtoys that will undo nine tenths of us
Leaving the leaving dead we call survivors
On a radiant waste. (42)

This is one trend, a quite substantial trend, in the structure of the poem, a trend towards death and total extinction. Reversely, the other trend, though muted, is also present, that is, the trend towards life, life's activities and life's strength, providing a wholesome dimension to the total structure of the poem. Life is and can be "good," the poet declares, and elaborates:

To sing, eat, swim, work, sleep, make love—to be
Breathing and out of pain, to have the arm
Of one's friend around one, or one's ears surrounded
By the deep quilt of music.... (43)

But the earlier strain, of death and extinction, remains as the most dominating strain in the poem, and "Close of Play" is both an exposition and a satire, of the great peril that faces mankind, which is their own doing, and from which they can escape by their concerted will and effort. Seth's continual probing into factors of life and death in *Mappings* is forcefully illustrated by "Close of Play," which, as has been said, remains as a singular and timely poem in the total oeuvre of Seth's poetry. *Mappings* was Seth's earliest poetry-collection, and though by his own admission, he was unsure about many of the poems later, and though many of the poems are of short length, yet together they advance a view of life which though on the one hand is hesitant, uncertain, and shows a deeply personal and lonely brooding, on the other, is full of joyous acceptance of life and a pleasure in living and many of the themes pursed in *Mappings,* such as love, relationship, sensitiveness to nature, sense of distress and pain, and social-awareness etc., have been further elaborated and illustrated in his subsequent volumes.

THE HUMBLE ADMINISTRATOR'S GARDEN

The Humble Administrator's Garden, dedicated "to my family, pictured within," contains 33 poems, in three sections—"Wutong", "Neem" and "Live-Oak", the names of three different trees, typically connected with the poet's differing associations, that is, China, India and America. They also suggest the poet's keen sensitiveness and intimacy with nature, which forms an important structural element in the poems here, as happened in the earlier volume too. They also continue the poet's habit of writing in rhymes, half-rhymes or in prose pattern, and with wide-ranging references though invariably with a strong personal point of view. The first poem, entitled "A Little Night Music", for example, refers to music, or more correctly, somebody playing music ("someone playing the erhu") and how the poet is drawn towards the place the music is being played. The poem begins with a reference to nature ("white walls, moonlight") and as the poet, a stranger, joins the player, he is easily welcomed, and the player continues to play:

> He pauses, tunes, and plays again.
> An hour beneath the wutong trees.... (79)

The music is for both, for "self and stranger", and the atmosphere leads the poet, in spite of differences (he, an Indian, and the player a Chinese) to a sense of commonality.

> ...as if all men
> Were brothers within the enclosing seas.

The music provides a strong sense of peace and relaxation ("The bow takes flight / And unwished tears come to my eyes").

The next two poems also, "The Master-of-Nets Garden" and "The Humble Administrator's Garden" as well as two other poems later, "The Tarrying Garden" and "A Hangzhou Garden" from the section "Wutong" have the same context each, that is, the garden and associated nature, and they project a similar attitude, that is towards peace, quiet and relaxation—almost a continuation of the first poem's projection. First, nature, as in "The Master-of-Nets Garden",

> Magnolia petals fall, pale, fragrant brown,
> Resting on moss within a square of white... (80)

then the mind moves to appreciate a whole world of fragrance —a combined fragrance of many flowers, and to a sense of quiet happiness.

> And jasmine and gardenias combine
> Their scent with that of closed magnolias.

Similarly, in "The Humble Administrator's Garden" the initial references are to nature,

> A plump gold carp nudges a lily pad
> And shakes the raindrops off like mercury. (81)

and then the quiet serenity, reminiscent of Matthew Arnold's "The Scholar Gypsy",

> He leans against a willow with a dish
> And throws a dumpling to a passing fish.

So too, in "The Tarrying Garden", an awareness of nature's aspects mix with a sense of rest and relaxation. Thus nature,

> Stand by the rock. The lotus and the fish,
> In still pale yellows, greens and fluid golds
> Startle the rainy sky.

and moving towards composing the senses to a quiet contemplation,

> The Tarrying Garden, piecemeal or entire
> Meander, tarry, amble, pause, admire. (84)

In "A Hangzhou Garden" the picture of the garden is brief and pointed, but the total movement is slow and relaxed.

> Wisteria twigs, wisteria leaves, mauve petals
> Drift past a gold-fish ripple. As it settles
> Another flower drops. Below, readily,
> The fish meander through the wisteria tree. (100)

In fact an awareness of nature's aspects, and resultant feelings of rest and relaxation can be seen in many poems of "Wutong" section—might have been inspired, one may surmise, because of the traditional contemplative Chinese conditions, where 'temples' abound. For example, the poem "Nanjing Night", that gives an account of the place, of students, of people, as well as references to nature and to the poet's 'dreams'. Thus first, the place, the condition of weather and nature:

> Full moon, the Nanjing walls, bicycle bells.
> Two children huddle in the 10 O'clock crowd
> Against the plunging cold...

and,

> It is the last month—the yellow plum is in bloom. (86)

A fine poem to that effect is "The Accountant's House". The context is the visit of the poet to the house of the accountant to clear up his income and expenditure account on the last day of his sojourn in China. In addition to the accountant there are references to his wife and two daughters ("His wife and two daughters smile as I come in") and also to the son who "died last Spring Festival",

> No one knows how he died. He came home from play
> And his head was hot, his nose bled, and he died.

The poem begins with a subdued reference to time and nature:

> We go in the evening to the accountant's house,
> It is dark and the road is slush.
> The fireflies flick silver.
> The ash flicked off by my companion, the barefoot doctor, is gold. (88)

The poet's account is routine, tone detached and observation disinterested. But what dominates the poem is a sense of deep pathos—naturalness of life and courage to hold on in spite of adversity:

> Yet they laugh, yet they laugh, these lovely people
> And he clicks his abacus and she gives me a towel and the two girls
> Smile shyly.... (89)

From a routine visit in connection with income and expenditure we move towards a point where differences in time and place are forgotten, and we realize how ordinary man lives through death and grows a healthy capacity to face it—a move towards peace and composure of the mind.

Similarly, in the poem "Research in Jiangsu Province", another fine poem, routine research details bring in human points of woe, happiness and the capacity to live through adversity. The poem begins with the detached routine questions related to the poet's research:

> The question bore in. How much is
> The cost and area of the house?
> I see you have two sons. Would you
> Prefer to have had a daughter too?
> And do your private plots provide
> Substantial income on the side?

The academic exercise mingles with the real misery of the common living:

> Forty square metres, sixteen cents.
> To save us from the elements.
> Miscarriage. Pickle with rice-gruel
> Three times a week. Rice-straw for fuel.

And the poet's attitude is one of the irony and disgust:

> Birth and fertility projections,
> Plans based on need and predilections.
> Oh needful numbers, and half true,
> Without you what would nations do?

The reality contrasts with that else which is only a speculative exercise and the irony leads to the realization of deep human sorrow and misery that lie underneath:

> And Mrs. Gao herself whose voice
> Is captive on my tape may choose
> Sometime when tapes and forms are far
> To talk about the Japanese war,
> May mention how her family fled,
> And starved, and bartered her for the bread,
> And stroke her grandson's head.... (90–92)

It is not just a contrast, here too, as in the earlier poem, reality supersedes all other details—a reality that also provides capacity to man, irrespective of where he is, to live through adversity, and hence Mrs. Gao's probable statement that, "such things could not occur today."

Two other poems from "Wutong"—"From a Traveller" and "A Little Distance", deal with companionship and communication, where past memory is linked with present reality and where emotions expressed are twofold. One is an assumption of intimacy, hence feelings of joy and happiness.

The other is a sense of distance, the extent of difference that has built up, hence feelings of longing and despair. And in each nature provides the background, and the structure of tone becomes both intimate and detached. "From a Traveller" begins with a reference to rural nature.

> The willows cut across the commune fields.
> Smoke pours from stacks, across persimmon trees.
> The afternoon light....

Though the reference is casual, it provokes the poet's emotion ("Provoke the familiar nostalgia of travellers"). In fact the trend is set by the communication received by the poet:

> Thank you for writing (again) and for the poem.
> It came a week ago and has been with me since.
> It made me happy. (94)

The rest is the poet's answer. First, the quality of the poem received ("Latinate and resonant, the words precisely lofted"). Secondly, a sensitive account of "Fall loveliness" at Nanjing ("The acorns, chestnuts and small sprouts of oak / On the unneedled ground beneath the pines / And a few pine-rats (squirrels) scampering around"). Thirdly, a throw back in memory (That those few days we spent in each other's company / in San Francisco,") where the observations register in detail ("I remember you in tastes—ice-cream, garlic soup, cinnamon rolls, pate"). But going back in memory was not that happy for the poet ("And I suppose it worried me, this affinity and ours") and he was unsure what it would be to revive the companionship together ("How would we face each other when I returned / Or revive those Vivaldian Beach-Boyish days / Endless summer...."). In fact the poet is aware of both "levity and gravity" of their "bond" and in spite of assertions his emotions remain divided and unfixed:

> And most of what I say is still inchoate
> Or irrelevant or evasive, take at least
> The 'I like you' you once skillfully prised from me
> As indefensible and true. (97)

"From a Traveller" is a perceptive study of relationship which may sustain or may not sustain. But the awareness that it is there, and can be recalled and relived, is strength by itself and nourishes the mind in spite of misgivings and hesitations.

In "A Little Distance" the sense of distance is used to link the past "companionable" days with the present reality, a reliving of intimacy that is no more, yet it remains:

> Just friends, reverting to a richer vein
> To what we were the way that we once were
> The way I hope, for a while, we may remain. (98-99)

The recollection of the past is one of excitement and pleasure—"You lie, beautiful, half-nude on the white pebbles, / Cream-coloured breasts open to the breeze and the sky." But the present reality is not so, the emotion is hushed, detached and the tone has a thin longingness for the past—"We do not / Even kiss goodnight yet wake to friendliness / It is perhaps the tiredness in my mind / Or the fear of a structure set." Thus the structure of the poem has elements of joy and hope along with despair and loss. The references to nature in the beginning suggest an easy intimacy and movement—a helpful background to human action:

> ...And near it azaleas grow
> And the shadows of thin fish fall
> Across the speckled stones, and a light breeze blows.

But that is not the case at the end. The nature continues to be the same, continues to provide the background. But the function is not one of nearness; the tone is detached, distanced:

> ...And the slopes
> That circumscribes our peace, and the warmth of the sun
> Melting us into the stones, and the azaleas
> Mauve against a sea of pine. (99)

The poet's emotions get "circumscribed", and he grows a sense of "unsettledness" ("Unsettledness / Is, what I have come to fear"). Yet the awareness of a point of happiness in the past, and reliving that point, is a matter of strength, and the term "a little distance" is metaphorically both a distance and not much of a distance.

Though the poems of the next section, that is "Neem" section, make references to India, yet they continue trends similar to that we have seen in the earlier one. Thus considerations of relationship and to what extent that can develop towards peace and relaxation of mind is an important factor. Then there are references to nature and to the passage of time. And then there are human details, references to family and juxtapositions of both intimate and detached tones. A few poems would be illustrative of our points. The poem "The Comfortable Classes at Work and Play", for example, as the title suggests is the picture of an affluent family in Delhi. The poem describes in detail the routine activities of the family ("at work and play") along with an eye on nature, and also with mild sarcasm. The poem begins with references to nature that provide the content to the account of the family that follows. Initially it is an open, free nature of flowers, little animals and birds, and the atmosphere is one of easy movement and contentment:

> Seven satbhai-champas chatter and burble below the bignonia trellis,
> The rat-ki-rani and malati and harsingar mingle their scent....
> While mynas frolic at the edge of the mango's shade
> And parrots flash across the sky. (107)

It is apparently the atmosphere of a garden, however free, and slowly the exact picture of the garden is conjured up, a garden trimmed and arranged. First the "peacocks" strutting,

> And down the lanes and across the garden hedges
> The peacocks themselves, turquoise-necked, turquoise-breasted....
> Walk primly to our neighbour's houses and ours. (107)

Next, the "pruned" nature of the garden,

> He prunes the rose the hedge, the champa, the two
> Lentana elephants....

And lastly, a leisured relaxation, in the midst of the garden,

> To walk, after drinking ginger tea against the chill...
> Or to sit on the large white swing
> And swing and stare or read. (108)

Thus the nature sets the tone and atmosphere, the context and entry into the family—the account of family members in their respective singularities. They are: (1) the elder son, with his apparent interest in music and dog ("And mumbles a snatch of Lalit, then hums and lapses... / To run Oscar down the red path / As far as the white-washed gate"), (2) the younger son, with his fads and girlfriend ("His girlfriend is feminist, and he is feminist"), (3) the daughter, with her socialization and sociology ("Immersed in sociology and social visits / Paid her at any hour by many friends"), (4) the mother, with her interest in law ("The mother takes a volume in half-calf / From off the wall, and wrestle with the judgement"), (5) the father, with his, interest in politics ("Inveighing against politicians and corruption") and (6) the grand mother, with her unhappiness against the restrictions put on her ("And complains that she is ignored, unloved / Her blood pressure is high, her spirits low / She is not allowed to eat gulabjamuns").

The accounts are given with sympathy, with a tone both familiar and detached, and with a tongue in the cheek attitude, with both humour and irony—humour in such a picture as the grandmother's and irony at the obsessions of the father and the mother. In fact, the whole picture of the family beginning with the suggestiveness of the title and the atmosphere provided by the circumscribed nature is one of humour and mild sarcasm—a mild sarcastic account how affluent people live in Delhi with their fads and superficiality, in comfort no doubt, but without much connection with the realities. In a way the poem can be compared with two other poems from *Mappings*; "Departure Lounge" and "Divali," where the poet speaks respectively, first, about his own relationship with his father, and secondly, about his own self vis-à-vis his family. The seriousness and the link related to the poet himself established in the earlier poems do not form a part of the poetic-structure here. It has different motivations and attitude—a type of seriousness joined with levity and not without sympathy and understanding, and one may say, with a social awareness how people in the upper crust of the society live. At the end we are again back to nature—again a garden, the Lodi Gardens, a famous one, where "Joggers thump", "Vultures nest," and "Arab domes" sit, "formed and fine" against the "exquisite morning sky," and,

> And neem and semal, ashok and amaltas
> And casuarinas lend the air freshness, the heart peace.

That is the poem's forte—moving from a mild sarcastic social account it goes on to show how a link can be established between the human beings and the nature, which would ultimately be beneficial to the former.

The next poem "From the Babur-nama: Memoir of Babur, First Moghul Emperor of India" is also a study of relationship but in a different vein, as among the human beings. We have seen how this forms an important preoccupation with Seth, the earliest of which was seen in "Departure Lounge". The present poem also deals with that and can be linked with the earlier poem "From the Memoirs of Babur, First Moghul Emperor of Hindustan", from *Mappings*. The earlier poem was a tale of endurance, the journey of Babur towards India through extremely inhospitable terrain. ("They had not found a soul / No sign of settlement / No wandering tribesmen, hill / On hill... and through snow and wind" ("That evening the wind blew / So sharply through the fierce / And fearsome drifts of snow"). But finally it was his endurance and determination that won, and he could find shelter in spite of extreme odds—"Thus we moved / From the inhuman cold / Into the warmth of the cave / Where all at length were safe."

The structure of the present poem is more elaborate. It is a fine, detached, yet intimate account related to the journey, the place and the purpose. The style, like the earlier "Babur" poem, is narrative, and tone impersonal, and there are frequent comments on the people of "Hindustan"; on animals, birds, particularly peacocks; and on kingship, and the intensity of father-son relationship. At the same time the poem has many human details as well as details about the surrounding, and on the whole its attitude is to evolve a good, disciplined, moralistic living. The poem has five Sub-sections. The first Section is given to a narration of Babur's young days, his young passion and love, and his state of mind thereto:

Sometimes, afflicted, I would roam alone
Over the mountains and deserts, sometimes I wandered
From street to street, in suburbs and in gardens. (114)

The second Section is given to an account of the journey ("At dawn we left the stream and resumed our march"), with references on the way to a garden ("I set down on a hillock on every side / The garden lay before me, shaped into beds. / Yellow on one side, the purple another / Laid out in hexagon exquisitely") to a drinking party ("On Saturday we had a drinking party") and to a peculiar situation arising out of the killing of a snake. Then the attention is changed, and is diverted to India. First it is a very disparaging and negative account of "Hindustan":

Hindustan is a land of meagre pleasures,
The people are not handsome....
They have no spirit, no comprehension, kindness
Or fellow-feeling—no inventiveness
In handicraft or skill in design—no method,
Order principle, rule in work or thought. (115)

Secondly, there are some good words about a "splendid bird", that is, peacock, particularly its colour and beauty:

... Its size is that of the crane.
The head of the male has an iridescent lustre;
His neck is a fine blue, his back is rich
With yellows, violets, green and blues and stars
Extend to the very extremity of his tail. (116)

The third Section is a reflective-meditative one, on life and death (reminiscent of *Omar Khayyam*), on life's powers, on fame and courage, as well as on purpose and determination. Thus on mortality:

Who ever tastes the feast of life must drink
The cup of death. The traveler at the inn
Of mortality sooner or later leaves
That house of sorrow, the world. (116)

On fame: "Let me have fame, since Death has my body"; on courage: "Should we now die the death of martyrs", on steadiness of mind: "Let us all swear then not to turn from battle / Nor desert the slaughter ensuing until we die." The fourth and fifth Sections together constitute the longest portion of the poem. They deal differently with Babur-Humayun relationship. First, the father's concern for his son ("To Humayun, whom I long to see, much health"), also the concern for the child born to his son ("To you a child, to me an object of love"), and gratefulness to God—"God from his grace and bounty has accomplished / Most unprecedentedly all our desires." Secondly, the father speaks of his son's invasions and injects courage and determination into his son—"This is the time to expose yourself to danger / Exert yourself, and meet things as they come / For indolence sits ill with royalty", and advises him to be liberal at heart—"Six parts are always yours, and five Kamrau's / Remember this, the great are generous." Thirdly, the father's advice to his son how to write a letter correctly and gracefully, about style, spelling, diction etc., (almost, one may say, Seth's own idea of how a piece to be composed well).

> ...write
> From now on, clearly, using words that cost
> Less torment both to your reader and to you.

Fourthly, the wealth of joy the son provides to his father: "His presence made / our hearts blossom like rosebuds, and our eyes, shine / like torches", and the high esteem with which the father holds his son: "...his conversation held / An inexpressible charm, and he realized / For me the very type of the perfect man." Lastly, the father's great sacrifice for his son—the story told how Babur sacrificed his own life for that of his son, taking up his illness to himself:

> I entered the chamber where my son was lying
> And circled his bed three times, saying each time,
> I take upon myself all that you suffer. (120)

In the poems of "Live-Oak" Section, a total 12, the poet generally reverts to California. But the earlier themes, more or less, continue, that is, the concern with aspects of the relationship and nature, as well as with such feelings as towards rest and tranquility on the one hand, and distress and destruction on the other. Then there are references to memory, to social situations, and to realities of life and death. The first poem, for example, "Curious Mishaps", is illustrative of a "mishap", how tranquility is cut by violence—interplay of life and death, what Wordsworth called nature in "tooth and claw". The reference is to a situation where a squirrel ("A squirrel came to look at me") was unexpectedly caught by an owl (..."and with a hybrid cry/— Half-dog, half-pigeon—fell upon his prey"). In a way, both the squirrel and the pigeon played their natural part. But the reaction on the poet is different—a reaction occasioned by the sudden interplay of life and death: "I stood too stunned to move / Indoors, or to continue clipping nails."

But such sentiments are muted in other poems, where the more expressed trend is towards feelings of rest and tranquility and towards aspects of relationship. Thus in the poem "Song: Coast Starlight", in rhymes and song, reminiscent of Tennyson, we have the reference to a journey and the poet's exultation that it is coming to a restful end,

> ...the Coast Starlight
> Will get me to the City by tonight
> Will get me to the City and my friend
> Will get me to my month-long journey's end
> Even references to nature provide an atmosphere of rest,
> The cattle rest among the mustard flowers,
> The Starlight circles past the prison towers.
> The golfers pull their carts along the green.
> The blackbird flies across the deep ravine.

At the end, the sense of restfulness goes beyond the desires of an individual and is expanded towards a general realization.

> Now darkness falls—the moon gives little light
> O Starlight, ride into the gentle night.
> O travellers, may Starlight see you home.
> O travellers, may you not sleep alone. (124-125)

The desires for rest and companionship also provide motivation in the next poem "From California", where emphasis is put on relationship and how it survives through time. The present situation leads to past memories, and both are seen side by side, and provide strength to the awareness of a human relationship that continues from the past to the present through fragments of memory. The poem begins with familiar pictures of home, suggestive of relaxed rest:

> Sunday night in the house.
> The blinds drawn, the phone dead.
> The sound of the kettle, the rain.
> Supper: cheese, celery, bread.
> Then memory sips in,
> All that I thought had slipped
> Through the sieve of long absence
> Is here with me again?

and the past details, of place and person, are recreated,

> The long stone walls, the green
> Hillsides renewed with rain.
> The way you would lick you finger.
> And touch your forehead....
> and then recollection of love and companionship;
> I walk with you again.
> Along those settled trails... (126-128)

Thus the present reality is aided by the recollection of the past, however fitful and temporary that may be, and metaphorically speaking becomes like the "parched" land being aided by rain ("The random rain outside / Rejuvenates the parched / Foothills along the bay"). The emotions, thus recollected, the poet points out, comes through time without passion ("The lack of hope or faith"), yet it becomes a part of experience and a matter of strength: "(Anaesthetized by years / I think of you today / ...Still worth my present while").

References to California can also be seen in the next poem "Between Storms", where in the context of nature's change, an awareness of distress and destruction is on the one hand and awareness for beauty and tranquility on the other could be seen arranged to present a personal point of view of joy and sorrow. The first references are to the working of an angry nature and the resultant condition of destruction:

> ...continual storms
> On California have washed away
> Houses, gouged the coastline,
> Stranded away walkers in aberrant waves...

A second storm which is predicted at night also brings in a lingering sense of distress ("And hears the squirrels chatter in distress"). But in the afternoon, after the storm, the incoming light brings in a sense of great joy:

> ...And transfigures
> Books, computer print-outs,
> The wooden seal the fruit sellers gave me,
> And my blue plastic poncho.
> Beautiful, beautiful light,
> Heavy as honey... (131)

Thus the two different situations related to nature, one of distress and the other of joy, also provide two different mindsets to the poet, one of a stunned condition ("And left a limpness in my brain"), and the other of a happy relaxation ("Drawing from the heart a music"). The change in nature mingles with the poet's changing attitudes, and the poem as a whole, a precisely, briefly organized piece, is a good example of the poet's frequent dependence on nature and on nature's frame to illustrate his own point of view.

The poem "Spring of Content" is another good example, where, as the title suggests, the trend is towards a sense of fulfilment and contentment. and that is aided by nature. From the beginning the nature indicates a change towards a throbbing fresh life:

> ...it has grown fresh and still,
> The blond hills have turned green...
> The ophthalmologist's almond tree is full
> No, swathed with frost-fine blossom, and the scent.

At the end the nature leads to the poet's mental condition and his attitude:

> ...And I lie hours
> Cat-curled and narcoleptic on the lawn
> And think of nothing—

This is the condition of complete relaxation, which is not disturbed by any extraneous consideration, not even by the memory of the past relationship ("not even that you are away"). Thus the nature provides the background, the frame, as well as motivation.

The next poem, "Moonlight" has similar motivation and point of view. But it is differently organized. The nature, though initiator, plays a minor role, and a greater emphasis is put upon the relationship that is no longer tenable as before. First, the nature—the moonlight's reference is brief and pointed: "Through pylons, as before, the moon tonight / Sears with a fire...," and again—"Most things have lost their power to hurt. A few / Exceptions, moonlight...." But the references to relationships are completely presented. First, how it was built up:

> It's I who built this bleached cairn, stone by stone
> The first time that you spoke to me by phone,
> Walks, Wordsworth, woodpeckers, Colombian heights...

Secondly, the present pain:

> I listen to the road outside. Despite
> Years, despite years, tears blur my steadied sight.

Thirdly, the feeling of a helpless acceptance of depression:

> I know there is not much I can do.
> I know that they will pass, somehow, somehow.

Fourthly, the wish that the lady ("my love of many years") should take the situation peacefully:

> I wish you what you have already, rest
> Of spirit.

And lastly, the conclusion that the memory of relationship is of no consideration—to both of them:

> ...to you memory appears
> Too little worth analysis or tears
> In my heart too I will if not to last. (135-136)

Thus, the moonlight that is a simple description at one point moves beyond it to acquire a complex presence related to emotions vis-à-vis human relationship.

The reference to moon, to moonlight, to sorrow related to memory and the capacity to overcome that, could be seen in another poem of "Live-Oak" section, with an interesting title, "Ceasing upon the Midnight," strongly reminiscent of Keats's famous line "To cease, upon the midnight with no pain" from "Ode to a Nightingale". Keats's references to life and death, and how the richness of one could help him to overcome the sorrows of the other, also forms a similar pattern in Seth's poem, except that in Seth it is tinged with irony and with a certain amount of casualness, joined with the details of a family surrounding. Initially the references are to household items, a routine list:

> The phone rings; he turns to reply,
> A smell of burning comes
> From somewhere. Something hums,
> The fridge....
> Then the awareness of nature—alive and bright:
> He walks outside. The breeze
> Blows warmly, and he sees
> A sky brushed clean of dust and haze.

The nature's aliveness, in contrast, brings in the memory, now relived unhappily ("Ah, tonight, / How rich it seems to be / Alive unhappily"). The sense of unhappiness provides the motivation — the desire to be free of memory ("...its force will rinse / The pus of memory from his mind, / Dispel the dust he's swept behind...") and to live freely and richly, in oneself, as well as linked with nature:

> He gets a bottle, pours a glass....
> Holds up its colour to the moon,
> Drinks slowly, listens to the tune
> The branches improvise,
> Drinks, pours, drinks, pours, and lies
> Face down on the moist grass and drinks
> The dewdrops off its leaves....

The poet speaks of three "shields" that protect him from the memory's "meandering"—wine ("alcohol"), nature ("the clear and intimate air") and poetry ("the rules of metre"). Hence the suggestiveness of the title "to cease upon the midnight with no pain" as in Keats "rich to die" is viewed differently, not ceasing at all, which would be a "joke":

...To cease upon
The midnight under the live-oak
Seems a too derisory a joke.

And the end is sound sleep and restfulness:

The bottle lies on the ground.
He sleeps. His sleep is sound. (142–45)

ALL YOU WHO SLEEP TONIGHT

All You Who Sleep Tonight has five Sub-sections, a total 53 poems, including 20 poems, 4 lines each, entitled "Quatrains". The other Sub-sections are, (1) "Romantic Residue" (9 poems), (2) "In Other Voices" (5 poems), (3) "In Other Places" (9 poems), and (4) "Meditations of the Heart" (10 poems). The structural trends are similar to what we have seen earlier, in the earlier poems, such as, related to love and relationship, to nature; and to feelings of distress, pain and death at one level, and happiness, playfulness and a sense of relaxation on the other. At the same time there is strong social awareness along with the mind's capacity to be reflective about situations, and to accept distress etc., as a part of one's living. The first poem "Round and Round", details a real situation, leading to the memory of relationship and again back to reality, in a rhyming pattern. It begins with the reference to a tiresome flight ("long and wretched")—"where babies wept and tempers shattered / And the plane lurched and whisky splattered," and flight over, at the destination, the poet comes to do the last routine job—to claim his bags from Baggage Claim. This is the first phase where the poet sticks to reality—the reality of a flight. The second phase begins at the Baggage Claim, where a throw-back in memory, arising from the sight of a "red and small" suitcase circling in the carousal, leads to a relationship in a similar situation—"I knew that bag. It must be hers / We hadn't met in seven years" and,

And as the steel plates, squealed and clattered
My happy memories chimed and chattered. (151)

But the end, that is, the third phase, is an anticlimax as well as an awareness how time moves and shatters both dreams and relationship—a coming back to the hard realities of the present when the "red and small" suitcase is pulled off:

> An old man pulled it off the Claim.
> My bags appeared; I did the same. (151)

The irony is obvious, and the quiet acceptance of the situation too, where almost imperceptibly, the happiness of memory merges with the distress of the present reality, and the young age melts into the old age in an awareness of time's passage.

Love and relationship, both the past and present, form an important aspect of most of the poems of the Sub-section "Romantic Residue". For example, in the poem "Protocols" the intimacy of a past love is contrasted with the distress of the present "broken" love—"Now that the facts are plain, the placid surface cracked. / The protocols of friendship broken," and in a linked reference to nature the poet wishes warmth and happiness to her independent of whatever may be his distress:

> May the sun burn away these footprints on the lawn
> And hold you in its warmth and keeping. (152)

Similarly in another short poem, "Across", the poet tries to keep his distress subdued, and views his love detachedly, from a distance, and wishes the lady well ("Across these miles I wish you well / May nothing haunt your heart but sleep"). Or in "Mistaken" the love between the two people, between the poet and the lady, is seen in a perspective, and is considered as a mistake on both their parts:

> ...And by and by
> We found we had been mistaken, all the while
> From that first glance, that first mistaken smile. (156)

Or in "Sit", while the lady is requested to give company for a while ("Sit, drink your coffee here; your work can wait a while"), the poet thinks, however temporary, it could be a panacea in a distressing world:

> The world is too opaque, distressing, and profound.
> This twenty minutes' rendezvous will make my day. (157)

Or in "The Room and the Street", the poet refers to an occasion of brief meeting and a parting, ("After a few short bars / You stop and look at me, / The last of our few hours / Is over. I am free") and considers their earlier relationship to have changed ("I see my younger grief / Accusing with your eyes / I cannot give relief / Nor can you give me lies") and shows how his love-emotion have become hesitant and uncertain:

> ... It's true
> That I may have light feet
> I'm not in love with you
> And yet with half my heart
> I wish I were— (159)

The poem "Walk", that also refers to love, has some distinct aspects. The occasion was a walk at night by the side of the "old" familiar "house":

> I walked last night with my old friend.
> Past the old house where we first met. (160)

The time, as the poet said, was "night", the place lonely, and the weather bad ("The moon shone, and the path was wet. / No one passed by us as we strolled") and these aspects of the situation got transferred to the mental conditions of the walkers—"...Though hand in hand / We did not speak. Our hands grew cold." Finally, the poet accepts all that—time's passage and the change in time, and admits how their relationship had been adversely affected:

> We did not deal in words or tears,
> At the dead light we did not rage
> What change had crept through our forked years
> We did not have the will to gauge. (160)

In the poem "Equals" a similar diffident mood continues. In the beginning the references to nature suggest a "still", inactive atmosphere:

> The sun has set behind the fogbound hill.
> The breeze has died, even the jays are silent.
> The lake is still.

This inert condition gets related to the mind:

> I sit down. I am tired.
> To speak my mind's beyond my power to do...

And the final impression as related to emotions and relationship is one of "cold" and distant:

> The concrete slab is cold. The arcing stars
> Pass too high overhead for easy grasping
> Even if ours. (155)

In "A Style of Loving", which as the title suggests, is about a "style" of love, the account is slightly different, not so much given to a mood of diffidence or uncertainty, as to an analysis of the same. The poem, like many other poems earlier, begins with references to nature, to a sunset time, a fading time:

> Light now restricts itself
> To the top half of trees;
> The angled sun
> Slants honey-coloured rays
> That lessen to the ground....

This is suggestive also of a fading time in love, and the poet refers to a condition of placidity they have reached in "years", and to routine activities in their relationship, short of sexual consummation:

> Picnic, movie, ice-cream
> Talk; to clear my head
> Hot buttered rum—coffee for you;
> And so not to bed

This is an account of the relationship of love, but the poet also goes to make an analysis of it, in a somewhat detached and impersonal tone, expressing a new dimension:

> And so we have set the question
> Aside, gently.
> Were we to become lovers
> Where would our best friends be? (153)

The poems from the Sub-section, "In Other Voices" are all third-person poems as against first-person we have often noted in Seth's poetry. That is, they are based either on a situation or an occasion and narrated by a person other than the poet and the content and conclusion grow out of those narrations. Comparable poems narrated earlier were two poems related to

Babur and the 'Memoirs' of Babur, from *Mappings* and *The Humble Administrator's Garden,* respectively. The present poems are, "Lithuania: Question and Answer", that relates the experiences of a rabbi and the brutality of Hitler's troops; "Work and Freedom" that relates the experiences of a Commandant in Auschwitz Camp; "Ghalib: Two Years After the Mutiny" is related to the poet Ghalib; "A Doctor's Journal Entry for August 6, 1945," related to the devastation caused by atom bomb; and "Soon", the soliloquy of a person on death-bed. Structurally the poems have almost a common trend—to express feelings related to pain, distress, devastation and death, variously linked with socio and socio-political awareness.

The poem "Lithuania: Question and Answer" narrates a situation that took place in Lithuania, during the Nazi atrocities in the Second World War, in connection with a Jewish woman who was raped by the Nazi troops, and who had tattooed on her arm "whore for Hitler's troops". The question arose whether in view of this it was done by consent or by force, and whether the woman's husband was religiously permitted to take her back. The poem begins with the Rabbi's narration of the case, whom the woman had come pleading for support—"She came to me / Eyes asking mercy. Tell me what to do." The Rabbi considers the case, the pros and cons, and comes to a conclusion—"This leads to the conclusion in this case / That she was forced." This is the first part of the poem—the Rabbi's judgement. The second part is the Rabbi's own deliberation about a commonly accepted social stigma, which, as for him should not be accepted as a stigma in such cases, which unfortunately some people do—"I know that some men have divorced such wives / Alas for us this happens in our times." The third part has broader dimensions that point to a strong socio-political distress and provides the point of view of the writer, where the narration sheds off its impersonal pattern and becomes a serious contemplation on human habits and activities. First, it is an intense anger against Nazi atrocities, and in general, by implication, all such atrocities and crime against humanity, taking place irrespective of time and place.

> ...yet we shall see
> The fall of the transgressors from whose face
> Is blotted any human semblance—wolves,
> Beasts of the forest and voracious wolves....

Secondly, the indictment is taken out of its social and political orbit and moves to a religious one, where the God's protection is assured for His faithful:

> Sing aloud, O you nations, of His people;
> For he avenges the blood of His servants, and
> Renders revenge upon His adversaries. (164)

Thus the poem "Lithuania: Question and Answer" has a number of dimensions, social, political as well as religious, and puts further the writer's point of view, how best man can live as a sentient being in spite of atrocious situations. The poem's narrative, conversational style shows a free flexible manner, and an elastic easy tone of both detachment and involvement.

The poem, "Work and Freedom" also relates to Nazi brutalities and to the infamous Auschwitz camp, where thousands were systematically exterminated. The account is through a third person, the Commandant in charge of the camp, and through his psychological response, in retrospect. First, there was a touch of irony, at his involvement in the work: "In Auschwitz truly / I had no reason to complain of boredom." Next, the horror of the situation—"The fire-pits, crematoriums, or gas chambers." Then how the horror affected him mentally,

> I would ride my horse till the terrible picture faded...
> At home my thoughts, often and with no warning.
> Turned to such things.
> and the mental restlessness related to the work done—
> How long will our happiness last? I was not happy
> Once the mass exterminations had started. (165)

As a parallel strain, in contrast to the camp's horror and death, there are references to his family, a unit of comfort and happiness: "My wife and children, true, were well looked after / Her garden was a paradise of flowers." ...Each Sunday / We'd walk to the stables, never omitting two kennels / Where the dogs were kept." Even the family's small kindness vis-à-vis the prisoners was a part of this happiness:

> My wife would have loved to give the prisoners presents
> And as for the children, they begged for cigarettes for them.

The contrast is also seen in two mental set-ups, the Commandant's and his wife's:

> My wife said, 'Think of us, not only the service.'
> How could she know what lay so heavily on me? (166)

Thus the use of the word "freedom" at the end ("But in the end I was glad to gain my freedom") is ambiguous, because the Commandant's freedom from his "excessive sense of duty" as well as from his "tasks and troubles" is not really possible, and the "freedom" is more in desires than in reality. Though apparently there is a veneer of sympathy, the implication of irony is pointed and telling. Seen from the angle of a person, an agent of Nazi brutalities, it is on the one hand a condemnation of the same brutalities, and on the other, a reference to a general proposition how man suffers mentally and at the same time, tries to be released from it.

The man's suffering—physical, social, political as well as mental, are all highlighted in the next poem "Ghalib, Two Years after the Mutiny". The reference is to a well-known political situation of resistance, suffering, torture and death—a whirligig of both heroism and destruction, and to a famous poet and his pain, loneliness and suffering. The poem is in the form of a letter, from Ghalib to his friend, Yusuf Mirza, and from the beginning it lists the poet's grief and sorrow ("Men have gone mad from cares far less than those I fight") and his helplessness ("What do I claim?— / For death, for parting, for my livelihood, my name"). It is an extremely dismal situation—politically ("I leave aside the stricken Moghal court") as well as socially, at the level of the family:

> Your uncle; Ashur Beg; and Mir Nasir-ud-din;
> My sister's grandson too, a mere child of nineteen;
> Mustafa Khan; his sons; the blood flows from my pen.

It is helplessness and grinding poverty, the poet's plight of loneliness, old age, sickness and the desire to be effective—pitiable picture of a great poet in throes of misery:

> Nor is my time my own. I have grown old. How can
> I bear this load? I am no giant but a man.
> I leave my sickbed; try to sit an hour or two
> To write, to plan, to think—but there's too much to do. (167)

The poet is aware of his poverty ("As for sustaining wine, my cash won't spill that far"), the negligence that is meted out to him ("They used to call me once. Will they do so again?"). Yet he persists in his desire to be effective in spite of all odds:

> I'm sending you an ode about my life, which night
> And day for two long months I've sweated blood to write.

That is the poet's strength—his creative ability that triumphs over his pain, distress and death:

> Another twenty months, and I too will be dust:
> My body to Rampur, my soul to light, I trust.
> What grief, joy, praise or shame afflict me in this spell
> I will find strength to face. Goodbye, May all be well. (168)

Thus the point of view is one of sustenance, as in the earlier two poems, so too here, it is the man's own strength, creative or otherwise, that can face extreme adversity and yet can remain in tact. The style too, as earlier, is conversational, elastic and like intimate communication.

Suffering related to a situation of complete destruction and devastation is seen in the poem, "A Doctor's Journal Entry for August 6, 1945". The situation refers to the dropping of atom bomb on Hiroshima, in 1945, as a result of which Japan surrendered and the Second World War came to an end. Seth has also another poem related to extreme dangers of nuclear explosions and their devastating effects on life as a whole on earth. The poem is "Close of Play" from *Mappings,* which we have already discussed. But the present poem is a specific one, and refers to the situation when the first atom bomb was dropped in Hiroshima. The narration is by a third person, a doctor on the spot, who narrates his devastating experiences. The context is calm, peaceful:

> The morning stretched calm, beautiful, and warm
> Sprawling half-clad, I gazed out at the form
> Of shimmering leaves and shadows.

Then it "suddenly" happened and "startled" him ("Suddenly a strong flash, then another, startled me"). Initially, it was a groping—what it could be? ("I saw the old stone lantern brightly lit, Magnesium flares?"...). Immediately after it was a matter of great devastation:

> The roof, the walls and, as it seemed, the world
> Collapsed in timber and debris, dust swirled
> Around me...
> A house standing before us tilted, swayed,
> Toppled and crashed. Fire sprung up in the dust,
> Spread by the wind. (169-171)

The general condition of devastation also affected the individual, first, physically—"A splinter jutted from my mangled thigh, / My right side bled, my cheek was torn," and then mentally, leading to an unnerving mental condition. First, panic—"Scared for my life, / I called out, panic-stricken, to my wife, / Pale, bloodstained, frightened, Yecko-san emerged." Then the vision of a place where dead and dismembered persons move, almost like that of hell:

> I saw the shadowy forms of people, some
> Were ghosts, some scarecrows, all were wordless, dumb—
> Arms stretched straight out, shoulder to dangling hand.

The situation is reminiscent of Eliot's such situation in *Little Gidding* also with a reference to a bomb-attack:

> In concord at this intersection time
> Of meeting nowhere, no before and after
> We trod the pavement in a dead patrol.

In Seth it is both—a complete physical devastation brought by the first-ever nuclear explosion in the world, and secondly, a complete mental anguish resulting thereto, and complete suffering, a tearful "silence" without any mitigation:

The face of an old woman on the ground
Was marred with suffering, but she made no sound.
Silence was common to us all. I heard
No cries of anguish, or a single word. (171)

But the fact that such things could be recalled, after a gap of time, and that too impersonally, detachedly, in a narrative style, shows the strength of human strength even to withstand the worst of calamities that may ever happen—a throw-back to his earlier poem "Close of Play" which also speaks of many strengths of life. Seth also refers explicitly to this strength:

My breath was short, but bit by bit my strength
Seemed to revive, and I got up at length
I was still naked, but I felt no shame... (170)

"A Doctor's Journal" is one of Seth's finest poems, that show a great calamity, its implications, and how that can be fought over—a situation which is local as well as universal.

The last poem of the Sub-section "Soon", in contrast to the earlier poems has no specific situation or a frame of narration. There is, of course, a situation, a person in death-bed, but that is not concretized, and the frame is provided by overlapping emotions—the type we have seen in the poems of *Mappings* etc. Sense of death as well as feelings of waste and pain are almost continuous:

I shall die soon, I know
It soaks my nights in sweat
And breaks my days in pain.
... ...
How am I to go on—
How will I bear this taste,
My throat cased in white spawn
These hands that shake and waste? (172-173)

Even love is a poor consolation, "He whom I love, thank God, / Won't speak of hope or cure". It is the sense of suffering and pain that dominates. In fact this repeated emphasis on pain and distress, without being related to any specific or local condition or situation, is a singular aspect of the poem "Soon", where "pain" is visualized as such, an independent unit of perception, and to that extent carries on the main trends seen in the earlier poems of the Sub-section—the trend towards suffering, waste and distress.

The next Sub-section, "In Other Places", has a total 9 poems, and the "other place" mostly refers to places in China. We again go back to strains in Seth's earlier poems, such as to descriptions of nature, a relaxed, playful attitude, and to a reflective mood, even at times to a sense of distress. The first poem "Hill Dawn", for example, is a brief description of the dawn in the Himalayan range of mountains. First, the coming of dawn:

Sudden and swift I hear
A distant avalanche,
The last stars disappear,
The blue shows flush and blanch.

Then, about the "mist"—"The rising mist now fills / The forest rifts below," and finally the trees:

Oak, rhododendron, pine
And cedar freed from night
Recede in a design
As visionless as white. (177)

The description is done detachedly, almost like a narration and the coming of dawn shows a calm, peacefulness. In many other poems too, the poet shows his perception of nature and nature's beauty, as well as a continuous feeling of joy and happiness. Thus in "Suzhou Park" an active nature, and relaxed human beings:

Magnolia trees float out their flowers,
A magpie flaps back to its pine,
A sparrow duet-rolls, fluffs, and cheeps,
... ...
The humans rest in a design!
One writes, one thinks, one moves, one sleeps. (178)

In "Night in Jiangning", a quiet, relaxed scene:

A glass of tea; the moon
The frogs croak in the weeds.
... ...

The whirr of winnowing grain,
The peace of loneliness,
The scent of imminent rain. (179)

In "The Scent of Sage and Bay" too, the nature's scene is visualized in a relaxed mood:

High on the hill I sit and watch an errant jay
Set a low twig of redwood swinging.
Wild columbines are here, the scent of sage and bay,
The slanting light, a cricket singing. (190)

The poem "Quingdao: December" has a slightly different design. It has, first of all, as in the earlier poems, a fine sensitivity to nature:

Here by the sea this quiet night
I see the moon through misted light
The pine-trees dense and earthward-bent
Suffuse the air with resin-scent. (182)

But the relaxed mood or the point of rest does not come automatically. It comes through a reflective mood and is motivated towards nature. Thus, first, the reflective mood—"Here all attempt in life appears / Irrelevant" and hence, we

Should yield our fever to the trees,
The seaward light and resined breeze.

Similarly, the nature is not seen independently, it is linked with the poet's sense of distress, a mood which we have seen in many of Seth's earlier poems. First, the hope that the quiet nature would "nullify the heart's distress", but, secondly, the realization that it is only partially so, in spite of nature, the mood of distress remains:

I see the light, I breathe the scent
I touch the insight, but a bent
Of heart exacts its old designs... (182)

Two other poems in the Sub-section, "Tourists" and "On the Fiftieth Anniversary of the Golden Gate Bridge" have different frames. In the former the present is contrasted with the past, particularly the present discomfort with the past happiness and the relationship is assessed. In the latter we have the account of San Francisco's Golden Gate Bridge and the activities thereon, given wittily, in a reflective mood. In "Tourists" the reference is to two persons—tourists to a particular place, the speaker and his companion, a lady, and their association; and secondly, the place itself. First, the persons—"she looked at him, he at the guide"..."They walked outside / To where confinement seemed less dense".... "They did not speak the language though"..."There on the Drum Tower, sipping tea / They watched the sunset lingeringly"..."They discussed / Their next day's pre-planned enterprise." Secondly, the place—"an old scene", and as it was in the past, and as it is at the present—in the past, as a recollection:

They'd lived here forty years ago
In hopeless times and cleaner air
And had been happy

and in the present as a reality:

They watched the sunset lingeringly
Across the black bricks, leaves and dust
That was the city. (181)

The account of companionship between two persons has been merged with the two different situations of the city—a pleasant past where times were "hopeless", yet the air was "clean", and the present when it is only "black" and "dust". The past is contrasted with the present, and both get related to the companionship of two persons, their past and the present, and the movement in time is through a "despair of change" towards a sense of uncertainty ("there glowed out an uncertain fire"). Thus the simple connotation of "Tourists" assumes a dimension where the nature of relationship is assessed and understood.

The occasion for the poem on the Golden Gate Bridge is its fiftieth anniversary, and the account is related to the recollections about the Bridge, and about its designers and builders. The initial reference is to the Pacific, and the location of the Bridge:

The grey Pacific, curved and old,
Indented, bare

Flings out, day after day, its cold
Breakers to, where
Marin and San-Francisco shore
The rapid strait
Christened a century before
The Golden Gate. (184)

Then the poet launches into its beginning ("Both counties know this still might be / A wistful view,") its obstructions ("Though courts twice threatened it, though storms / Once washed away"), how the work progressed ("Two forms / Inched day by day / Closer...."), its massiveness ("Two towers hold the cable; ton / on ton of it..."), its crowd in the morning ("Breathing against a neighbour's face / Gasping for air") and the Bridge's association with life and death in general:

How much of life has passed above,
Below, upon
How much of hatred and of love
Has come and gone! (186)

and speaks of soldiers who have "sailed out to war", and many of whom have not "sailed back beneath the bridge", of lovers who "have stood and kissed" under the cloak of mist on the bridge, and people who in "unsupported grief have thrown / Their lives away." This is one aspect. The other aspect is not as general as this. It goes beyond the Bridge to a specific reference to its designers and builders, a couple of husband and wife, a matter tinged with grief, because of an act of discrimination it holds out:

The plaque upon his tomb displays
The bridge; on hers
The bridgeless strait, as if she says
That she demurs. (189)

The next Sub-section "Quatrains" contains 20 short poems, 4 lines each, on varieties of topics such as, "Telephone", "Pigeons", "Pomegranate", "Pendulum", "Door", "Night Watch", "Promise", "Passage" etc., and often with an ironical twist. The themes are, as we have often seen in Seth, related to relationship, particularly love, and such moods as uncertainty, restlessness, distress, grief etc. The references to nature could also be seen, as well as comments on the art of writing. On the whole the poems are pointed, intelligent and witty pieces and finely illustrate Seth's skill in writing. For example, love, which provides motivation in many poems, is often linked with varying moods. Thus in "Telephone" where the conversation almost shows a physical proximity ("And feel the moisture of your hair / And smell the musk of your cologne") is suddenly resolved into nothingness—"Hello Is anybody there?" or in "Condition", the lover, in spite of his eagerness to speak ("I have to speak—I must—I should—I ought") hesitates because he thinks it is too soon ("well, it might be too soon"), or in "Prandial Plaint" the lover's attraction for the lady's body ("I love your breasts, I love your nose. I love your accent and I love your toes") is playfully disapproved because of the lady's way of sipping coffee ("don't slurp your coffee in that way") or in "Passage", the sad feeling that everything is subject to loss and decay ("Your eyes, my understanding, all will rot / The trees we see, the books we read, will go") is ironically approved and accepted ("and we are fortunate that this is so"). Even differently, in pieces that do not refer to love, moods vary from uncertainty and restlessness to grief. In "Dark Road" the poet speaks of darkness and distance ("The road is dark, and home is far") and hopes to be free of sorrow ("Wake free from fear, half-free of sorrow"), in "Southward Bound" metaphorically the journey is from lack of happiness towards happiness ("For each train-hour towards Nanjing / Is two-days' journey into spring"), in "Door", again metaphorically, the door is seen as the life's door through which the poet entered long ago ("At which he knocked and entered years before") but it ends in nothingness, nowhere, in futility:

> But now no street or city comes to mind.
> Nor why he knocked, nor what he came to find. (195)

Similarly, in "Night Watch" nature brings no consolation or respite to the vacantly obsessed mind,

> Awake for hours and staring at the ceiling
> Through the unsettled stickiness of the night. (195)

where the sense of distress continues even after the night is over: "that dawn has come and gone and brought no light." The poems of "Quatrains" are short and pithy as well as sharp and exciting, and as has been pointed out, good illustrations of Seth's skill and awareness.

The last Sub-section, "Meditations of the Heart" has 10 poems, on varying titles, but have one dominant strain, an awareness of distress and death in life, the capacity to go through and accept all that, and finally to acquire the strength to live. Often the mood is reflective, and references are to relationships that life can provide. The title poem "All You Who Sleep Tonight" is an illustrative one. The first reference is to people who live in a distressing loneliness, away from those they love: "All you who sleep tonight / Far from the ones you love / No hand to left or right / And emptiness above." Next is an element of sympathy, commonness in distress:

> Know that you aren't alone
> The whole world shares your tears. (213)

Similarly, in another poem, entitled "How Rarely These Few Years", we note the pain in living which one has to accept and go through. First, it is a reference to separation from one another—"How rarely these few years, as work keep us aloof / Or fares, or one thing or another...", the next, the realization that the separation is inevitable, particularly the end-separation, and hence reference to 'death' ("All five of us will die..."). Yet, the "hard" fact is to be accepted and one has to go through it:

> What's hard is that just one of us will be the last
> To bear it all and go on living. (207)

In another poem, "The Wind", as the title suggests the content is provided by nature—"The bay is thick with flecks of white / The freezing air is honed and thinned." But the context remains separated from the speakers, from his distress and mood of loneliness, and the end is an acceptance of the designs of life, and its obstructions:

> Against the wind, as it should be,
> I walk, but in my solitude
> Bow to the wind that buffets me. (212)

"Poet" is a singular poem, having a different strain from other poems of the Sub-section, more comparable to the poems of the

Sub-section "In Other Voices," particularly to a poem like "Ghalib". It has a narrative style, where the trial and tribulations of a third party other than the poet have been narrated, where the suffering was of extremely painful nature ("She lived for six years in a cage"..."Cabbages and bread, rotten and stale, were food"..."Years of her youth / Were sickened for no crime"). Yet what motivated the poem was not the suffering, but the capacity and strength to live through extremely adverse situations:

> ...I think
> Of her who through long cold and pain did not
> Betray the ones she loved or plead for mercy. (203)

A similar motivation is also found in "Adagio", the next poem, where the strength lies in sustaining oneself despite distress. The reference is to music—the adagio of the clarinet Quintet, that communicates sorrow, yet one gets strength by listening to it:

> ...Yet to hear him is
> To suffer all heartbreak, to assume all sorrow
> And to survive. (204)

The comparison with Nightingale, done latterly in the poem, also shows the same strength—the strength to sustain oneself in life's adversities:

> In the clear supple lilt of one who like
> The nightingale, his breast against the thorn,
> Sang jubilantly in sorrow.... (205)

To live through the system of life, and to accept whatever is given or whatever is our due, and to go on living without much complain, is the type of attitude which is also projected in other poems of this Sub-section, such as in "Voices", "Heart", "Things", and "Mist", for example. In "Voices", a short poem, the division is clear. First, the pattern of life—"Kisses, Bread. / Prove yourself. Fight. Shove. / Learn. Earn. Look for love." That is the dominant force, the primary motivation. But the other trend, the "lesser voice", is also there, quieter but equally forceful:

> Breathe in peace, and be
> Still, for once, like me. (210)

In "Heart" too, first the awareness that the life's process continues, exemplified even in one's body, in such attributes as heart and blood, both of which continue to function, whatever the situation may be, day and night—one beats "all night and all day long," and the other drives "Through / My arteries, my veins, my lives." That is how the poet maintains; one goes on living without forethought and afterthought:

Above all, to my heart I'm true,
It does not tell me what to do,
It beats, I live, it beats again.
For what? I wish I knew it knew. (211)

In "Mist" it is viewed slightly differently, in a general reflection on life that has its own circuit of movement, which the poet admits, vis-à-vis the problem of mist on the road they are driving through, in contrast to the clear road they have passed through. First, the reference to an easy movement, done comfortably, without any obstruction:

In the bright valley that we left,
Each needle leaf, and cone distinct,
In clarity's excessive heft. (206)

This is, metaphorically, the easy, comfortable passage through life. But obstructions come along, also metaphorically, through "mist":

The wires sink into the mist.
The red madrone trunks blur to grey.

And finally, the reflection, of what life is and would be:

Here on a lesser planet's crust
How may we hope that we exist
To mark a vision in our trust,
Too bright for us and dim for mist? (206)

Hence it is heartening if we accept whatever is given to us, the design and system we live through, and that would be peaceful and enduring. One good aspect of this attitude is to develop communication with whatever other creatures we live along. The poet illustrates this in the first poem of the Sub-section, "The Stray Cat". First, the pranks of the cat ("He tries to wedge / His nose indoors"..."He turns his topaz eyes / Upon my eyes"..."He ventures forth an easy paw"....). But finally a live communication and relationship is established with the cat:

I fetch a bowl, and watch him gnaw
The star-shaped nuggets he likes best.
He is permitted food, and I
The furred indulgence of a sigh. (202)

THREE CHINESE POETS

Next in the series of the anthology is *Three Chinese Poets*, a Section of poetry by the titular poets Wang Wei, Li Bai and Du Fu translated into English by Vikram Seth. The three poets were contemporaries and are considered to be amongst the greatest Chinese poets, though Du Fu did not receive much recognition for his poetry during his life. The three have been described as Buddhist recluse, Taoist immortal and Confucian sage respectively. Though this trichotomy has been criticized as simplistic and artificial, it can act as a guiding figure. They lived near the end of the Tang Dynasty and the political strife at that time affected all of their lives very much and this impact is evident in the poetry of all the three. It is not clear whether Wang Wei and Li Bai ever met, but they had a mutual friend in Meng Haoran. Li Bai and Du Fu did meet and in fact Du Fu greatly admired Li Bai.

In the introduction of *Three Chinese Poets*, Seth talks about the influence of translations on his life and work; that while sometimes he has been so moved by a translation that he learnt another language to read the original, he doubts that he would ever be able to do this as much as he wished to. However, he says that Charles Johnston's translation of Aleksandr Pushkin's *Eugene Onegin*, Richard Wilbur's translation of Molieiere's *Tartuffe* and Robert Fitzgerald's translation of the *Iliad* have helped him enter worlds without which it would have been out of his reach. He states that he avoided the style and philosophy of the famous translations by Ezra Pound which was to read and deeply understand a poem, then to create an approximate translation inspired by the original—the judge of the merit being whether the new poem is a good poem in the new language. Instead, he wanted to follow the example of the translators mentioned above to retain a greater fidelity and to try to preserve structure such as rhyme. He stresses that while he has tried not to lose meaning, he has often failed, explaining that because each word is much more important in poetry, the problem of losing associations of words is much greater than when translating prose. He also makes note that any satisfaction derived from the tonality of the poems is necessarily lost because of the non-tonality of English. However we will omit Seth's translations as they are not relevant for our practical discussion, and move on to Seth's next original poetry-collection, *Beastly Tales from Here and There.*

BEASTLY TALES FROM HERE AND THERE

Beastly Tales from Here and There (1992), as the poet points out, is a "group of ten animal fables in rhymed couplets". The fables are in the grand tradition of *Panchatantra*, the incomparable work by Pandit Vishnu Sharma, where philosophy, psychology, politics, music, astronomy, human relationship etc., have all merged together, to stand their test for millions of readers—children, youngsters and adult—for the last more than 2000 years. The other work to which the affinities of the *Beastly Tales* can be traced is T.S. Eliot's *Old Possum's Book of Practical Cats* (1939). In both Vishnu Sharma and Eliot, animals in general in Sharma, and cats particularly in Eliot, have been humanized, and they share the same characteristics of love and hatred, compassion and wit, courage and cowardice, and generosity and meanness with human beings as a whole, and provide a picture of life, viewed with great sympathy, humour and insight. The tales in the *Beastly Tales* are also humanized, as was done in the earlier tales. Additionally, human details are also put in, such as, human habits, conversation, relationship, behaviour, mindset etc., on the whole, the content and the frame. Thus the beasts are not only humanized, they become by themselves, human beings, with all their multiple activities and manners and with all their involvements in the daily process of living. The tales have often an implied moralistic attitude. But what really dominates the accounts is the humanistic frame, in a tone which is both witty and humorous, and in a pattern of narration which is both racy and bantering, and involved and detached.

The first tale, entitled "The Crocodile and the Monkey", is the well-known story of the crocodile and the monkey, their initial friendship, and subsequent estrangement because of the crocodile's betrayal and bad motive. The implied moral is also the traditional moralistic attitude of the ancient tale, that is, not to trust those who are not trustworthy. But its distinctive aspect lies in its organization, in integration of prose and verse. Providing a pattern where elasticity of verse has joined with the strength of prose, in its racy conversational movement with a lot of wit and humour and with an attitude of joyous playfulness, and in a tone that has detached impersonality. The poem begins with a simple reference to the crocodile, in a non-personal manner:

> On the Ganga's greenest isle
> Lived Kuroop the crocodile;
> Greeny-brown with gentle grin,
> Stubby legs and scaly skin.... (279)

The reference is almost like that to a human being ("gentle grin"..."stubbly legs"). Then the crocodile's characteristics are described, that is, how avaricious he was, how cruel towards his prey and how docile to his wife. This is the first phase—about the crocodile. In the second, we note the relationship between the crocodile and the monkey—a friendly one, with a panegyric on mangoes, almost like a divine fruit gifted to man:

> Eat, my friend, and take your wife
> Nectar from the tree of life—
> Mangoes ripe and mangoes rare,
> Mangoes, mangoes everywhere. (281)

In the third phase the friendship changed to deceitfulness on the part of the crocodile, and he tries to lure the monkey towards his death, again, in a humanistic context:

> Then Kuroop the crocodile
> Gazed up with a gentle smile:
> Monkey, you are far too kind,

But today, if you don't mind,
Dine with both of us, and meet
Her whose life you've made so sweet. (281)

In the fourth phase the matters turned to be topsy-turvy. The monkey became deceitful, the crocodile stupid, and the end became a hilarious anti-climax, again, in a criss-cross of human behaviour, gullibility and readiness to act in situations:

...and as for you,
Here is my parting gift'—He threw
Mangoes—squishy, rotten, dead,
Down upon the reptiles head,
Who, with a regretful smile,
Sat and eyed him for a while. (285)

The poem "The Crocodile and the Monkey" can be considered as a typical poem among the poems of the *Beastly Tales,* particularly as regards the organization and the narrative skill. Also a play of wit and humour as well as a detached playfulness, characterize almost all the tales. At the same time the purpose remains to entertain and edify. But the messages differ, though some of them have a general similarity. Thus "The Crocodile and the Monkey" and "The Louse and the Mosquito" have one message, a warning, that is, not to trust those who are not trustworthy. Similarly, "The Mouse and the Snake" and "The Eagle and the Beetle" have one message, to instill hope and courage, that is, a weak being with determination can fight out the strong and win. Also, in "The Bat and the Ox" and "The Frog and the Nightingale" we can note a similarity, making people aware of a social situation that often exists, that is, the cunning and the sly can always corner the innocent and the gifted, and can win the day against truth and honesty. Then there is the practical advice to help people in their day-to-day living, that is, as in "The Goat and the Ram", that the pluckiness and intelligence always helps, or as in "The Cat and the Cock", in a situation of tit for tat, it is pointed out that clever people always remain steady and balanced and at the end succeed, whereas the foolish and the flippant who try to show off always come to grief. But two tales, "The Hare and the Tortoise" and "The Elephant and the Tragopan" do not give the messages so succinctly. The former has social implications, and the latter socio-political, and both convey pungent irony, integrated in the situations, more in the latter than in the former, against the prevailing modern dispensation. The two tales can be analyzed a little further.

"The Hare and the Tortoise" has seven phases. First, the place and the type of characters involved—locating the situation with a tinge of humour:

> Once or twice upon a time
> In the land of Runnyrhyme
> Lived a hare both hot and heady
> And a tortoise slow and steady. (304)

Secondly, the account of the hare and the tortoise, just like two human beings, with their individual habits and manners. The hare first:

> When at noon the hare awoke
> She would tell herself a joke
> Squeal with laughter, roll about,
> Eat her eggs and sauerkraut,
> Then pick up the phone and babble,
> —'Gibble-gabble, gibble-gabble'— (304)

Next, the tortoise:

> But the tortoise, when he rose,
> Daily counted all his toes
> Twice or three times, to ensure
> There were neither less or more.
> Next he'd tally the amount
> In his savings bank account.
> Then he'd very carefully
> Count his grandsons: one, two, three— (305)

The accounts are humorous, and have social aspects. The hare is like a gay, young lady, restless, and given to pleasures, and the tortoise is circumspect and extremely calculative. Next, in the third phase, the two meet:

> One day by the Fauna Fountain
> Near the noble Mammal Mountain
> Where the ducks and ducklings dabble. (305)

and the hare laughs at the tortoise's speed of walking:

> Inch by inch by inch he's crawling
> How pathetic! how appalling!
> … … … … … …
> Teddy Tortoise, go and grab,
> Tram or train, or taxi-cab! (306)

The tortoise gets angry, and throws out a challenge:

> Madam, you are rash and young
> And should mind your mindless tongue.
> Doubtless, Madam, hares exceed
> Tortoises by far in speed,
> But, were we to run a race,
> I, not you, would win first place. (306)

Then the race was run, and the upshot is a well-known story.

But what is interesting is the way the poet describes the hare's habits—an account full of humour as well as irony too. First, the hare's manners in replying to the press, like a modern young woman's:

> Pouting out her scarlet lips,
> Swiftly wiggling head and hips,
> Making wolves feel weak inside,
> Languidly Mrs. Hare replied. (307)

Then her habits; completely indifferent to the race—her "satin shorts" ("cut for fashion more than sports"), her "yawns" ("Yawning softly,") and her two O'clock "sleep" ("Two O'clock! My beauty sleep,") when she "stretched out in the sun." Even the hare's sudden attraction for the "field of mushrooms" even after she had started running was like a modern lady's flippancy for intoxicating things:

> 'How delicious! What a treat!'
> Said the hare: 'I will stop and eat'
> So she did, and very soon
> She was singing out of tune. (309)

When the race ended the tortoise's reaction was predictable. It was for steadiness, and that is the inherent message:

Now she'll learn that sure and slow
Is the only way to go—
That you can't rise to the top
With a skip, a jump, a hop—

That should have been the end. But it is not. What comes after the race becomes more important than the race itself. The hare, though defeated, gets maximum attention and publicity ("Thus the hare was pampered rotten / And the tortoise was forgotten").

That is the second message—pungent irony at the system of modern society that pampers the unworthy, against the people of real worth, through publicity stunts:

...the hare
Suddenly was everywhere
Stories of her quotes and capers
Made front page in all the papers—
... ...
Soon she saw her name in lights,
Sold a book and movie rights,
While a travel magazine
Bought the story, sight unseen,
Of her three hour expedition
To the wood—called "Mushroom Mission." (312)

The hare ceases to be a hare; she becomes a modern overreacher, and fits in with the tastes and preferences of the modern society and modern living.

"The Elephant and the Tragopan", the longest tale in the group (about 26 pages, and 800 lines), goes a little further — it combines social expediency with political manouvers. The first reference to the context is an account of rich, luxuriant nature—a picture of great calm, peace and happiness.:

In Bingle Valley, broad and green,
Where neither hut nor field is seen,
Where bamboo, like a distant lawn,
Is gold at dusk and flushed at dawn,
Where a cold river, filmed with ice
Sustains a minor paradise.... (337)

But the "minor paradise" was going to be destroyed by man's actions, and the elephant and the tragopan who get the first information of this were disturbed:

> That man had hatched a crazy scheme
> To mar their land and dam their stream
> To flood the earth on which they stood
> And cut the woods down for their wood. (337)

They decided to convene a "full meeting" of the "Forest Folk" to discuss how "they might outmanouver man". The meeting was convened to which they all came ("Gibbons and squirrels, snakes, wild dogs / Dear and macaques, three types of frogs / Porcupines, eagles, trout, wagtails / Civet cats, sparrows, bears and quails / Blood sucking leeches, mild-eyed newts / And leopards in their spotted suits....").

That ends the first phase of the poem. In the next phase we have the meeting of all "forest folk", the discussions that ensued, the elephant's long address, and the decision taken thereafter to meet the atrocities in a rally. The elephant's address is a crucial pointer in the poem that reflectively points to man's true nature and character, and his propensity to destroy everything for his selfish ends, almost one may say the writer's own point of view on such subjects. Thus, this is how the elephant speaks about the man:

> He is a creature mild and vicious,
> Practical minded and capricious,
> Loving and brutal, sane and mad,
> The good as puzzling as the bad. (342)

And again, referring to man's selfishness:

> He sees the planet as his fief
> Where every hair or drop or leaf
> Or seed or blade or grain of sand
> Is destined for his mouth or hand. (342-343)

So too, is man's enormous greed, and his enormous capacity to destroy environment:

> For nowhere lies beyond man's reach
> To mar and burn and flood and leach

A distant valley is indeed
No sanctuary from his greed. (344)
....
Think what will happen when his scheme
To tame our valley and our stream
Begins to thrust its way across
These gentle slopes of fern and moss
With axe, explosive, and machine. (343)

It would be illuminating to compare this view of man with Alexander Pope's famous view of man, and his reference to man occupying the middle position in the "Great Chain of Being" (1734):

Created half to rise, and half to fall;
Great lord of all things, yet a prey to all;
Sole judge of truth, in endless error hurled:
The glory, jest and riddle of the world!
(*An Essay on Man*, Epistle II)

Pope's view is the 18th century view of man, and has philosophical dimensions inherited from the Middle Ages. But the elephants belong to the present time, showing how man in his tendency towards greed, selfishness and deceit has fallen to a position below the beasts, and is no longer the "glory", "jest" or "riddle", but a transparently mean creature. That is why the conclusion of the elephant's speech takes a political twist, and calls all the "endangered denizens of Bingle" to unite— "We must unite in fur and feather— / For we will live or die together."

In conclusion a decision was taken to take out a rally, and next, we get an account of the rally:

And so it happened that a rally
Meandered forth from Bingle Valley
A few days later, up and down
The hills towards the human town. (346)

It was even "cheered" by the villagers on the way, who came out "in scores",

So stunned and stupefied were they,
They even cheered them on the way
Or joined them on the route to town. (347)

The next scene brings in man to the scene—the negotiation between the beasts on the one hand, headed by the elephant and his secretary, the Tragopan—the aggrieved "people", and the elected ruler of the town, the Great Bigshot Number One, "Sri Padmabhushan Gobardhan", and his associates—the rulers. The negotiation continued, Tragopan exposed the motivated, selfish doings of the rulers, and the Bigshot Number One tried to cajole, persuade and intimidate the beasts. In the negotiation the Bigshot Number One remained stubborn, used all his deceitful tactics, and maintained that whatever decisions would be taken should be to the benefit of the rulers, conducive to the prevailing politics, however corrupted that may be. The Bigshot Number One was candid about this as well as in general, about the politician's ways—a pithy admission of how things shape:

> I think you fail to comprehend
> What really matters in the end.
> The operative word is Votes,
> And next to that comes Rupee-notes. (354)

He again refers to the political reality, how to sustain oneself in power and continue administration:

> It's not just water that must funnel
> Out of the hills through Bingle Tunnel.
> Do animals have funds or votes—
> Or anything but vocal throats?
> Will you help me get re-elected? (355)

The sudden jutting in of Smallfry, the Number Three and the Bigshot Number One's son, was a jolt to the latter. In comparison he was much more transparent and more akin to the demands of the beasts, and in support of keeping the environment intact ("As the roads come, the trees will go."). But he was rudely stopped by his father, who decried his upbringing, the attitude of younger generation, and most important of all, maintained that the son should inherit the father's political legacy, willingly and smoothly:

> One day all this would have been yours—
> These antlers and these heads of boars,
> This office and these silver plates,

These luminous glass paper weights,
My voting bank, my Number Game,
My files, my fortune, and my fame. (358)

The whole account is full of ironical twists, and forward devastating comments on the politicians and their deceitful ways of sticking to power without any consideration of the welfare of people who have elected them or any consideration of the good of the country—a good account of politics and politicians, particularly in India, and to that extent, the beasts' protest, rally and negotiations with the powers to be, to save themselves, the environment and the country is symbolic of the prevailing state of affairs.

The end was both an anti-climax and a climax. The Smallfry and the Elephant were silenced, the Tragopan was killed. The conclusion took up different dimensions, also a reflection of what happen at times. The Tragopan became a martyr, and his death achieved what could not be achieved while he was alive—the whole country took up his cause—the cause of the aggrieved:

For it undoubtedly was true
That suddenly the whole state knew
Of Bingle Valley and the trek
That ended in the fatal peck. (361)
....
The water problem in the state
Became a topic for debate.
The Bigshot struggling with the flood,
Was splashed with editorial mud. (361-362)

In fact, the tale of "The Elephant and the Tragopan" has a special significance. Unlike other tales of the *Beastly Tales* it is not just humanized, in character, spirit and motivation, it is by itself a human drama—the type of situation we often see around, particularly in India, between an autocratic, self-motivated administration and the people's resistance to that—a typical case in the underdeveloped and developing countries where politically powerful try to rule the roost indifferent to general will or woe. A pertinent case, comparable to the Bingle

Valley situation, it may be recalled, was the Silent Valley case in Kerala some years ago, which was almost going to be devastated and was finally saved by stiff public resistance. In "The Elephant and the Tragopan" the writer has offered no resolution to the problem ("The resolution of their plight / Is for the world, not me, to write"). He has only highlighted, and dramatically, the inevitable destruction of environment in the name of so-called "development", and has suggested how best that can be averted. To that extent the account of the tale of "The Elephant and the Tragopan" has continuous ironical dimensions—irony at the expense of projects, Governments, and motivated rulers, and has implicit symbolical bearings to suggest how best man can live in this planet and how fruitfully. In a way, all the tales of the *Beastly Tales* aim at that end and highlight different moods, levels and activities of man and his propensity more towards negative aspects than the positive. In that sense it is a continuation of the *Panchatantra* tradition, and an improvement on it, improvement in the sense that it is more related to the factors of reality as available at present.

Conclusion

Critical discussions on Vikram Seth's writings are limited. Particularly on his poetry it is very much so. To some extent his verse-novel *The Golden Gate,* which received Sahitya Akademi Award in 1988, got some critical attention. But his other poetry books, 4 in number, that were published in a period of 11 years, between 1981 and 1992, such as, *Mappings* (1981), *The Humble Administrator's Garden* (1985), *All You Who Sleep Tonight* (1990) and *Beastly Tales from Here and There* (1992), received very limited attention. Even when *The Humble Administrator's Garden* received the Commonwealth Poets Prize for Asia in 1985, the attitude did not change much. Yet Seth's poetry is a substantial part of his total creative act, and contributes very substantially to the Indian English poetry written in the last 25 years. Apart from stray references to his poetry here and there, some consistent references, though short, can be noted by critics and in books as under: (1) *Modern Indian Poetry in English*, Revised Edition, by Bruce King, 2001; (2) *An Illustrated History of Indian Literature in English*, edited by Arvind Krishna Mehrotra, 2003; (3) *Indian English Literature, 1980–2000: A Critical Survey,* by M.K. Naik and Shyamala A. Narayan, 2004.

King's discussions of Seth's poetry is sympathetic and to some extent wide-ranging. He first refers to *Mappings* and points out that it records dual feelings of "nostalgia" for India and his continuing attraction to the "notes of other birds". Additionally, the poems show "youthful restlessness" and "ambivalent feelings" towards his family, especially his father, and he quotes from "Departure Lounge" to make his point. Then he points out how many of the poems are very "anti-romantic" and proceed from a "rational and hedonist" philosophy, to rhyme, form and a low or mixed diction are used to deflect deep feelings into "tongue-in-cheek" humour—Such self-conscious, self-mocking, self-deflating art rejects the high cultural seriousness and elitism of modernist literature" (King 2001: 227). Many poems in "The Humble Administrator's Garden", King points out, are metaphorically about the nature of art, and many others refer to his "loneliness", "sense of being continually on the move", naming three sections in the names of three different trees—Wutong, Neem and Live-oak, suggesting three different countries—China, India, and America. King quotes from the poem "Abalone Soup", and says how California poems particularly, "are of interest for their mixture of amused enjoyment, witty defensiveness, sense of danger, comic incongruities and feelings of loneliness." (228). King maintains that Seth's aesthetic is as distinctive as those of Nisim Ezekiel, Dilip Chitre, Arvind Mehrotra and Jayanta Mahapatra, and he speaks of his "highly original poetry" referring to poems such as "Ceasing upon the Midnight" and "Unclaimed". "Seth's acceptance of and delight in exile" says King, "combined with a highly self-conscious traditional poetic form and prosody result in surprisingly original poetry. Like most good art, it is very much of its time.... Seth's poems offer a sense of being uprooted, lonely and of needing to enjoy the moment (not just because this is all there is) because there are no lasting deeper relationships available and life is an adventure abroad" (229-230).

An Illustrated History of Indian Literature in English is a comprehensive account, in 24 chapters, of the development of Indian English Literature, since early 19th century till today, and one of its chapters, entitled "Poetry since Independence" by Rajeev S. Patke, of the National University of Singapore, deals as a part of it with Seth's poetry. Patke speaks of Seth's poetry as "energetic and cheerful kitsch", and refers to the wide success of his "narratives". Then he refers to Seth's "metrical propensities" and calls him a gifted "pasticheur of styles", and points out that his facility turns out to be a "mixed blessing: the reader can be swept on a flood mixing doggerel, banality, romanticism and sentimentality with much else that is fascinating" (Mehrotra 2003: 273). Seth's poetic styles, Patke continues, are a "curious mix of the modern and Victorian. His forte is light verse; his true métier is a Victorian narrative" (273). At the same time he admits that "to have restored the drive of narrative to verse is Seth's principal contribution to poetry" (273).

Indian English Literature, 1980-2000 contains eleven chapters, of which the 7th chapter entitled "The Cygnets of Poetry—II" deals partly with Seth's poetry. The chapter is written by M.K. Naik, formerly of Karnataka University, Dharwad, and author of *A History of Indian English Literature* (1982). Naik refers to Seth's first book, *Mappings* as a "bright young man's attempts at self-scrutiny, the mappings of his diverse selves" (Naik 2004: 171), but points out that his love poems seem to betray a "strange lack of intensity", though the "most successful" poems are those with a "dramatic element" in them, and he cites Seth's poem "Party for the Retirement of the Oldest-Serving British Museum Reading Room Book Attendant" as a "very fine dramatic monologue" touched with a "delicious irony". He further cites the poem "Departure Lounge", and points out how against irony the "baffling complexities of the love-hate relationship between father and son are delicately probed" in the poem (171). Similarly, with reference to the poem of Seth's next book *The Humble Administrator's Garden,* Naik maintains that they are mostly "descriptive" and have a sense of "immediacy" in many poems. So too in *All You Who Sleep Tonight* the monologues ("In

Other Voices"), and epigrams ("Quatrains") are most rewarding, and he hopes that as "monologues show a sure grasp of situation and character, one hopes Seth will turn more often to this form" (173). Referring to *Beastly Tales from Here and There,* Naik says that the "style has an easy flow and the rhyming is effortless and impeccable. But one is disappointed to find that the poet generally fails to invest these traditional tales with a new, contemporary significance" (173).

As can be seen, the references to Seth's poetry are brief and to a large extent sympathetic. As the same time the critics pinpoint many of the important aspects we have discussed with reference to Seth's poetry much more elaborately. For example, Seth's narrative and descriptive skill as well as his capacity for effortless and impeccable rhyming is well-taken. Seth's narrative skill, best seen in his *Beastly Tales*, can also be seen in many other poems including "Babur" poems, and his descriptive skill in many places and portions of the poems in creating an atmosphere, or making out a picture, or even concentrating on references to nature. Mr. Naik's point in this connection, that Seth excelled in providing dramatic elements to his poems and shaping dramatic monologues is very relevant. Similarly all the three critics point out the presence of wit, humour and irony in Seth's poetry. King speaks of 'amused enjoyment' and 'tongue in cheek humour,' Patke of 'energy' and 'cheerfulness' and Naik of 'delicious irony'. In fact, wit, humour, irony etc., along with an ingenious capacity to integrate them in the total context as substantial parts of the total attitude are what characterize Seth's poetry, and that is aptly recognized. As part of one's own being, as a matter of attitude, understanding and condition of living, Seth's poetry provides a strong trend towards self-scrutiny, of a sense of loneliness and uprootedness, as well as a rationalistic and a self-deflating way of viewing things around him. The critics admit that in various ways. It may be pointed out that the critical attention given to Seth's poetry, though brief, yet to a large extent goes to the core of Seth's poetry, and at the same time, it is interesting to note that the attention is guarded, cautious, and for whatever reason may be, gives a reluctant praise.

WORKS CITED

King, Bruce. *Modern Indian Poetry in English*. Revised Edition. Delhi: Oxford University Press, 2001.

Mehrotra, Arvind Krishna, ed. *Illustrated History of Indian Literature in English*. Delhi: Permanent Black, 2003.

Naik, M.K. and Shyamala A. Narayan. *Indian English Literature, 1980–2000: A Critical Survey*. Delhi: Pencraft International, 2004.

Seth, Vikram. *The Poems 1981-1994*. New Delhi: Viking, 1995.

3 Poems 1981–1994: A Study in Style

Seth's poetic style has many singular features. Some of these may be listed for a brief assessment. First of all, though he has a strong trend towards organizing his poetic pieces in a prose pattern, yet he freely employs rhyme, half-rhyme, even the pattern of a song, whenever the occasion comes. Thus as in the following examples, we can note the end-rhyme, in a mix of prose and conversational trend:

> The old man in grey reproves the women's tears
> And shouts from dock to dock. The sailor hears
> Smiles, flings a cigarette to a store bound mate,
> The Wuhen steamer hoots—two minutes late— (101)

Or, as on the page 279, in describing the crocodile and its habitat:

> On the Ganga's greenest isle
> Lived Kuroop the crocodile:
> Greeny-brown with gentle grin,
> Stubby legs and scaly skin.

Or, as on the page 151, in describing the strain of a flight:

> After a long and wretched flight
> That stretched from daylight into night,
> Where babies wept and tempers shattered
> And the plane lurched and whisky spattered...

Elsewhere, in the poem "Song: Coast Starlight", in a nature-sensitive account the rhymes almost pattern into songs:

> The cattle rest among the mustard flowers.
> The starlight circles past the prison towers.
> The golfers pull their carts along the green.
> The blackbird flies across the deep ravine. (124)

Or,

> Now darkness falls—the moon gives little light.
> O Starlight, ride into the gentle night.
> O travellers, may starlight see you home.
> O travellers, may you not sleep alone. (125)

But whatever may be the rhythmic arrangement, there is invariably a mix of prose pattern which is often conversational and at times argumentative. At the same time it may be pointed out that this integration of prose and poetry is completely achieved, and the prose aspect adds a very pleasant dimension to the total aesthetic appeal of Seth's poems. An early example, and a very apt and successful example, could be seen in Seth's long, fictional work in verse *The Golden Gate* (1986), where aspects of narration, observation and speculative ruminations mingle, along with a mocking tone, in a structure impeccably organized, to provide both the feel of prose and verse together, in an atmosphere which is both intimate and detached. A good, beginning example is the first verse of *The Golden Gate* (1.1):

> To make a start more swift than weighty,
> Hail muse. Dear Reader, once upon
> A time, say, circa 1980,
> There lived a man. His name was John.
> Successful in his field though only
> Twenty-six, respected, lonely,
> One evening as he walks across
> Golden Gate Park, the ill-judged toss
> Of a red Frisbee almost brained him.
> He thought, "If I died, who'd be sad?
> Who'd weep? Who'd gloat? Who would be glad?
> Would anybody?" As it pained him,
> He turned from this dispiriting theme
> To ruminations less extreme.

The poems of *The Poems 1981–1994* exhibit these aspects extensively.

Thus as in *Mappings*, as the poet addresses a fellow traveller ("To a Fellow-Traveller"), the address is both light and serious, has distinct prose connotations in describing a situation and arguing out an issue, along with a mocking tone:

Dear Madeleine, I dip my Pepperidge Farm
Cookie into tea and think of you
And how you laughed and held me by the arm
On Shattuck when I left. Though I'm one who
Believes that between strangers there should be
A proper distance kept— (17)

Or, a little later, in the same poem, urbane, routine descriptions of the flight, with a tone of disgust, almost like a prose-statement:

The pilot is obtuse, the plane is late,
The flight attendants flighty and the sheer
Monotony of a sedentary state
Maintained for seven hours will likely drive
You into lunacy... (18)

There are a number of examples; from *Mappings* as well as from other poetry-collections where a trend towards a prose-statement relating to different situations, but integrated all the while with the total poetic-structure, adding strength and new dimensions, could be seen. Some examples would be apt. Thus in the poem "From the Memories of Babur" describing the ordeals of Babur's people:

Four days passed: they returned
They had not found a soul.
No sign of settlement,
No wandering tribesmen; hill
On hill, and that was all. (25)

In the "Party for the Retirement..." the reply-statement of the person who retires is in an easy conversational tone:

Yes, yes, thank you, thank you, yes, it has been
A very pleasant forty...fifty years.
Quite so, sir, how time does fly. I have seen
So may changes that the world appears
Peculiar now. (45)

A similar, almost a bald statement in "Divali":

Five? Six? Generation ago
Somewhere in the Punjab

My father's family, farmers,
Perhaps had a small shop
And two generations later
Could send a son to school... (65)

In "The Accountant's House" too the account given by the poet of his meeting with the accountant is matter of fact and straightforward:

I want to clear up some questions on the income and expenditure account,
His wife and two daughters smile as I come in,
They pour tea. Their son died last spring festival.
We smile and discuss electricity fees. (88)

In "From a Traveller" the reply of the poet to a letter he has received—a direct tone of communication, and a normal, friendly appreciation:

Thank you for writing (again) and for the poem:
It came a week ago and has been with me since,
It made me happy. It is very fine—
Latinate and resonant, and words precisely hefted. (94)

In "Sit" the atmosphere of companionship and the desire to be drawn together in a quiet conversational mood:

Sit, drink coffee here; your work can wait a while.
You're twenty-six, and still have some of life ahead.
No need for wit; just talk vacuities, and I'll
Reciprocate in kind, or laugh at you instead. (157)

But the poem "Protocols", also related to companionship and in a conversational mood, shows emotion and a suppressed excitement:

What can I say to you? How can I now retract
All that that fool, my voice, has spoken—
Now that the facts are plain, the placid surface cracked,
The protocols of friendship broken? (152)

Differently, it may be noted in the poem "Mappings", how a routine narration and a quick combination of almost disjointed references bring in a conclusion of personal emotion and reflection:

The light has lapsed, I strip and swim towards
A wooden raft.... My wake,
The wine, my breathing, the recovering stars,
Venus, bright as a plain, Jupiter, Mars,
My pulse, my vagrant selves, my poetry,
Seen here to inhere in a seamless me. (63)

Or, differently, it may also be noted, how the prose text of a statement, almost like a bland academic discourse, could be turned into a poetic structure, as in the poem "From a Traveller":

For the obtuseness you diagnosed with such acuity
Had in it an element of intention.
Apart from the aspect of physical difference,
As exciting to me as that of similarity,
And beauty that I always am a sucker for.... (96)

A remarkable aspect of Seth's style is his frequent use of epithets, which are to be found in large numbers and almost in every poem, a use which merits favourable comparison with such practice in the poems of Keats. Some of the examples may be listed, such as "grimy-margined bay" and "high-octane breath" (23), "lawn's cropped-edge" (31), "pain-dense track" (40), "the apple-blossomed earth" (43), "highwayed plain" (47), "gold-shot hair" and "red winged blackbirds" (55), "house-shadowing tree" (56), "blue-battered jays" (59), "cool enveloping lake" (63), "snow-drowned" (69), "fire-crossed sky" and "disquieted heart" (70), "moss-trunked tree" (83), "shoulder-borne" (87), "cloud-busy, far-blue air" (92), "embanked trees" (95), "roach-frequented kitchen", "predictable week", "self-inwardness", "Vivaldian Beach-Boyish days", "sun-spoilt denizens" (96), "slow-cooling cycles" (97), "blue-tailed lizard" (98), "turquoise-necked, turquoise-breasted" (107), "dew-soft dew-grayed lawn" and "whitewashed gate" (108), "enamel-striped domes" (110), "the weathered past" (128), "resin-scented right" (137), "forked years" (160), "a sparrow dust-rolls" and "the stenciled stone" (178), "the pool-pierced maze" (180), "group-contained" (181), "resined breeze" (182), "the furred indulgence" (202), "the acred land" (208), "tender-hearted" (287), "dream enriched" (288), "venom fanged" (290), "topsy-turved" (293), "hare-brained hare" (306), "shell-shocked" (311), "sundown snack" (328), and "sleep-deprived" (335) etc.

The epithets provide compact and concentrated images by themselves. Additionally, Seth also creates images through a combination of words and phrases. They have limited contexts, but provide suggestive pictures and enrich the poetic structure generally. Some interesting examples of image making can be seen in an early poem "To a Fellow Traveller" (17). First, a declaration of love which the poet feels would be rejected as a piece of pompous act, as an "overripe Parnassian pretence" (17). Subsequently, in the same poem as he refers to the flight, he initially points out how evening light falls on the white clouds in the sky—"the snow-fluffed cloud-terrain heavy with evening light", and then how the sunset is quickly followed by night—"the chased sunset merging with the night", the "cloud-terrain" and the "chased sunset" making out appropriate images. In "After Three Years" (31) the picture is of the sunset across the steep hills towards North Wales—"The sunset, reddens steeply towards North Wales", and in "The Sultan's Turret" (35) the lovers are inside the quilt, like fotuses being inside the mother's womb—"wombed in the quilt with you". The suggestion of warmth provided by "quilt" is related to music in "Close of Play" (43), in the image "deep quilt of music". Other images that can be noted in the connection are—"the sky / splintered with wakes of light" ("Divali", 65), "the peaks / snow-drowned—permanence" ("Divali", 69); "The Yangtze flows on like brown tape", and referring to research work—"Each figure like a laden boat / with white or madder sails afloat" ("Research in Jiangsu Province", 91); referring to the light of the afternoon-sun falling through trees in the orchard—"changeable as the sieved light that falls / upon this page from beyond the embanked trees" ("From a Traveller", 95); referring to a sense of joy in Babur and his wife in Humayun's sudden appearance—"our hearts blossom like rosebuds, and our eyes shine / like torches." ("From the Baburnama...", 119); referring to loss in love "through the sieve of long absence" ("From California", 126); referring to the contentment that the late afternoon light after a storm brings to the poet's room —"Beautiful beautiful light / Heavy as honey, redolent / of Cotswold stone / And of lemon groves on drier hills" ("Between Storms", 131); referring to the coming of dawn, like a man who shows himself partially in the beginning—"Dreaming, while dawn's left hand is in the sky" ("Abalone Soup", 137); speaks of "the pus of memory" referring to the unwanted memories to be cleansed from the mind, and compares his mental condition to a "dead river" that "meanders" nowhere—"Down a dead river on a plain...Leads to no open sea" ("Ceasing upon the Midnight", 143); referring to the light at sunset—"The angled sun / slants honey-coloured rays" ("A Style of Loving", 153); speaks of "forked years" referring to the uneven past life ("Walk", 160); speaks of "uncertain" glow of fire as "smoke-red and unentire" ("Tourists", 181); speaks of human race as "over-salted pie", and morning traffic on the Golden Gate Bridge as "frail lemmings on the bridge / Jammed in so tight" ("On the Fiftieth Anniversary of the Golden Gate Brigade", 187); speaks of the affection between the child and the man as "this web of tenderness" ("Adagio", 205); speaks how the bright light of the valley affected their eyes—"Like baffled owls we winced and blinked" ("Mist", 206); speaks of a passage through life as "To hack a route through rotten woods" ("Things", 208); referring to the movement of mosquito away from the room in the morning—"Let me sleep here for one night / And I'll catch the morning flight / Thus the sad mosquito pleaded" ("The Louse and the Mosquito", 287); and referring to the behaviour of shy politicians—"So he changed the inclination / Of his musical temptation / And, like prince or politician / Tried to split the opposition" and to the voice of the cat—"Murmuring—and now his voice / Purred like a well-oiled Rolls-Royce" ("The Cat and the Cock", 317, 322).

Even plain use of words, with adjectival and otherwise nuances, with a view to co-ordinate the meaning, provides an important dimension to the totality of Seth's style of writing. Some such words and their use may be listed by way of reference, such as:

Punjab, pandits, panir
Panipat and paan,
Family, music, faces
Food, land, everything
Draw me back.... (3, 4)

The tin stack, the Mussourie store,
Hunger, the freezing rain, (10)

After you went it became an effort to water,
Weed, mulch, replant, even harvest.... (22)

Blight, change, recurrence—I am at it again.
Yours illness; meaning; the old neurotic search. (31)

You blink, I smile, we kiss, 'your turn', I nod. (35)

To where you live, jog, laugh, toke, talk— (39)

My mappings of these selves—despondent, witty,
Calm and uncalm, lost in self-doubt or pity....
The courtier, soldier, scholar— (62, 63)

The Tarrying Garden, piecemeal or entire:
Meander, tarry, amble, pause, admire. (84)

...The air foretells
Snow, moonlit snow, low-voiced, dog-eared,
heads bowed,
Students seep out from libraries into the cold. (86)

...no method,
Order, principle, rule in work or thought;
No good flesh or bread in their bazaars,
No ice, cold water, musk-melons, grapes, no horses; (115)

...of the four A's
Of California—asparagus,
Ale, avocado, artichoke—you raise
Our palates to the most vertiginous
Conception of sublimity... (138)

A piece of gristle catches his eye.
The phone rings, he turns to reply
A smell of burning comes
From somewhere, something hums. (142)

Drinks, pours, drinks, pours, and lies. (144)
Unconsummated, therefore
Unjaded, unsated,
Picnic, movie, ice-cream;
Talk, to clear my head
Hot buttered rum-coffee for you, (153)

But grief and cares for what? You ask—
What do I claim?—
For death, for parting, for my livelihood, my name. (167)

As shadows, then as mass,
The mountains of Garhwal
Serrate and curve by pass
And peak towards Nepal. (177)

A magpie flaps back to its pine,
A sparrow dust-rolls fluffs, and cheeps,
The humans rest in a design:
One writes, one thinks, one moves, one sleeps, (178)

...He stares
In contemplation at a face,
Cold, calm, unsorrowing, that bears
Pain, age, death, vandals, and disgrace. (183)

Voices in my head,
Chanting, kisses, bread,
Prove yourself. Fight. Shove
Learn. Earn. Look for love? (210)

In a different vein the words have also been used to pinpoint a context, a situation, even a mood or an atmosphere. Thus as in "The Hare and the Tortoise", the hare and her companions, like restless young chaps given to pleasure, almost like social Americans, in a restless conversational manner:

Hay, girls, did you know the rat
Was rejected by the bat?
'Good for her! The rat's a fool!'
'Oh, I think his kinda cool.'
'Too bad, darling, now his dating
Lady Lemming's maid-in-waiting.'
'What—that hamster? You don't say!'—

> Gibble-gabble every day!
> Gibble-gabble every everywhere!
> Went the mouse and mole and hare—
> Gibble-gabble, gibble-gabble.
> Oh, what riffraff! Oh, what rabble! (304)

An atmosphere of fear, panic, horror, and great devastation is created in the poem "A Doctor's Journal Entry for August 6, 1945":

> ...While I debated it,
> The roof, the walls and, as it seemed, the world
> Collapsed in timber and debris, dust swirled
> Around me—...Alarmed, I gave a shout,
> 'Where are you, Yecko-san?' My blood gushed out.
> The artery in my neck? Scared for my life,
> I called out, panic-stricken, to my wife.
> Pale, bloodstained, frightened, Yecko-san emerged,
> Holding her elbow ....There we stood, afraid.
> A house standing before us tilted, swayed,
> Toppled, and crashed. Fire sprung up in the dust,
> Spread by the wind. (169-170)

Atmosphere, context, mood and attitude, all mingle in a spirit of abandon, and through multiple creation of images, all related to sea, in the fifth Section of the poem "Bagatelles". The passage has echoes from Homer, Greek Mythology, Shakespeare and Yeats, and tries to establish a serious point of view about life. But at the same time what may be noted is a subtle play of humour and an ingenuous use of words, phrases and epithets that combine together to provide a fine poetic texture. The whole passage may be quoted.:

> O luminous, dark and serpent-haunted sea,
> O ever-hooded, tragic-gestured sea,
> O dolphin-torn, O gong-tormented sea,
> And thou, thou unplumbed, salt, estranging sea,
> O snotgreen sea, O scrotumtightening sea,
> Incarnadined and multitudinous sea,
> O finny-tribed, much-described sea,
> How weary of description must thou be. (48)

Expressions of wit, humour, irony, satire etc., also constitute important aspects of Seth's poetic style. They are integrated in the poetic structure as a whole, and provide motivations to the poet's understanding and attitude. In fact, it is not so much expression of wit and satire as humour and irony, particularly an ironical-cum-humorously mocking tone, can be seen in many poems. A few examples may be listed. Such as humour:

> I'd always hoped somehow, sometime, somewhere
> I'd meet someone like you. I also deemed
> Such visions built on vodka and on air,
>
> ("To a Fellow Traveller", 18)

> Our spiders are much blacker and much thinner,
> Patrol their webs with greater frequency
> And seem perpetually anxious about dinner,
>
> ("A Morning Walk", 71)

> The father sits in bed reading the 'Indian Express'
> Inveighing against politicians and corruption.
> 'India could do so much....' he says.
> 'Even in the time of the British...' he says,
> 'Can you believe it—on every bag of cement—
> And still he continues to be a minister!
> The rot has gone too deep. Let's go for a walk.'
>
> ("The Comfortable Classes at Work and Play", 109)

Likewise the humorous account how the whole tribes of bugs just like human being eat into the King's blood ("The Louse and the Mosquito"):

> Once the signal came from Creep
> That the king was fast asleep,
> Quietly, discreetly, they
> Nipped and sipped and drank away.
> Sons and grandsons, sisters and brothers,
> Great-granddaughters, great-grandmothers,
> Second cousin and their wives
> Thus pursued their gentle lives
> Lives of undisturbed delight—
> Growing plump and smooth and white. (186)

Similarly, the account of the tortoise's steadiness and carefulness is equally humorous—a tongue and cheek account of people who claim to be steady and balanced ("The Hare and the Tortoise"):

> But the tortoise, when he rose,
> Daily counted all his toes
> Twice or three times to ensure
> There were neither less or more
> Next he would tally the amount
> In his savings bank account.
> Then he'd very carefully
> Count his grandsons: one, two, three—
> Ed, and Ned, and Fred by name
> And his sermon was the same... (305)

So, too, the account of beasts and their meeting, touched with humour, like an account of different groups of people getting together in a meeting ("The Elephant and the Tragopan"):

> And so, that evening, all the creations
> —With tusks, or grills or other features—
> Met at the river's edge to plan
> How they might out manoeuver man.
> Gibbons and squirrels, snakes, wild dogs,
> Deer and macaques, three types of frogs,
> Porcupines, eagles, trouts, wagtails,
> Civet cats, sparrows, bears and quails,
> Blood sucking leeches, mild-eyed newts,
> And leopards is their spotted suits—
> Stated their stances, asked their questions,
> And made their manifold suggestions. (340)

The use of irony too, a part of the total account, suggesting motivations and attitudes, both in short references as well as in larger contexts, is almost pervasive in these poems. Even on many occasions the mix of humour and irony illuminating both the context and the point of view, has been deftly achieved. Thus as in the poem "Bagatelles", illustrating the rake's progress, mild, yet sharp irony:

'Cars, women, beer—there's nothing else in life.
This is the tripod of my youth, said Swill.
Ten years—and now the tripod is the wife,
The television and the sleeping pill.

Or, speaking in praise of urban green illustrating the people's attitudes:

When every park becomes a highwayed plain
Cemeteries and golf courses remain;
For every thinking man who is not red
Reveres the rich; and next to them, the dead. (47)

In "A Morning Walk", sting of irony contrasting individual affluence with collective misery:

How fine it is to share the world and not
Its need when, there are those who weep for food.
Their children's limbs will atrophy, brains rot
Swollen for lack of it, while 'all things good',
Food, shelter, health are mine; interests; loves;
The time to work though avocado groves. (72)

In "Research in Jiangsu Province" the reference is to research and statistics data on which socio-administrative decisions in general depend, but how futile such exercises generally are:

Statistics where none grew before
And housing estimation galore,
Diet, and wealth and income data,
Age structures and a price inflator,
Birth and fertility projections,
Plans based on need and predilections,
O needful numbers and half true,
Without you what would nations do. (92)

In "Work and Freedom" the nature of work in Auschwitz, the infamous Nazi concentration camp given to mass-killing is spoken of as a generally relaxing work—"no reason to complain of boredom" (165). Similarly, in the quatrain "Passage" the considerations of loss and decay are viewed in a stingingly ironical attitude:

Your eyes, my understanding, all will rot;
The trees we see, the books we read, will go;

> The way that we use words, as like as not;
> And we are fortunate that this is so. (197)

Or, in a separate quatrain ("Prandial Plaint") the projection of love has a subtle element of irony all through:

> My love, I love your breasts, I love your nose.
> I love your accent and I love your toes.
> I am your slave. One word and I obey.
> But please don't slurp your coffee in that way. (196)

So too, for example, in "The Rat and Ox", in such work as how commissioned reports on important national issues are prepared—where the nature of work becomes more important than the purpose itself, the ironical twist is pervasive:

> So the deity descended,
> And, until his task was ended,
> Workaholically obsessed,
> He took neither food nor rest—
> But with undiminished vigour
> Questioned every fact and figure
> —Size of sunspots, times of tides,
> Weights of white fish—and, besides
> Cross-examined train-commuters,
> Crunched the data in computers,
> Tested truths, refuted guesses,
> Curved his Ts and crossed his Ss...
> Grilled the sages of six nations
> And to the celestial court
> Made his interim report
> After three and thirty years. (294)

Differently, in "The Hare and the Tortoise", the usual habit of media in the modern times to give excess amount of attention to motivated clever people is satirized:

> ...the hare
> Suddenly was everywhere,
> Stories of her quotes and capers
> Made front page in all the papers—
> And the sleepy BBC
> —Beastly Broadcast Company—

Beamed a feature with the news:
'All the World Lost for a Snooze'.
Soon she saw her name in lights,
Sold a book and movie rights.... (312)

And in "The Elephant and the Tragopan", an ironical account of the deceitful talk of politicians in power—one may say, in India particularly:

'Of course, my friends, it slipped my mind.
But then, these days, I often find
'I have so many files to read,
So many seminars to lead,
So many meetings to attend,
So many talks, that in the end
A minor fact or two slips by. (351)

Similar element of deceit can also be seen in tragopan's death, the deceitful behavior of people responsible for its death trying to lift it to the level of respect and honour—a motivated action apparently humorous no doubt but sharply ironical:

He had the body laid on ice,
Draped in the state flag, end arrayed
With chevron, scutcheon and cockade—
....
Four bugles played "Abide with Me";
Four matrons wept on a settee;
Four brigadiers with visage grim,
Throw cornflakes and puffed rice on him;
Four school girls robbed the tragopan
Of feathers for a talisman;
And everyone stood round and kept
Long vigil while the hero slept. (360)

Thus Seth's poetic style has many facets. Beginning from the use of prose and prose-pattern as a part of poetic structure, to the use of appropriate phrases, epithets, images for providing necessary suggestions and embellishment, to incorporating wit, humour, irony as parts of attitude and points of view, we move to many other aspects, such as, defining a situation or atmosphere, providing a portrait through detai' observations, developing a tone varying from flippancy to reflectiveness and from personal involvement to impersonal detachment, and exhibiting competent descriptive and narrative skill. A few examples may he listed. Thus in "Night in Jiangning" the account provides a quiet, relaxed atmosphere:

A glass of tea; the moon;
The frogs, croak in the weeds,
A bat wriggles down across
Gold disk to silver reeds.
The distant light of lamps.
The whirr of winnowing grain.
The peace of loneliness,
The scent of imminent rain. (179)

An equal picture of peace and relaxation with an eye to detail observation is provided with reference to Lodi Gardens and its morning atmosphere ("The Comfortable Classes at Work and Play"):

There against the exquisite morning sky
The Arab domes of the tombs sit formed and fine
And neem and semal, ashok and amaltas
And casuarinas lend the air freshness, the heart peace,
On the enamel-stripped domes the vultures nest,
Along the casual paths three joggers thump.
A group of eight old citizens wearing safas
Gossip in the growing sun and laugh with abandon. (110)

A graphic picture of the "splendid bird" peacock with a keen observation of details is given in the poem "From the Baburnama..."

...Its size is that of the crane.
The head of the male has an iniridescent lustre;
His neck is a fine blue, his back is rich
With yellows, violets, green and blues and stars
Extend to the very extremity of his tail.
The bird flies badly, worse indeed than the pheasant. (116)

Differently, a situation is defined as a fearsome situation with all its gruesome details, as an aftermath of atomic explosion, in the poem "A Doctor's Journal..."

...There we stood, afraid.
A house standing before us tilted, swayed,
Toppled, and crashed. Fire sprang up in the dust,
....

and,

A splinter jutted from my mangled thigh,
My right side bled, my cheek was torn, and I
Dislodged, detachedly, a piece of glass,
....
I saw the shadowy forms of people, some
Were ghosts, some scarecrows, all wordless, dumb—
Arms stretched straight out, shoulders to dangling hand.
(169-170)

The tales of *Beastly Tales* are each fine narrative pieces where tales have been told with racy sequence of events and situations as they developed, with references to the activities of the characters and their mutual contacts, with a good deal of humour, irony and wit. In fact Seth's poetry shows both the skills, that is, both narrative and descriptive, in equal competence. Thus a racy narrative account is in "From the Memories of Babur..." showing adversities of a journey:

The snows near Chiraghdan
Covered the roads. Our guide,
Like us, was lost. We sent
Out men to find the road.
And still it snowed and snowed.
Four days passed: they returned.
They had not found a soul. (25)

In "Between the Storms" the account is one of destruction, narrated detachedly, like submitting a report:

The hills are green again, the lake
Murky. Continual storms
Over California have washed away
Houses, gouged the coastline,
Stranded bewildered seals,
Swept away walkers in aberrant waves... (131)

Or as in "The Mouse and the Snake", the fight between the mouse and snake is narrated in quick excitement:

Swift as rage the little mouse
Rushed towards the killer's house,
Bit his tail once, twice, again,
Hissing wrath, the snake backed out,
Swerved his body round about
Lunged towards the mouse and tried
Swallowing her—but she leapt wide
Every time he lunged, till, he,
Wriggling back, exhaustedly
Slid inside his hole once more. (291)

Similarly, good descriptive skill can be seen in many other poems. Thus the poem "A Little Distance" opens with a graphic account of a place—sunny, pleasing and restful, a veritable abode of nature:

A little distance from the waterfall
By a small pool the yellow beachtowel lies
On a long warm rock, and near it azaleas grow
And shadows of thin fish fall
Across the speckled stones, and a light breeze blows,
Rippling the skin of the pool, first this way, then that.
A blue-tailed lizard suns itself. (98)

A similarly intense descriptive account of nature can also be seen in the poem "Spring of Content", a picture of happy, free movement:

The blond hills have turned green, the winter rain
Has pressed the dust back to the earth again,
The ophthalmologist's almond tree is full,
....
Grapes of wistaria are every where
Usurping walls where climbing roses aren't
Jostling each other in the breeze and sun;
Wild oats and barley intersperse with grass.
And boisterous dandelions— (134)

And in "Hill Dawn" too, the description of the day breaking—a joyous, exciting time:

The rising mist now fills
The forest rifts below:
Peninsulas of hills,
And lakes of fluid snow.
Oak, rhododendron, pine
And cedar freed from night
Recede in a design
As visionless as white. (177)

Finally in this connection, an apt and fine example would be the first stanza of "The Elephant the Tragopan", a fine descriptive account of a nature-rich place that is Bingle Valley, a place of trees, flowers, streams and animals which we have already referred to. The passage is in balanced rhymed couplets, providing a musical context, and builds up an atmosphere of calm joy in a relaxed, restful mood, and related to the situation creates a state of happy, emotional acceptance:

In Bingle Valley, broad and green,
Where neither hut nor field is seen,
Where bamboo, like a distant lawn
Is gold at dusk and flushed at dawn,
Where rhododendron forests crown
The hills, and wander halfway down
In scarlet blossom, where each year
A dozen shy black bears appear,
Where a cold river, filmed with ice,
Sustains a minor paradise. (337)

At the end, another interesting aspect of Seth's style may be noted. It refers to many echoes from the past poets that lie interspersed in many parts of his poetry. These mainly relate to British poets, such as, T.S. Eliot, Keats, Wordsworth, Arnold, Fitzgerald, Donne, Yeats, Shakespeare, Larkin, as well as to European authors Homer and Dante, and an Indian English poet like Ezekiel. We say 'interesting', because they do not actually constitute an influence on Seth's style. They come lightly and casually, and aid in illuminating the particular context. The echoes from Eliot are more pervasive than the echoes from other poets. The composition of Eliot's *Book of Possum Cats* can be compared with the composition of Seth's

Beastly Tales. But that is in general. There are other specific echoes elsewhere in the poems: from Eliot—"Of corrugated sheds, the times / Of Sutro Tower, bill boards, wires, / The airport, scrap, discarded tyres" (23), "The errant Coffeeman gets out of bed" (35), "He gets a bottle, pours a glass" (144), "My colleagues untrustworthy, those above me / Reluctant to understand or even to listen" (165). Similar is Fitzgerald's translation of *Omar Khayyam*—"Wake up! The smudge of dawn / Low on the hills has shot / The bay with light" (33), in the title "The Sultan's Turret" (35), "The Traveller at the Inn..." (116); Keats—in the title "Ceasing upon the Midnight" (142), "Ah, tonight / How rich it seems to be / alive unhappily" (143); Wordsworth—"Duty, stern Daughter of the Voice of God" (35); Arnold via reference to "Scholar Gypsy"—"He leans against a willow with a dish / And throws a dumpling to a passing fish" (81); Donne —"What can I say to you? How can I now retract / All that that fool, my voice, has spoken" (152); Yeats—"O dolphin-torn, O gong-tormented sea" (48); Shakespeare—"Incarnadined and multitudinous sea" (48); Larkin—"Hearing the water's roar as it churns past / The ancient brewery" (13); Homer—"O luminous, dark and serpent-haunted sea" (48); Dante—"A hope abandon, ye who enter here" (18) and Ezekiel, in the title, "Party for the Retirement of the Oldest-Serving British Museum Reading Room Book Attendant" (45).

WORKS CITED

King, Bruce. *Modern Indian Poetry in English*. Revised Edition. Delhi: Oxford University Press, 2001.

Mehrotra, Arvind Krishna, ed. *Illustrated History of Indian Literature in English*. Delhi: Permanent Black, 2003.

Naik, M.K. and Shyamala A. Narayan. *Indian English Literature, 1980-2000: A Critical Survey*. Delhi: Pencraft International, 2004.

Seth, Vikram. *The Poems 1981-1994*. New Delhi: Viking, 1995.

4 The Golden Gate

In 1986 Vikram Seth wrote *The Golden Gate*, a novel in verse, composed entirely in rhyming tetrameter sonnets. The novel was said to be "Byronesque" (Perry, 549-551), and was a satirical romance describing the stories of young professionals in San Francisco through their quests and queries to find, and then deal with love in their own lives as well as in each other's. *The Golden Gate,* simply put, is a verse narrative about San Francisco written in rhyming sonnets. This was a bold project considering that poetry today mostly consists of free verse. And the incredible volume of rhymes (over 7000 lines) is astounding. This metrical feat alone makes the novel interesting reading. We are given the key to what prompted Seth to attempt a verse-novel in a "comical authorial intrusion" (Patel, 2000), at the beginning of Chapter Five, and also we are informed about his poetic concerns:

A week ago, when I had finished
Writing the chapter you've just read.
And with avidity undiminished
Was charting out the course ahead.
An editor—at a plush party
(Well-wined, provisioned, speechy, hearty).
Hosted by (long live!) Thomas Cook
Where my Tibetan travel book
Was honored—seized my arm: "Dear fellow,
What's your next work?" "A novel..." "Great!
We hope that you, dear Mr. Seth—"
"...In verse," I added. He turned yellow
"How marvelously quaint," he said,
And subsequently cut me dead. (5.1)

And again,

How do I justify this stanza?
These feminine rhymes? My wrinkled muse?
This whole passé extravaganza?
How can I (careless of time) use
The dusty bread molds of Onegin
In the brave bakery of Reagan?
The loaves will surely fail to rise
Or else go stale before my eyes
The truth is, I can't justify it. (5.3)

Seth, an ardent admirer of Charles Johnston's translation of Pushkin's masterpiece, *Eugene Onegin* (1977) ("Like champagne / its effervescence stirs my brain."), uses the complex and flexible tetrameter structure that marks Pushkin's composition. A really interesting choice considering, as Seth admits, that the "once —noble meter capers before the proud pentameter, Tyrant of English." Seth's meter appears to be more syllabic and the scheme matches Pushkin's, down to the masculine and feminine rhymes. *Eugene Onegin* is one of the classics of Russian Literature and its hero served as the model for a number of Russian literary heroes. It was published serially from 1823-31. The first complete edition was published in 1833.

The Golden Gate comprises 594 sonnets, all written in iambic tetrameter (which also includes the acknowledgements, table of contents and author's biographical note), and follows the fourteen-line stanza pattern of *Eugene Onegin. Eugene Onegin* is (almost wholly) written in verses of iambic tetrameter with the unusual rhyme scheme 'aBaBccDDeFFeGG' where the lowercase letters represent feminine rhymes and the uppercase represent masculine rhymes. This form has come to be known as the 'Onegin stanza'. Unlike (for example) the Shakespeariean sonnet of 'abbacddceffegg' the Onegin stanza does not divide into smaller stanzas of four lines or two in an obvious way. There are many different ways the sonnet can be divided, for example the first four lines can form a quatrain or instead join with the 'cc' to form a sestet. The form's flexibility allows the author more scope to change how the semantic sections are divided from sonnet to sonnet, while keeping the sense of unity provided by keeping a fixed rhyme scheme. Vikram Seth used this stanza in his novel *The Golden Gate.* There are thirteen chapters with an average of forty-five sonnets. Seth's rhyme scheme differs from the traditional sonnet forms. The traditional sonnets were written in pentameter, and the rhyme scheme employed were abba abba cdecde (Petrarchan) or ababbcbc cdcdee (Spenserian) or ababcdcd efefgg (Shakespearean). Seth's rhyme scheme is very much unlike these, and goes ababcdcd in the octave and effegg in the sestet, and this is rare in the sonnet form. For Seth the sonnets function as interlinked units which gradually progress with the narrative pace of the novel:

> Soothed by such counterfactual reason
> Phil's thoughts turn from his homely face
> To the crisp features of the season:
> The straw-gold hill, this oak-strewn place,
> With her the flutter of a dusty
> Sparrow, and there the encroaching rusty
> Lichen upon the rock where Paul
> Sits singing to himself, and all
> The hillsides burred with skeletal thistles
> And thornbush, and the clear cool air
> Presaging winter rain, and there
> A mockingbird with chacks and whistles
> Liquidly aviating through
> A sky of Californian blue. (3.4)

Here we can also quote a section of Pushkin's original stanza form (translated by Charles Johnston) to accentuate the similarities between the two books:

> How early he'd learnt to dissemble,
> To hide a hope, to make a show
> Of jealousy, to seem to tremble
> Or pine, persuade of yes or no,
> And act the humble or imperious,
> The indifferent or the deadly serious!
> In languid silence, or the flame
> Of eloquence, and just the same
> In casual letters of confession—
> One thing inspired his breath, his heart,

And self-oblivion was his art!
How soft his glance, or at discretion
How bold or bashful there, and here
How brilliant with its instant. (39)

But, *The Golden Gate* has more in common with *Eugene Onegin,* than merely the form. Pushkin's novel, just like Seth's *The Golden Gate* is also "about a specific space in a specific time, and the characters' attitudes to love" (Multani, 61). In *Eugene Onegin,* as in *The Golden Gate* says Angeli Multani, "The characters' attitudes to love underscore their attitudes to life, to issues that are outside or beyond the private question of romantic or sexual love" (61). Seth, like Pushkin, removes the boundaries that are built in most modern societies between the public and the private by probing and then revealing a person's options in love and in life. In both the books, there is also a latent orientation towards a "preferred" and "more correct" way of life and loving.

In *Eugene Onegin*, Pushkin depicts the story of Eugene, "a jaded member of the St. Petersburg's elite and Tatyana Larina, a young country girl. Tatyana falls in love with Eugene, who is something of a dandy with nothing interesting to occupy his mind. In later years the character of Eugene came to represent that famous Russian character—the "superfluous man, the individual who could find no productive role in the society, despite intellect, education and wealth" (Multani, 61). But Eugene doesn't reciprocate Tatyana's love and is forced to leave the provinces after a senseless duel in which he kills another man. Tatyana, on the rebound marries a prince, and becomes a member of the high society group of St. Petersburg. Eugene, on his return to St. Petersburg meets Tatyana again and instantly falls in love with her, but now it is her turn to reject him, either because she doesn't want to or is unable to reciprocate to him now.

Angelie Multani commenting on this says, "Just as Eugene's inability to respond to Tatyana when there was the space and opportunity for them to have a future together characterizes his weak and self-indulgent nature, the various choices made by the different characters in *The Golden Gate* represent their ability or inability to lead personally happy or fulfilling lives" (62). Again, in both texts, the landscapes of the locations, the social settings, the values, politics and customs, food, atmosphere and weather play important roles in the lives of the characters.

The pivot character is John, whose acquaintances fill out the multitude of San Francisco. His conservation, it seems, fits well with his job as a computer programmer, working on nuclear projects, though not with any of his friends. Liberals, homosexuals, bisexuals, and anything that remotely concerns a bit of thinking eventually irritate him. Liz Dorati, the love interest, is a lawyer who eloquently protests against Lungless Labs and nuclear bombs and has an "anti-nuclear cat", Charlemagne, who is completely territorial and who vehemently dislikes John. Bisexual Phil is John's alienated, witty, long-time friend, who is also a liberal and has an affair with the guilt-ridden homosexual Ed, Liz's brother. The only person John can really seem to get along with is Janet Hayawaka, the delightful and funky sculptor—punk drummer, and who intermittently appears as John's confidante-ex-lover and would be the present and future love interest.

These are the five central figures in the book. Each of them is defined within the parameters of his profession, personal life and whims and family and social conditions and connections. By the end of the narrative, all of them have interacted with each other at some level or the other.

Twenty-six year old John Brown is a graduate of Berkley. He is a successful but extremely lonely computer executive in Silicon Valley. He is employed in the high-tech computer and electronics industry and works in the area of nuclear research. A workaholic, John "Kneels bareheaded and unshod / Before the chip, a jealous God (1.9):

> John's looks are good. His dress is formal.
> His voice is low. His mind is sound.
> His appetite for work's abnormal.
> A plastic name tag hangs around
> His collar like a votive necklace.
> Though well paid, he is far from reckless,

Pays his rent promptly, jogs, does not
Smoke cigarettes, and rarely pot,
Eschews both church and heavy drinking,
Enjoys his garden, likes to read
Eclectically from Mann to Bede.
(A surrogate, some say, for thinking.)
Friends claim he's grown aloof and prim.
(His boss, though, is well-pleased with him.) (1.3)

Gray-eyed, blond-haired, aristocratic
In height, impatience, views, and face,
Discriminating, though dogmatic,
Tender beneath a carapace
Of well-groomed tastes and tasteful grooming,
John, though his corporate stock is booming,
For all his mohair, serge, and tweed,
Senses his life has run to seed.
A passionate man, with equal parts of
Irritability and charm,
Without as such intending harm,
His flaring temper singed the hearts of
Several women in the days
Before his chaste, ambitious phase. (1.4)

He follows conservative politics and is open about his opposition to the anti-nuclear war peace campaigner. He refuses to realize the implications of the kind of work, he is involved in until the end of the book when he faces moments of self-doubt. "John does not question the ideological apparatus that constructs his consciousness," says Mala Pandurang (78). Along with the other nuclear plant employees ("Those who devised these weapons, decent / adjusted, family minded fold"), he could be considered as an ideal co-opted subject, John feels that what / He chooses to ignore can't hurt him / Some things are his concern, some not. / His politics have strongly, slowly, / Rigidified" (2.14). There are however other reasons behind John's psychological history. Seth offers "compressed insights" (Hill, 89) into John's childhood. His present condition induces sympathy when we learn that it does not "...wholly stem from his tenure in Defence. / It's a reflection, in a sense, / Of a rigidity deeper-seated. / A bit of an emotional waif / Since, a small boy, he used to chafe / Against the fate that he'd been meted, / The mother's love he'd never had. / He'd clung to "standards", good or bad (2.14).

Janet Hawakaya is of Japanese descent and the only ethnic presence in the novel. She was John's girlfriend in the past, becomes his confidant and in due course once again becomes his lover. The sensitive and artistically gifted Janet is passionately involved with her sculpting of "Ma Hen, her maiden work in stone" (12.16). She is also a drummer in the punk band "Liquid sheep". Jan plays a pivotal role in the narrative. The day is set in motion when she takes the initiative to place a personal advertisement in a newspaper with the intention of easing John's loneliness. It is to the message written by her that Liz responds. More importantly, Jan strives towards a possible re-conditioning of John's narrow perspectives. She reacts angrily to John's demeaning sexist remarks by reprimanding him for his intolerance of women and gays ("Johnny Boy, your mind needs cleaning / Of the debris of prejudice") (1.33).

> John stands beside his phone, recalling
> Janet's warm beauty, smiling calm,
> Her dark eyes, high-boned features, falling
> Black ponytail, her vagrant charm.
> He thinks, "I guess I'll be the wiser
> For talking to a sound adviser. (1.18)

Liz Dorati is a 27-year old, high-powered ex-Stanford Law School attorney. She is a beautiful, vivacious, blue-eyed, "well-rounded" blonde, who is from a family of Italian immigrant vine-growers (2.27). John is impressed by her handwritten reply that Jan forwards to him, and invites her to meet him. They share a passionate, whirlwind romance that is soon destroyed by personal prejudice, political differences and a pet cat called Charlemagne. Invited to a protest meeting by anti-nuclear demonstrations, Liz arrives at the gathering with her cat Charlemagne in a pram, and eloquently speaks against the Lungless Labs and nuclear bombs. Initially she is unwilling to commit and to risk her career, but eventually gives a spirited reply in court on behalf of the protesters:

Her gold hair's fashioned, not severely,
Into a bun. From a gold chain
A single pearl, suspended clearly,
Allures his eye. John, once again,
Can't speak for wonder and confusion:
A woman, or divine illusion?
He overcomes his vertigo
And stands. He mutters, "Liz, hello.
I hope... was it a hassle finding
This place?" His voice fails.
He sits down. Liz says, "You're nervous,
Mr. Brown. Don't worry: I too need reminding
That this is real." In an unplanned
Gesture of warmth, she takes his hand. (2.43)

Twenty-eight year old Phil, the least conventional of the characters, is John's former room-mate from Berkley. Once a nuclear engineer in Datatronics and a computer expert, his "self accepting psychic bounce" and "moral vision" forces him to get out of the rat race that John is caught up in and to devote himself to the anti-nuke movement as a "peacenik" (4.25). Phil is Jewish and has a six-year old son named Paul. For the most part of the earlier sections of the text, we find him trying to recover from the traumatic experience of his wife Claire leaving him for another man and returning to the East Coast (3.15). Claire's protestant family had never approved of her marriage to "a good atheist Jew" (3.17). What Phil wants now is—"to live / Without this emptiness—to give / A little love, to get a little" (9.35). Open and non-conservative minded Phil has a brief homosexual affair with Liz's brother Ed, but he eventually has a marriage of convenience—and also for affection and companionship—with Liz who has by this time ended her relationship with John:

Such thoughts melt through the frozen river
Of his sad mind, and yet loud,
Seeing Paul quietly weep and shiver,
He says, taut featured, head half bowed,
"No, Paul, she's gone away." "Forever?"
"I just can't tell you, son—but never

Think you are alone. You've got me." "When
Will you leave me?" Phil, shocked, stares, then
Holds Paul (still snot-nosed) to him tightly,
And says, "Don't say that. You are all
And everything I care for, Paul.
I'll never leave you." Then, more brightly,
"In fact, you know, you'll be the one,
When you've grown up, to leave me, son. (3.19)

Ed Dorati is twenty-three, "intense, athletic, / silent" (4.24), and caught in a dilemma between his religious beliefs and his natural homosexual preferences. He shares a tender relationship with Phil, but is unable to come to terms with his feelings of guilt, a consequence of his Catholic upbringing. He ultimately breaks away from the relationship. But as long as it lasts it is clear to the reader that the Phil-Ed relationship has all the love, warmth and sharing that truly characterizes the best man-woman relationship. In spite of the rather lighthearted reference to censors, the reader can feel the purity and almost elevated quality of their relationship. What Seth has tried to establish over here is the fact that, in a relationship it is not the sex that matters nor the sexuality, but how far one is compatible and comfortable with the other person.

As Phil talks on, his eyes grow radiant.
Ed thinks of the first time they met.
The weeks have warped the placid gradient
On which his even wheels were set.
Neither the sense, at every meeting,
Of his heart's full and rapid beating,
Nor the abrupt and scalding rush
Of redness to his face, the flush
When he feels Phil's eyes resting on him,
But something infinite and slow
And tide-like holds his life in tow.
The salt of human love upon him,
To it his leached will yields control,
Whether it stings or heals his soul. (8.7)

In *The Golden Gate* Seth portrays San Francisco in its manifold charm the way Pushkin does for Russia. The breadth of life is exhibited from its most trivial aspects to its more contemporary, disputed and moral standards. Friendship, love, work, play, sexuality, the nuclear age, single parent child rearing, death and the city are just some of the topics included. And then there are the wonderful light touches of scrabble and chess, symphonies and art critics, interesting party scenes and personal resolution through personal dating advertisements. Such insignia's like the bumper stickers and billboard slogans seen while driving down a freeway are artfully and engagingly rendered in verse. If anything ties Seth's work together, it is the rootless, detached quality of the narrator. "It is a total, unparalleled pleasure to wallow in the seductive cadences of Seth's poetic novel, and then marvel at the no doubt obsessive and somewhat twisted brain which has come up with the words, rhymes and humour in this book. In the style of long, long ago, this book is the only one that I have ever read which brings poetry totally and absolutely to life. It is poetry which details and narrates, talks about punk rock bands, and watches love come and go. This is a great experience" (an anonymous reviewer from Silicon Valley, California).

San Francisco has often been a magnet for America's counterculture. During the 1950s, 'City Lights Bookstore' in the North Beach neighbourhood was an important publisher of beatnik literature. During the latter half of the following decade, the 1960s, San Francisco was the center of hippie culture. Thousands of young people poured into the Haight-Ashbury district of the city during 1967, which was known as the 'Summer of Love'. At this time, the 'San Francisco sound' emerged as an influential force in rock music, with such acts as the 'Jefferson Airplane' and the 'Grateful Dead' achieving international prominence, blurring the boundaries between folk, rock and jazz traditions. 'The Church of Satan' was founded and made its headquarters here in 1966. During the 1980s and 1990s San Francisco became a major focal point in the North American and international punk and rave scene.

Although he says he is not interested in literary theory ("and calls the deconstructionists and other university litcrit types, the mad critics"), (quoted in Knorr, 1999), Seth is part of a contemporary trend among poets towards formalism. He was at Stanford at the same time as Dana Gioia, whose *Can Poetry Matter?* (1991) recorded the public estrangement from the confessional, anything-goes poetry coming out of American universities along with various other things. Seth informally studied with the poet Timothy Steele, who has published a book on metre and versification.

"Trends in poetry are even in a sense more rigid than trends in fiction," Seth said, "Because at least in fiction, if something sells, then editors will publish it, but in poetry –poetry lists are the preserve of people who don't expect to sell and they don't expect their poetry list to make a profit, so they just leave poetry editors to publish their friends and their fellow poets in their particular school of writing." *The Golden Gate* which combines humour and sadness in sonnet form, "is a wholly successful linking of formal poetry to modern dilemmas," says Katherine Knorr (1999). Once he had seen Steele's verse Seth said, "I realized that one could write about one's own times with a modern sensibility and yet use these forms which have existed in the language for hundreds of years, full of the resonance that they had and the clarity that they almost forced upon one." After his early schooling in India, Seth went to Oxford, then Stanford. "I thought, oh my God, thick-headed beach boys and no intellectual conversations. But then I met people who were both very intelligent and interested in things of the mind, and also who would think nothing about teaching you to swim butterfly. For me it was like a revelation in a wonderful way. That's why *The Golden Gate*, in a way, for all its tragedy, it's a happy book" (Knorr, 1999).

"There is a sense of conviction about the writer, of purpose, that has enabled him as a writer to take the road less travelled and arrive triumphant" (*The Guardian*, April 7th, 1999). Even as he was writing *The Golden Gate* friends and editors scoffed at the idea, but he was confident enough to incorporate their comments into the text—"Drivelling in rhymes all very well.

The question is does spittle sell?"—And was rewarded when the book sold very well and received glowing reviews. Seth manages to sustain throughout the length of the novel a demanding verse form that allows him to demonstrate a high degree of technical dexterity and poetic wit. More important he tells a tale which demonstrates a deep sympathy with all his characters. Seth pardons all because he understands all. The story is not pushed forward by vignettes, but rather by the characters that inhabit the novel. "Once one reads the story for the plot, one can then savour the many felicities of language and, pervading all, nothing less than a philosophy of life based on the acceptance of other and value of friendship and love."

The Golden Gate has an all-American cast of characters and it offers a perceptive look at the 1980s Yuppie lifestyle in northern California. The term 'yuppies' has now come to be referred to more than just a demographic profile: it is also a psychographic profile. It describes a set of behavioural and psychographic attributes that have come to constitute a commonly believed stereotype. According to this stereotype, yuppies are more conservative than the preceding hippie generation. Dispensing of the social causes of their more passionate parents (who themselves shed traditional values), yuppies tend to be 9-5 professional workers. Yuppies tend to value material goods (especially trendy new things). In particular, this can apply to their stocks, imported automobiles (e.g. BMW, Lexus, and Mercedes-Benz), sport utilities, development houses, and technological gadgets, particularly cell phones. Unfortunately, the fast-paced pursuit of these material goods has unintended consequences. Usually in a hurry, they seek convenience goods and services. Being 'time poor', their family relations can become difficult to sustain. Maintaining their way of life is mentally exhausting. Sometimes, they will move every few years to where their job goes, straining their family. The fast-paced lifestyle has been termed a 'rat race'. Heavily influenced by a competitive corporate environment, they often value those behaviours that they have found useful in gaining upward mobility and hence income and status. They often take their corporate values home to their spouses and children.

According to the stereotype, there is a certain air of informality about them, yet an entire code of unwritten etiquette can govern their activities from golf and tennis to luncheons at cocktail and sushi bars.

Seth has made every effort to portray an intimate Californian lifestyle. He has said that "...it was not his detachment but rather his love of California that was the most valuable to him in writing the book. One can't come with a cold and objective eye from outside and then write with affection about a place. One must have lived years in that place and not just observed for years" (Leslie, 1986:4). There are a number of details that range from the seemingly inconsequential to more serious social issues open to debate such as contemporary sexual mores and nuclear armaments. Socializing activities include housewarming parties, winemaking picnics, weekend jaunts followed by sumptuous breakfasts, and gestalt group parties.

Seth's players share exclusive relationships with their pets, which include a Siamese cat called Charlemagne and an iguana called Schwarzenegger. Past-times range from a child's addiction to the star wars, to art exhibitions and classical symphonies, as also performances of a raucous punk rock band called "Liquid Sheep". Seth has worked hard to include as many culture-specific indicators as possible so that the reader may have no reason to suspect that this is a non-Californian doing the writing:

> Anne Gunn, who draws delight from sketching
> The unearthlier products of the earth,
> Decides that Schwarz is "rather fetching".
> The others give him widest berth.
> Some leave to play football or footsie,
> Some for a matinee of *Tootsie*,
> To watch a high school tennis match
> Or tend their vegetable patch,
> Study statistics, skunks, or Serbia,
> Shop, sail, or swive, stretch out and snooze,
> Or smoke a joint, or strum the blues,
> Repair the doodas of suburbia,

Plan out the Lungless Labs campaign,
Or dream of real estate in Spain. (5.27)

Commuting to and from work on the highway, John Brown, one of the central characters, notices policemen chasing "little Bugs and harmless Hondas", and sensational headlines that scream "the President is a lesbian spy". Billboard slogans and bumper stickers convey requests to motorists to "Honk for Jesus" and "to hug your whale today". Leslie suggests that the text is filled with details about California "that natives sometimes overlook because of excessive familiarity" (4), and Craig Tapping comments if the work might be considered in terms of Seth "returning the gaze that has so often found India exotic, on that most exotic hothouse of late 20th century capitalist culture—California (1992:294).

The novel portrays the contemporary Californian lifestyle through the story of the relationships of a group of young professionals. It is a life of love and lust, told with wit, restraint and intelligence and deals with white American characters with just one character of partly Japanese descent. There are no Indian characters at all and Seth seems completely at home in white American culture. It is an America where people from all over the world – and not just from Western Europe—shed their ethnic dimensions after sometime and acquire a new American identity. When Seth was asked why he writes about it, his reply was "one can't quarrel with inspiration".

The novel is basically the story of a man who is unable to sustain love and companionship in his life and ends up much the same way as he begins—a lonely and depressed human being. Yet, at the end we realize that catharsis and enlightenment has taken place for John. Although he is still lonely and depressed, the loneliness and depression is not the same as that we find in the initial few pages of the novel. His life has come full circle and his bittersweet experience of life has made him a mature and better human being. There is every hope that a new chapter to his life might still yet begin:

To make a start more swift than weighty,
Hail Muse. Dear Reader, once upon

A time, say circa 1980,
There lived a man. His name was John.
Successful in his field though only
Twenty-six, respected lonely...
...Across the pine-serrated sky,
Dragged from his care, not knowing why,
He feels an urgent riptide drawing
Him far out, where, caught in the kelp
Of loneliness, he cries for help. (1.1)

When the novel opens, we realize that John's mother is dead and he is "caught in the kelp of loneliness" (1.2).

The novel deals with personal relations, love, loss and morality with an acuteness and delicacy of perception, a humorous yet compassionate and a very healthy understanding of human beings—particularly in difference in generations—not conflicts but just stances, desires Seth deals with two sorts—the older, modern kind of living, feeling and thinking, and the sometimes crippling freedom of the post-modern period, where the old monogamous love between sexes are now a part of a rosy past. It is different and heartless. *The Golden Gate* is witty—but it is all heart.

The influence of Pushkin is exceedingly strong as regards the meticulous reflection of the social fabric, individual characters, interaction, and above all, the pervasive irony directed often (as Alexander Pope's is not) against the author himself. Seth himself is like Goldsmith's Chinaman, a balanced, wry outsider who considers this society from the inside. He is critical, but (like Pushkin) never sets himself to be a judge, only an amused commentator. He shows us how messed up their loves, their art, and publicity are—but he is Kim Tarvesh in anagram, "the alcoholic, thesis-bedeviled foreigner on the fringe" (Bobb and Digirolamo, 1986). Tarvesh is like Chaucer the pilgrim, narrower and more naïve than the omniscient Vikram Seth. The unbroken use of the Pushkin stanza form, the tetrameter sonnet, enhances rather than impedes the poised style, the sophistication of diction and the effortless yet persuasive rhythm of the lines.

In relation to this Tabish Khair says, "poems written in iambic tetrameter are by no means a novelty in English verse and one can even come across entire narrative series written in that form. Take for example, chapter six of John Fuller's novel in verse, *The Illusionists* (1980), what distinguishes Seth's sonnets, from Fuller's more pensive sonnets, is probably their speed and lightness of wit. These characteristics are sustained or highlighted not only by the diction and the short conversational sentences, but also by the fact that syntactical endings do not always coincide with line endings and by the use of feminine rhymes and enjambment. The use of both catalexies and hypercatalexis also reinforces the conversational, at times flippant, rhythm of the lines. Of course, the iambic tetrameter helps too, by imparting a skipping lyric quality to the poems and shortening the sonnet line by one foot. As does the ironic distancing use of poetic conventions" (2004:55-56).

> Unnoticed, Janet leaves, abstracted
> By her abortive coffee break.
> Back in the café, Liz, attracted
> By John's absorption, nibbles cake,
> Sips tea, doffs her defensive armor
> And, laughing, thinks, "This man's a charmer.
> I like him, and he likes me, though
> I can't imagine why it's so."
> (O nightingales! O moon! O roses!)

In talk as heady as champagne:

> "A wondrous cat!" John laughs, proposes
> A toast: "The King and Queen of France
> And England. Far away they advance. (2.40)

Anita Desai commenting on this verse form of Seth has said that too much is being made of the fact that the verse form used is the tetrameter sonnet employed by Pushkin: "The analogy is unfortunate. For all its technical achievement, *The Golden Gate* is essentially light verse closer in spirit to John Betjeman and Ogden Nash than to Pushkin's ferocious and satirical wit" (1993:22).

The Golden Gate offers an amusing yet sensitive look at the 1980s yuppie lifestyle in northern California. Young and prosperous but bored and lonely, the characters in the novel search for meaning and happiness. Bisexual Phil is attracted towards gay Ed, but Ed, a devout Catholic is tormented by sexual guilt. While Phil is gradually learning to understand and accept his sexuality, he gets attracted towards Liz, Ed's sister, and they marry. Lurking beneath the novel's gentle satire on the Californian ethos is Seth's message that sexual self-acceptance, meaningful-commitment, sincere love and stable friendship are the basis of an authentic life. In *A Suitable Boy* (1993), where Seth projects an epic vision of the Indian life of the 1950s, homosexuality is merely hinted at—in one of the novel's numerous subplots, there is a suggestion that two male characters —Maan Kapoor and Firoz Khan were once lovers.

While the idea of a novel in verse may be initially off-putting, readers of this tour de force are in for a treat. Using the sonnet form throughout, and varying his language from lyrical elegance to "timidly vernacular", Seth's tale of four California yuppies is as fully dimensional as a good novel, and twice as interesting. In this witty, compressed style he gives us "fully delineated characters"; John, a Silicon Valley executive seeking solace in a meaningful amatory relationship; his friend and ex-lover Janet, an artist and musician in a raucous rock band; Liz, whose parents produce superior Californian wine; her brother Ed, floundering between sin and religion; and John's Pal Phil, abandoned by his scientific career at Lungless Labs, a scene of anti-nuclear protests and rallies. It is an engaging story of the pangs and passions of love, interlaced with serious ruminations on homosexuality and religion and on the future of the earth in the atomic age, and some comic scenes of feline behaviour, bumper stickers, responses to "personal ads, and other facets of the contemporary scene, as refracted through Californian life-style."

The bard does not hesitate to interrupt history time to time, to explain a change in the course of events or to comment upon the structure of his narration, as he defends himself against critics who would accuse him of folly in writing an entire novel in the sonnet form. Inspired by the marvelous swift metre of Pushkin's *Eugene Onegin*, Seth performs imaginative acrobatic jests, quips and sums, delivering his social commentary with spirit and verve. In spite of some passages where he veers towards the maudlin and bathetic, Seth's experiment is a resounding success:

> John notes the late September showers
> Have tinged the blond hills round the bay
> With a new pre-winter bloom. The way
> That, when he was a child, the mysteries
> Of San Francisco's restless history
> Kindled in him an answering spark,
> It strikes him now, as through the park,
> Wrested from old dunes by the westward
> Thrust of the green belt to the slow
> Pacific swell, his footsteps go
> But it is late. The birds fly nestward
> Toward the sunset, and the arc
> Of darkness drifts across the park. (1.5)

The novel ranges through all the important facets of human life: love, marriage, birth and death. An exploration of these vital issues brings to the fore problems still by and large peculiar to affluent societies of the West, the Americans in particular; such as unhappy marriages, broken homes, single parenthood, divorce and homosexuality.

Yet, these problems are gradually coming out of the closet in comparatively conservative Eastern societies also, particularly in the Indian scenario. Unhappy marriages, broken homes, homosexuality etc., are no longer taboo in our country. Gradually they are coming to the fore and bringing along with them an awareness and acceptance that was not there a few years back. Globalisation and economic liberalisation and a growing multinational culture, both in literal corporate terms as well as the availability of certain goods, jobs and opportunities in India's urban centres have led to a lifestyle that worships material consumerism, comfort and freedom. "At this point of our history, certain classes and groups in urban India are no longer as removed from the yuppie culture of California as they may have been a couple of decades ago", says Angeli Multani (62).

John, robbed of a mother's love, devoid of a family to "cushion his solitude", no spouse, no sibling, no children, he is advised by his former love Janet who is still a friend to him to insert matrimonial advertisements in the papers. The responses it evokes from various women, the events that follow thereafter provide a touch of comedy along with wit and irony. After interaction with a couple of women, John literally falls for Elizabeth Dorati, "Sweet Liz", who is also a little lonely except for her infamous cat Charlemagne, who has remarkable similarities with another famous and notorious cat who goes by the name of Garfield (the well-known cartoon character). With her "golden hair" and "vibrant verve", Liz charms John who in his elation cannot figure out whether she is woman or "divine illusion".

The loving pair is enveloped in an "amorous mist" for a time, their heads surrounded by a halo of rosy light. John has at last found a new home, and someone to love in "life's brief game". He and Liz cohabit for a while enjoying the bliss of togetherness until the storm blows that makes them realize that "all life's a shaky dream". All the quirks that had amused John first later aggrieve him. He can't get over the feeling that Liz loves the cat more than she loves him: Constant friction between the two on account of the cat and Liz's sudden decision to marry Phil (a good kind man who makes me laugh), drives John to an "embittered brooding / against the cosmos". Pain "mangles" John who believes he is "duped" by love. "So all her talk of love was spurious", he laments. Hurt by Liz and Phil's "breach of trust" he rejects all their attempts at reconciliation. "Lonely and injured in his pride / His sorrow festers." "He is lost in savage transportation of grievance." Then proceeds to lead a life of wastage, "sifting bars each night / For cute chicks". Then follows a time when he even gets "resigned / To loneliness".

"But Liz herself, torn between conflicting emotions and to loyalties, is somewhat like the poor little bird which keeps yearning between her winter and summer home in A.D. Hope's *Death of a Bird*", says Ragini Ramachandra. It is when John's friendships have all dissipated that he thinks of his former love, Janet Hawakaya whom he has treated "less than ideally". Jan who at one time was "mad" about him and, "could hardly think of life without him" responds to his friendly overtures and makes an attempt at a comeback. The two slowly slip back to their old days of "fire and smoke". Now a "quilt of peace" surrounds John, he dreams of nothing and is even "free of all volition". It astounds him to think how little the enmity of the crass world, its fickle illness bothers him.

As time passes, Janet, intent upon patching up differences between erstwhile friends John, Liz and Phil, invites the latter home to a party. But as destiny would have it, even as the guests are arriving for the night's revels, news of Jan's involvement in a car accident reaches John, leaving him absolutely shattered. Jan succumbs to her injuries in a hospital where John, not being related to her, is not allowed inside to see her in the dying moments of her life. In his intense despair he broods that, had he managed to say a word to her she might have survived. Jan's friends, the Lammonts too die in the crash leaving their little son the sole survivor of the accident. Both the sorrow of an orphan and the anguish of a bereaved lover are movingly portrayed and it is in the handling of these crises that the whole novel achieves a new depth and dimension:

Phil, more distressed by the calamity
Than he himself shows, sometimes sees
His son and Chuck, in quiet amity,
Playing—and Chuck abruptly freeze
And—gasping, sobbing, wheezing, crying—
Relive again his mother's dying:
The blood, the broken sleep, the scream:
Was that, or is this now, a dream?
One day Phil, shattered by his pleading
To "take me back home," drives him down
To his old house. The grass is brown
In patches, and the flowers want weeding;
But brilliant in their summer bloom
Geraniums mass outside Chuck's room. (13.5)

... ...

Sitting in the small Cessna, flying
Along the algae-tinted shore

Of the long bay, Chuck squints down, trying
To make his house out. Then with awe
He points: "that's it back there. I see it—
With the red flowers. That must be it,"
And laughs out loud with sudden joy.
When Mrs. Craven gives the boy
A hug, he once again grows quiet.
She says, "Look, Chuck, life's tough! When you
Are lonely, or just feeling blue,
Come over – we two'll stage a riot.
How does that sound?" Chuck, somewhat bleak,
Replies, "I might be blue next week." (13.9)

John who is completely shattered by this unexpected disaster becomes a nervous wreck. Haunted by the images and memories of Jan, it seems as if he can't outlive this pain. The reader feels for him as "he tries to wring / Meaning from things that have no meaning / And scrapes at rusted words that yield / Few glints of insight" (13.26). In his grief John indulges in meditations of a philosophical nature which have an echo of Hamlet's ruminations and even allows himself to an expression of "prayer" so as to find a pattern in or cure for Jan's death:

As if some random psychedelic
Drunkard or lunatic or child
Had left a daubed and reckless relic
On his mind's walls, with bright and wild
And unaccountable lucidity
—So forcible in their vividity
That his perceptions seemed unhinged—
Old images of Jan impinged
On his dimmed life. At work, or driving
To work, or after work, at home,
She seemed to be with him, to come
To him (thus brokenly surviving)
Like a rich revenant of life—
Seizing a chisel or a knife. (13.14)

But life must go on and so Liz requests him to be the godfather to her newborn son whom she has chosen to call John.

The novel ends with John poignantly hearing Jan's voice saying to him, "I am with you John. You are not alone. / Trust me, my friend; there is the phone. / It isn't me you are obeying./ Pay what are your own heart's arrears. / Now clear your throat; and dry these tears"; thus bringing John's "explorative voyage" to an end. The wheel has come full circle. "What did not last in life has now possessed John wholly." "It looks as if the invisible bridge is the only kind of bridge man is destined to build...to reach out...to reach across...to people and not any concrete one that the city of San Francisco boasts of," suggests Ragini Ramchandra (1997:107).

The setting of the novel, as mentioned earlier, is San Francisco, the city of Saint Francis, "the loveliest city in the world"—"light pearled", "fog fingered", "pinnacled" with its famous bay—the "unruffled daughter of the pacific", glimmering in the evening with light from the golden globes of its street lamps—"like sequins on black velvet robes". In short, San Francisco comes alive in this novel in verse. Along with these vivid touches and beautiful descriptions, the milieu and ethos of life lived there, of yuppies and urban officials, or artists and ordinary people, also gets successfully evoked. Seth has vividly captured the people and the places in this city—especially its "Yuppiness" that has since multiplied. The novel is an acute portrayal of an educated, hip, typically San Franciscan circle of friends and their highly entangled love affairs:

Patron of your beloved city,
O San Francisco, saint of love,
Co-sufferer in searing pity
Of all our griefs, whom from above
Birds would alight on, singing, feeding
Within your hands—hands pierced and bleeding
With Christ's own signs—who, stigmatized
As dupe and clown, apostrophized
The sun in its white blistering starkness
As brother, and the blistered moon
As sister, and who, blind at noon,
Opened your heart and sang in darkness—

And where it was, sowed light, look down.
Solace the sorrows of your town. (13.4)

It is interesting to note here the acceptance of *The Golden Gate* by American reviewers who acknowledge the text as an "American product", recognize its "American qualities", and read it as being very much "American in intention" and a "quintessential California novel" (see Bobb and Digirolamo, 1986). Gore Vidal states (on the dust jacket) that the book is "the Great Californian Novel", while a *New York Times* reviewer calls it "a splendid achievement" and "a thoroughly Californian novel peopled by unmistakably Californian characters".

Rowena Hill comments: "Judging by his novel, *The Golden Gate,* it is hard to see how Vikram Seth can be considered an Indian writer, except by accident of birth. There are few Indian references in the text such as the "taste of honey", and the charioteer metaphor, and the non-violent attitude of the peace marchers has obvious Gandhian connections...but there is nothing that California has not possessed for a long time" (87). The shifting of the location of Seth's own creativity from his place of birth to the USA (Bay Area of San Francisco) is read as an act of de-territorialisation. Hill goes on to add that the book, "...is, in fact, a totally Californian novel but what does perhaps result from the author being an adopted son of that state is a dose of gloating (the insistence of the accepted outsider on his belonging) in his celebrations of the Californian way of life, which can be irritating to anyone who has been exposed to the Californian claim to represent the vanguard of humanity in awareness and know-how".

But according to Makarand Paranjape, the "microcosm" of Seth's moral world is not only of California, but, as Seth would have it "of our brave new world itself". He says, "Those who are not on the correct side of the correct causes are corrected by life itself and hence the moral standard that form the underlying framework of the book are projected to be universal and absolute" (1986). He again suggests that, "central public theme of the book is world peace and therefore the seventh chapter, wherein members of an anti-nuclear movement organise a peace protest march against the 'Lungless Labs', the centre for Defense Research, has the best claims to be considered as the climax of the book".

Although *The Golden Gate* is all about American characters and American identity, Izeth Hussain in an outstanding paper dealing with Vikram Seth's *The Golden Gate* finds the Indian sensibility at work (quoted in Sastry, 1991):

> However the content of his book, as distinct from its technical aspects, shows more clearly an Indian sensibility at work. This could raise questions about what exactly is uniquely or distinctively or specifically Indian when we are speaking about a country noted for its cultural diversity. What can be said is that Seth is an Indian and what seems non-western about his work shows the pull of ethnicity, the power of his own cultural background. (156)

And again he goes on to add:

> An Indian sensibility and outlook is shown in several ways, one of which is in the attitude to marriage, seen as a relationship requiring for its success sensible accommodation between two people for the founding of a family. John and Liz are brought together through the advertisement column implying that marriage is a question of matching two people on the basis of their personalities and circumstances, and not a question of inexplicable chemistry drawing them together. (157)

Commenting on Seth's virtuosity, Hussain sees it significant for revealing something Indian, or at any rate non-English and non-American:

> There could be something Indian or oriental about Seth's virtuosity.... In Seth's case, one thinks of the Indian predilection for the ornate and the elaborate which is to be seen for instance in Hindu architecture and sculpture, and in the unimaginably complicated rhythmic sequences of some Indian classical music. (157)

Central to the plot of the novel is the advertisement for a companion for John; this is sent to the Bay Guardian by Janet.

She sees it as a means of solving John's intense loneliness as he verges on "the brink of Thirtydom" (1.35). Seth has spoken of how the idea occurred to him after a conversation with a friend on the advisability of using such advertisements to find romantic partners (in Leslie, 1986: 6). John, at the outset vehemently criticizes the idea of advertising for love and companionship, and dismisses it as "a meat market"—"Goats and monkeys, bears, bulls, bidders / Buyers grab me while you can" (1.34). Janet however pursues the matter and receives eighty-two responses from equally lonely souls ("From dulcet Deborah to foxy / Farah—a world of tendered joys, / A passion play of pleas and ploys" (2.5). Janet forwards these replies to John, and after six unsuccessful attempts, the seventh letter that John replies to is that of Liz Dorati.

Rukmani Bhaya Nair has given a very interesting and apt analysis of a series of personal relationship / marriage advertisements in *Gender, Genre and Generative Grammar: Deconstructing the Matrimonial Column* (1986). Nair has made use of data of matrimonial advertisements from *The Times of India* and *Hindustan Times* as also advertisements from the *New York Review of Books* and the *New Statesman* and *Society* to arrive at "a linguistic nexus", and "a cultural place and pressure-point where studies of gender, genre and grammar meet." Nair says that, "while the putative genre label of marriage advertisements may be superseded by terms such as 'heartsearch' and 'person-to-person' in personal columns in American and British newspapers and magazines, the underlying commonality of purpose of such advertisements is to seek companionship".

But in the Western context, the purpose of such advertising need not always necessarily be for a long-term relationship. Nair points out that advertisement differ from newspaper in India to those in Britain and America, "Although dating advertisements in personal columns share several of the structural features of the Indian advertisement, multiple differences do emerge upon a close reading" (234). For example, "prototypes of the desirable female and acceptable male emerge, separate and certainly unequal from both Indian and western representations" (234).

Nair demonstrates, "the embedding of social ideologies and cultural presuppositions in this particular form of discourse. In the Indian advertisements, for instance, the potential bride and groom are embedded, if not marginalized, within powerful familial frames. One family seeks out a compatible other with a view to mutually satisfactory union" (226).

According to Nair, Indian matrimonial advertisements consist of a passive structure with agent deletion, while Janet's insert has an active structure with the agent as the subject noun phrase:

> Young handsome Yuppie, 26.
> Straightforward, sociable, but lonely,
> Cannot believe that he's the only
> Well-rounded and well-meaning square
> Lusting for love. If you, out there,
> Are friendly, female, under 30,
> Impulsive, fit and fun, let's meet.
> Be rash. Box... (2.3).

The text itself is used here as an invitation to initiate an interaction between two potential partners. This is suggestive of direct contact between two individual parties. Nair comments that such freedom would rarely be allowed in the Indian context, where the dignity of family and community is at stake (243). Nair also points out at adjectival modifications in the Indian advertisements based on parental / familial assessments as the continual references to caste and family status indicate. Such go-betweens in the guise of families and friends or the "negotiating parties" (237) are not present in *The Golden Gate*. The "active agent" is a "grammatically singular person" unlike the varied protagonists in *A Suitable Boy*. Indian advertisements essentially consist of a collective relationship between two sets of families and their children. Compatibility between large units of families and friends, of which the individual is only a part of the whole, is what is sought after. In *A Suitable Boy*, this is what Mrs. Rupa Mehra hopes to achieve through the marriage of her daughters Savita and Lata. On the other hand, the interaction in the West is established between individual people who stress on the details of their personal preferences and characters which differentiate them from the other members of their larger social group. This is Liz Dorati's reply to John's advertisement:

> I'm friendly, female, 27.
> Well-rounded too, and somewhat square.
> I've not yet known romantic heaven.
> But harbor hopes of getting there.
> I'm fit—at least, "I'm not convulsive;
> And fun, I hope, though not impulsive
> To match the handsomeness you flaunt
> (I do not mean this as a taunt;
> I find immodesty disarming),
> I have heard several people say
> I am good looking, in my way.
> So if you'd like to meet, Prince Charming,
> That shows discernment. If you flout
> My charms, you are a tasteless lout. (2.27)

Commenting on this, Nair says that in the Western inserts, personal characteristics are expanded or are over-specified, whereas in the Indian advertisements personal characteristics are severely restricted. "It is here that manifestations in the two cultures radically diverge. While advertisers in the West aim at starting up a conversion, Indians begin a negotiation which could include discussions of dowry and horoscope predictions (243). The encompassing family, so pervasive in the Indian advertisement, is quite factored out in the Western mode or representation (242). Nair continues: "The recurrent pattern in the Western column is the classic literary motif of the quest (heart search) for a romantic partner; the Indian theme, on the contrary, is that of the request, the solicitation. Indian advertisers ask for a "suitable match"; Western advertisers for a "perfect mate" (243). Nair concludes by saying, "to draw a literary analogy, the Western advertisements seem to be Beckettian texts, where individuals are revealed in isolation while the Indian matrimonies appear to be Brechtian texts, with all the society milling around" (250).

The central motif in both *The Golden Gate* and *A Suitable Boy* is the quest for a companion in life. Mrs. Rupa Mehra initiates the search in the latter, while Jan sends the advertisement on John's behalf. Mrs. Mehra performs the role of a traditional matchmaker, which is nowadays being increasingly played by matrimonial columns of national newspapers, especially among the English educated Indian middle- and upper-middle-class people.

But in Janet's draft, a question is used as an invitation to initiate a conversation between potential partners. This is suggestive of direct contact between two individual persons. There is also a willingness to mention negative personal attributes, which is completely taboo in Indian matrimonial advertisements. On the contrary, in Indian advertisements the tendency is to exaggerate the positive personal attributes rather than downplay them. But exaggeration again is so common to the Indian psyche that in the long run it does not hold a lot of significance. Exaggeration, rather than understatement, is an Indian way of life, which is known and understood by all.

Critics have really tried hard to find ways of making Seth's epic verse part of Indian English writing or have berated him for not conforming to notions of Indianness (Gupta 1990, Narasimhaiah, 1991 etc.). *The Golden Gate*, however, is not Indian at all except in so far as it has been written by an NRI, nor is it for that matter as its cover boasts, "The Great Californian Novel" save that California is the place in America for migrant and expatriate multi-culturalism (as the party joke has it: "Hey, look everybody! I just met someone who was actually born in California!"). The book is, however, very much a Diasporas narrative seen from the point of view of an Englishman who has gone to Stanford to get a Ph.D. and moves in the yuppie circles of second generation Japanese artists, Hungarian economists, Jewish atheists, green activists, women lawyers and gay advertising executives from Italian wine-growing families and high-tech researchers in Silicon Valley. "The society, like the poetry, is poised, self-aware, even slick, and the point is that style (or lifestyle) is part of the brittle protective barrier erected by an atomized, secularized community against, disquieting invasion—not from foreign culture, since that is all part of the multi-national post-modern pot-pourri—but from uncool angst of loneliness, passion, commitment and above all morality" (Sharrad, 1993).

It is under the structure of Diaspora that we can assemble such different works as *Bye-Bye Blackbird* (Anita Desai, 1971), *The Golden Gate* and *Wife* (Bharati Mukherji, 1975). Vikram Seth's bridge and his detailed signs of the social and physical landscape constitute structures that simultaneously suggest belonging and distance, continuity and the mortality of the individual. Dimple Dasgupta's submission before T.V. ads—icons of the West that capture a civilization in its liveliest but most fixated form, "making a point of heightened desire (love/life) coincident with the promise of instant gratification of such desire (death)—is part of her 'erratic' life; shallow at its start, unstable at its end, but consistent with the kind of experience and artistic logic outlined here" (Sharrad, 1993). Continues Sharrad; Dev (*Bye-Bye Blackbird*) consults the moribund oracles of empire and finds them monstrous until his displaced desire encounters the emotionally compatible but totally over-whelming natural monument of England's countryside, the "green and pleasant land" that overshadows, but co-exists with the "green and grisly" one already experienced.

According to Leela Lakhsmi Narayen, the title of the book appears to have escaped critical attention, except as an identifying feature of the landscape (1993: 174). An engineering marvel in steel, the majestic Golden Gate Bridge is a suspension bridge that carries its weight with no visible means of support. In the novel, the bridge functions as more than just a connector between two geographical locations in the Bay area. It provides an opportunity to the characters to connect to their natural surroundings and with each other. Ed drives across the "tall-spanned bridge" after a fight with Phil, and as he observes the city from the bridge, "a benediction" steals over his heart, and he decides to write to Phil (5.8). After Phil has a bitter argument with John, he and Liz drive out together on to the bay, and walk across the bridge:

> They park the car by the Marina.
> The surface of the cobalt bay

Is flecked with white. The moister, keener
October air has rinsed away
The whispering mists with crisp intensity
And over the opaque immensity
A deliquescent wash of blue
Reveals the bridge, long lost to view
In summer's quilt of fog: the towers,
High-built, red-gold, with their long span
—The most majestic spun by man—
Whose threads of steel through mists and showers,
Wind, spray, and the momentous roar
Of ocean storms, link shore to shore (9.28).

While on the bridge, Phil and Liz confide in each other their difficult relationships with Ed and John respectively.

The background against which the novel's plot is set is modern day America (timed clearly in 1980). This is a world of advertisements and consumer products that have little to do with human emotions. This dichotomy between private emotions and external milieu is evident throughout the book, the best example of which could be seen in Chapter V, sonnet 6, when Ed has his first disagreement with Phil. His anguish is to be countered by the best "media strategy". The choice—between available brands (*Encore or Savour*)—seems quite unrelated to the essential product, i.e. coffee. "The sheer absurdity of the situation underscores its impossibility: after all, one cannot fight an emotional crisis with a cup of coffee, no matter what its brand name", suggests Sahana Das (1998).

The Nature, the landscape, is another character in the novel. Although not given center-stage, the novel is full of descriptions of natural sceneries of the Californian horizon which serves as a backdrop to quite a few emotional dramas. The landscape is always there in the novel, now smiling, now berating, outstretching and dwarfing the human drama played out before it as on a stage:

It's spring! Meticulous and fragrant
Pear blossoms bloom and blanch the trees,
While pink and ravishing and flagrant

Quince bursts in shameless colonies
On woody bushes, and the slender
Yellow oxalis, brief and tender,
Brilliant as mustard, sheets the ground,
And blue jays croak, and all around
Iris and daffodil are sprouting
With such assurance that the shy
Grape hyacinth escapes the eye,
And spathes of Easter lilies, flouting
Nomenclature, now effloresce
In white and Lenten loveliness. (12.5)
... ...
Day's pass, and on the golden birches
The mocking birds sing lucidly.
A soft sun shines. A blue jay perches
High on the knotted pepper tree.
The whales move southward. Snail tracks harden
In Matt and Joan's unguarded garden,
And wrinkling unplucked olives thrive
Along the curve of Campus Drive.
Magnolias shed their vein-bruised petals.
The vineyard turns a fiery red.
In John's yard, each untended bed
Grows thick with weeds. Inside, dust settles
Through his disordered rooms. He holds
A note he stares at, then unfolds. (13.50)

In the above-cited sonnets, both love in the air and loss in the mind are portrayed movingly and vividly and each sonnet in its own way helps in furthering the storyline.

Seth's manner of presenting this emotional drama is such that the reader can never quite sympathize with anyone completely. The rejection or fear of love and emotional commitment shown in the text is, obviously, not an inevitable consequence of modern American life. The opening chapter introduces John as a byproduct of modern conservatism leading an apparently successful life. In close contrast to the description of the artificiality of John's life are lines which describe the natural beauty available all round him. In Chapter 1, sonnet 2,

John deliberately turns his mind to thoughts of electronic devices. Yet the awareness of silhouetted birds that "move cawing / Across the pine serrated sky" serves to emphasize the sterility of his life. It is precisely because there are alternatives present that he recognizes the emptiness of his life and "cries for help". Yet the support for John is far from being unqualified. Reader sympathy is controlled and limited by a critical insight into John's psyche:

> Lost in a savage transportation
> Of grievance, he won't own that he
> Helped generate this new equation
> Selective sensitivity
> To his ills, blindness to their feelings
> Of Equal injury, his dealings
> With Phil and Liz to him seem just
> Reprisal for their breach of trust. (11.27)

In a letter to Robert Conquest, published posthumously in his selected letters, Philip Larkin called Seth's work "a load of crap" and wrote a not entirely fair pastiche: "Outside, a dog barks / swinging from your prick I muse / On Wang-Lei's lyrics." But to Seth he wrote, "a very nice letter, pointing out what he didn't like, but also with words of encouragement, nice things I won't repeat. It kept me going for five years". In California, too, after the introspective worlds of boarding school and Oxford, Seth discovered a happiness he had not known before: "I loved the sunshine, so diverse ethnically and in terms of lifestyle. The freedom, the sense of ease in the personalities. I learned to have fun." Quizzed further on this, Seth is deliberately vague, as he is generally about his personal life, but there are clues in his writing which seems deliberately to invite speculation.

In *A Suitable Boy*, he writes how his alter ego Amit rebuffs "all the efforts of his female admirers or their mothers to get to know him better". He had remained faithful to Jane Austen. He appeared to be content to lead a life of contemplation. But in California Seth wrote a poem, "Dubious", which he refers to whenever he is asked about his private life and even read out on the Omnibus television profile of him a few years ago: "Some men like Jack / and some like Jill. / I'm glad I like / them both." In *The Golden Gate*, too, there is a bisexual character that is generally believed to be another loose self-portrait. "The humour and friendly satire in *The Golden Gate,* as much as *A Suitable Boy*, owes a debt to Indian fiction in English, so much of which, like the Malgudi chronicles of Seth's great favourite, R.K. Narayan, is characterized by low comedy and the affectionate pricking of pomposity ("A Suitable Joy", *The Guardian,* April 7th, 1999).

R.K. Narayan, on his part has this to say about *The Golden Gate*: "It is a novel in verse form, three hundred and odd pages, written by a young Indian, and it seems to me no small achievement...it is an extraordinary work. I have never come across any other modern writer who has ventured almost recklessly to narrate a story in verse...weeks later, the author, Vikram Seth, appeared in a TV interview and I realized, here was a genuine writer with the right values, gift and outlook, not writing in order to blow off steam or to reform society but a genuine artist who takes pleasure in writing. Here I found rhyme, reason and humour, and above all sensed a rhythm which 'vibrates in the memory' even after the book is shut and put away. Vikram Seth shows absolute mastery of the English language and has created a unique literary alchemy. Yes, this is a book fit to be kept beside Palgrave's *Golden Treasury* for frequent literary refreshment" (1999).

Seth's own reaction to the different critiques is predictably caustic: "*The Golden Gate* got, by and large, generous reviews. But there was one school of thought who said that stylistically speaking it was deliciously avant-garde; and another school which said it was dreadfully reactionary because it goes back to Pushkin and rhyming metre. As far as content went, some people said it was wonderful, it talks about gay rights and women's rights and the anti-nuclear movement. And yet, another school said it had the happy families of the typical antiquated, silly Victorian novel. So whether it is reactionary or distastefully trendy, who cares?" (Field, 1993:46).

The Golden Gate, in short, is Seth's San Francisco novel—all alternative lifestyles, gender breakdowns and anti-military protests. It uses a fresh, unusual and extremely interesting experiment to look back to the ancient epic tradition, and bring it right up to date in modern California. It is a vibrant, absorbing novel, notable for its vivid characterization (human and feline), as well as for its linguistic dexterity. "Set in the affluence and sunshine of Silicon Valley in the years immediately before the dot.com boom, *The Golden Gate* manages to be at once romantic, pleasantly sentimental and yet deeply satirical about the spaced out hedonism of California's beautiful Yuppies. When it was published *The Golden Gate* was singled out as a remarkable tour de force and praised for its light comic touch, its parodist elegance and its speedy way with narrative. Now a generation later, it reads like a strangely elegiac portrait of a lost world of innocence before the corruptions of the Nineties boom and the psychological devastation of 11 September 2001" (*The Sunday Observer,* 27th January 2002).

Gore Vidal has dubbed *The Golden Gate* as "the Great California novel" (on the dust jacket). The action in the verse-novel might be labeled as "a slice-of-life gone amorously awry." It has got two dimensions: one relates to America, particularly Californian socio-cultural conditions in the 80s, the second to Indian social norms and Indian sensibility, and written with wit, humour and detachment, and is a mix of English verse narrations and Indian Kavya, with focus on an individual's predicament in an alienated world related to instability, uncertainty and loneliness. In relation to this it would be interesting to quote Chandrasekhar Sastry who has said that, "sometimes the expatriate Indian swings to an extreme. Completely shedding his old identity he tries to invert a new himself repeatedly. Transformation for him is not just letting the old self die, but strangling it in a deliberate act of killing. And from that corpse of his former self he hopes to resurrect a new man, indistinguishable from the people he lives amongst. He discards all his old history, turns away from other people like him and simulates all possible outward features that he thinks appropriate to his newer self. He celebrates his assimilation and adopting the idiom and accent of the white man around him he commences to think and act like them—even in relation to his own people" (1991:155).

WORKS CITED

Bobb, Dilip and Vincent Digirolamo. "I am Looking Forward to Non-Entityhood." Interview with Vikram Seth. *India Today,* 15 June 1986: 152-155.

Das, Sahana. "The Reader and the Point of View: The Narrative Technique of *The Golden Gate.*" Nilufer Bharucha and Vrinda Nabar, eds. *Mapping Cultural Spaces: Post-colonial Indian Literature in English.* New Delhi: Vision Books, 1998.

Desai, Anita. *Bye-Bye Blackbird.* Delhi: Vision Books, 1985.

——. "Sitting Pretty." *The New York Review of Books*, 27 May 1993: 22-26.

Field, Michele. "Vikram Seth." *Publishers Weekly,* 10 May 1993: 46-47.

Gupta, Santosh. "*The Golden Gate*: The First Indian Novel in Verse." Viney Kirpal, ed. *The New Indian Novel in English. A Study of the 1980s.* New Delhi: Allied Publishers, 1990: 91-100.

Hill, Rowena. "Vikram Seth's *The Golden Gate:* A Quick Look." *The Literary Criterion*, 21.4, 1986: 87-90.

Khair, Tabish. "No Golden Gate for Indian English Poetry? Reading Vikram Seth's Novel in Verse in the Context of Indian Poetry in English." In G.J.V. Prasad, ed. *Vikram Seth: An Anthology of Recent Criticism.* Delhi: Pencraft International, 2004: 49-59.

Knorr, Katherine. "Vikram Seth Plays to His Truest Judges." *International Herald Tribune,* 23 April 1999: Online. http://www.iht.com/IHT/KK/00/kk042399.html

Leslie, Jacques. "Rhyme and Reason." *Los Angeles Times Magazine,* 8 June 1986: 16.

Mukherjee, Bharati. *Wife.* New Delhi: Penguin, 1987.

Multani, Angelie. "A Metrosexual Lovestory." G.J.V. Prasad, ed. *Vikram Seth: An Anthology of Recent Criticism.* Delhi: Pencraft International, 2004: 60-76.

Nair, Rukmani Bhaya. "Gender, Genre, and Generative Grammar: Deconstructing the Matrimonial Column." Michael J. Toolan, ed. *Text and Context: Essays in Stylistics.* London: Routledge, 1992: 227-254.

Narasimhaiah, C.D. "Introduction." *The Literary Criterion*, 26 (1), 1991: 1-11.

Narayan, R.K. Interview with *India Today,* 5 April 1999: Online. http://www.rigzin.freeservers.com/jhumpalahiri.htm# NARAYAN.

Narayen, Leela Lakshmi. "The Golden Bridge is Falling Down, Falling Down, Falling Down: A Study of Vikram Seth's *The Golden Gate.*" *Critical Responses, Commonwealth Literature.* Department of English, Osmania University, Hyderabad. New Delhi: Sterling Publishers, 1993.

Paranjape, Makarand. "*The Golden Gate* and the Quest for Self-Realization." ACLALS Bulletin. Eighth Series, No. 1. *Contemporary Commonwealth Fiction.* Ed. John Thieme. Aarhus, 1989.

Pandurang, Mala. *Vikram Seth: Multiple Locations, Multiple Affiliations.* Jaipur and New Delhi: Rawat Publications, 2001.

Patel, Devesh. "Vikram Seth: A Poet in Exile." *Contemporary Poetry Review*, 25 Sep. 2000: Online. http://doononline.net/highlights/seth/contemporary.htm.

Perry, John Oliver. *World Literature Today*, 65 (Summer, 1991): 549-551.

Ramachandra, Ragini. "Vikram Seth's *The Golden Gate*: Some First Impressions." V.N. Narendra Kumar, ed. *New Perspectives on Indian Writing*. New Delhi: Prestige Publications, 1997: 102-107.

Sastry, Chandrasekhar. *The Resident Indian: From Non-Being to Being.* Bangalore, India: Panther Publishers, 1991.

Sharrad, Paul. *Journal of the South Pacific Association for Commonwealth Literature and Language Studies.* No. 34-35, 1993.

Seth, Vikram. *The Golden Gate.* New Delhi: Penguin Books in association with Faber & Faber, 1986.

Tapping, Craig. "South Asia writes North America: Prose Fiction and Autobiography from the Indian Diaspora." Shirley Geok-Lin and Amy Ling, eds. *Reading the Literatures of the Asian American.* Philadelphia: Temple University Press, 1992.

5 *A Suitable Boy*

Vikram Seth's book *A Suitable Boy* (1993) that made history as a publishing phenomenon heralded the change from an economist-poet to a full-time writer, making millions in pounds. The media dwelt on its 700,000 words and 1,349 pages, the longest novel published in England since Richardson's *Clarissa* (1744-48) and longer than Tolstoy's *War and Peace* (1865-69)—and on Seth's advance of more than 2 million pounds. More relevant are the artistic comparisons made to Jane Austen, George Eliot, Tolstoy and Dickens. The pre-release publicity and the "superbly orchestrated public relations campaign" (Kagal, 1993: 50) that accompanied *A Suitable Boy* had never ever remotely happened to an Indian author. Publisher Arthur Cheetham of Orion, who had gambled on Seth with the huge advance, went on to reap rich rewards as the voluminous book outsold John Le Care and Wilbur Smith and the critics were reminded of Tolstoy and the Victorian novels. Vikram Seth's new book, he said, "had given him immense pleasure." "This was the kind of book that reminded him of why he came to publishing", he said. He was very disappointed after the Booker judges ignored *A Suitable Boy*. Subsequently, *A Suitable Boy* won the Commonwealth Prize and Britain's Channel Four is to serialize the novel.

Seth views the Indian edition with pride, as marking "a watershed in Indian efforts to be part of mainstream of world publishing". He explains that since he felt that *A Suitable Boy* was a distinctly Indian novel, he wanted the novel to be published initially in Indian and to be typeset here. "I was in Calcutta, and I knew I wanted the novel to be typeset once only. I couldn't bear to proofread a book of this length for three different English language publishers. I would have hated it by the end. I decided to do it in India to show that we could" (Field, 1993: 47). It has also been written that while working on *A Suitable Boy* he wrote as many as 12,000 words a day in longhand. But Seth, in one of his interviews refuted this and said that, "may be it was true for a day or two. But there were weeks when I didn't write a word. The first time I've written any of these novels, I've just had a straight first draft without looking back or publishing. Normally, I don't show it to anyone while I'm writing the first draft, then I send it out to friends to gauge their opinion on what works and what doesn't, which characters make sense, and so on. Then I mull over what they have said and read the book myself. And then I leave it for a few months because I don't want to revise by committee, so I leave it until I think I'm ready".

It was about another five years before Arundhati Roy's *The God of Small Things* (1997) received international hype of a similar degree. However, this excessive media publicity also has its own adverse effects. As Rukun Advani points out, "It has darkened the qualitative work of a book beneath a breath-taking façade of quantification—crores of rupees, millions of words, hundreds of pages: ergo (and this "truth" is drummed into us with temple cacophony), the book is bound to be as those statistics" (1993: 172). *A Suitable Boy* won the Connect Award in 1993 and launched Seth into a slew of interviews, talk shows and book signings on his book tour.

A Suitable Boy is set wholly in India. The main plot line, like that of *The Golden Gate* (1986), centres on the question of finding a suitable partner, and here it assumes an Austenean form. Will the heroine Lata submit to her mother Mrs. Rupa Mehra's arrangement or will she follow her own spirit, even if that means defying not only her mother, but also barriers of caste and religion. Three candidates present themselves: Kabir, a cricketer, dashing and handsome, but a Muslim; Amit Chatterji, Bengali poet and novelist, sophisticated, rich and a Brahmin, and Haresh, an energetic and bright young man determined to make a career for himself in the shoe manufacturing industry. "Lata finally settles for Haresh, not implausible because unromantic, an index of Seth's own pragmatism and of the direction in which India is, probably, heading," says D.C.R.A. Goonetilleke.

But the main strength of the novel lies not in the business of matchmaking, but in the depiction of the social panorama of the decade after Independence. Seth manages to interweave in a credible way all the larger themes of political, social and religious conflicts, with the day-to-day ordinary human emotions of his true-to-life characters, who have a strong resemblance to Dickensian characters, over whom countless readers have laughed and cried. A multitude of characters and events throng the novel, the setting moves back and forth between the cities of Brahmpur, which is fictional, and Calcutta (a world by itself), with excursions to New Delhi, Kanpur and Lucknow and to a remote village in the north, where Mann Kapoor spends a month in exile. Brahmpur represents a geographical area whose North Indian identity is stretched out to make it a representative of India as a whole. The wide sweep of the novel gives Seth a chance to portray life in the fictitious northern State of "Purva Pradesh" in its various aspects:

> ...This little fire was indeed the center of the universe. For here it burned in the middle of this fragrant garden, itself in the heart of Pasand Bagh, the pleasantest locality of Brahmpur, which was the capital of the state of Purva Pradesh, which lay in the center of the Gangetic Plains, which was itself the heartland of India... and so on through the galaxies to the outer limits of perception and knowledge (16).

Seth offers a huge, thick, and multi-layered slice of Indian life that, in its veracity, serves to counter the widespread false views of India and improve the world's understanding of our country. The historical scale of Seth's novel invites comparison with *War and Peace*. Like Tolstoy, Seth writes the history of the recent past from the point of view of individuals whose lives are affected by the great historical events of the time and also crosses the boundary between the invented and the historical. Nehru is his equivalent of Napoleon.

"In contrast to the fierce magic realism of Salman Rushdie, Seth writes in a 19th century realist mode with a vein of 18th century sentiment, flat at times but generally eminently readable and engaging (but not quite equaling his great predecessors of the sparkle of *The Golden Gate*). Seth's novels show that it is wrong to privilege modernist or post-modernist modes of innovation; tradition endures, sustains, and can provide for major achievement," suggests D.C.R.A. Goonetilleke. This also suggests that in spite of the fascination for Magic Realism in recent times, fiction of social realism still flourishes, and will perhaps always flourish, because the novel, born of social reality, may deviate from it, but will always continue to find external reality an eternal source of substantial artistic material. It is therefore hardly surprising that in the heyday of Salman Rushdie and Magic Realism, we have an equally strong school of social realism led by Vikram Seth, whose *A Suitable Boy* won almost as much attention on its publication as *Midnight's Children* (1980) had done a dozen years earlier.

Seth's book is original, rich and real, and it is a realism that is humorous and tender by turns. Life moves through its vast frame as it does in the world with a "charged aimlessness" (Basu, 1993), and the scenes unfold both elements of laughter and pathos, strongly reminiscent of similar situations in the Victorian novels, particularly in Dickens. *A Suitable Boy* owes a lot to Victorian novel-writing tradition in general and to Jane Austen in particular. Seth himself has acknowledged that his book is, in a sense, a novel of manners, in the Austen mould, and not just a showpiece for his considerable literal ability: "My great heroes are the Victorian novelists: Charles Dickens, George Eliot, and Jane Austen" (Goswami, 1993).

Like Austen, Seth's irony, far from being gentle, is savage in its condemnation of the extremists, the hypocrites, and the snobbish; his humour is razor-sharp in its exposure of human weakness in a morally flawed society. His characters are set painful lessons in personal knowledge and moral self-discipline, as a result of which rationality triumphs over any sort of obsessive or passionate indulgence. His characters may suffer, but they also understand and their understanding derives from a proper exercise of rational thoughts rather than from emotional or subconscious enlightenment. Seth, through his characters, proposes that we deny passion and remain, as far as possible, in control of ourselves.

Affinities to *Middlemarch* (1867) also exist. Just as George Eliot examined the great political and social changes in an earlier England, so Seth writing in the 1990s recreates the period of transition (1951-52), after Independence (1947)—but without Eliot's demanding critical dimension.

A Suitable Boy focuses on the experiences and entanglements of four moderately rich Indian families connected through marriage or friendship, at a period of time when India was experiencing her post-Independence turbulences. It is primarily about the social, religious and familial customs of India and her people with the numerous characters serving as tools to illustrate the veracity of these customs. It is structured into nineteen well-crafted sub-sections that allow Seth to move back and forth while telling the story of four families—the Mehras, the Kapoors, the Khans and the Chatterji's who are related to each other by marriage and friendship. Each family has a minimum of four members who in one way or the other experience a series of turbulent emotions, which slowly season them towards life and its adversities. In addition to these individuals, there are also hordes of other characters who contribute, either in a major or in a minor way, to the development and the progress of the plot line. And to work out an appropriate alliance, Mrs. Rupa Mehra must take into serious consideration issues of religion, caste and social standing.

Seth does an admirable job handling the enormous cast of characters. Even the most minor characters are easily distinguishable from each other, and by the end of the book it is hard to avoid the feeling that you know these characters intimately, Seth deals deftly with the dizzying complexity of India's historical background. The title of the book itself is quite revealing. The main plot of the story revolves around the search for "a suitable boy" for Lata, Mrs. Rupa Mehra's younger daughter. Seth is most proud of his vibrant Mrs. Mehra, who is based in part on Seth's grandmother, also named Rupa Mehra and whom Seth calls the "muse of the project" (Bemrose, 1993). Seth sees *A Suitable Boy* as a plea for religious tolerance, among other things. He says, "it is an insult to Hinduism that these people, have hijacked what it means to be Hindu." He said, "It is tolerance, understanding—not just trying to bash your neighbour over the head because he is Muslim. These things need to be said."

The title of the book suggests that an "Indian sensibility" is at work. This term "suitable boy" is actively used in the Indian market of arranged marriages, where the search is always on for suitable boys and girls. Meenakshi Mukherjee points out that the subject of finding a husband is not new in Indian fiction and cites the examples of Budhadeb Bose's *Tithidor,* a massive novel in Bengali woven around the theme of a girl choosing a suitable husband out of limited options. She also suggests that *A Suitable Boy* can also be related to the voluminous trilogy by Ashapurna Devi and Bimal Mitra (1998:93). Mukherjee states: "Reading the MS. before publication, I remember having wondered if anybody except a reader like me who shares the same regional background would get so completely involved in the nuances of the story of those interlocked upper middle-class families in UP, Bihar and Bengal." She adds: "We know that the author is familiar with Austen, Dickens and Eliot, but his novel might just as well have been written in Bengali where a tradition exists of long three Decker realistic stories about families" (1998: 91).

The search for Lata's husband expands into a richly detailed and exotically vivid narrative that criss-crosses the fabric of India. Seth's panoramic scenes take the readers into law courts, religious processions, riots, and academics—even the shoe trade. Portraits of actual figures are incisive; the cameo of Pandit Nehru, for example, captures his high-minded, well-meaning indecision. In one of the rare authorial asides unaffected by any outside elements, Seth gives an assessment of Nehru:

> And thus his [Nehru's] meeting ended, and on he went to the next one, always late, always impatient, a man whose greatness of heart won the hearts of others, and whose meandering pleas for mutual tolerance kept a volatile country, not merely in those early and most dangerous years

> but throughout his own lifetime, safe at least from the systemic clutch of religious fanaticism (1355).

Seth's point of view is both wry and affectionate and his voluble, palpably atmospheric narrative teems with chaotic, irrepressible life. Woven into the main plot is the story of the troubled times of the 1950s, the rift in the Congress, the abolition of the Zamindari system, arduous efforts by a country trying to stand on its own feet, religious strife, communal riots, strands of cultural life, many chunks of academic life etc. In other words, it is an absolute wholesome picture of a secular India, giving an experience to the reader what it is to be an 'Indian'. As Thomas Blom Hansen says:

> The secular state in India, in other words, not merely produced public spheres full of reason and science, as is sometimes suggested (see India, 1995). On the contrary, the public spheres in secular India remained full of religious signs and practices, packaged and represented as culture, making up a nationalized cultural realm represented as a political, pure and sublime. Now a Friday prayer, a mosque, or a Hindu procession and temple were no longer manifestations of community and sectarian strength, but picturesque and awesome manifestations of Indian culture and the Indian nation. (Blom Hansen, 1999:53)

But, in spite of the fact that the book was first published from England and America, Seth has made no effort at making the milieu accessible to the foreign readers. Hindi and Bengali words remain untranslated and Indian references are not explained. In this connection Vikram Seth explains—"When I wrote *The Golden Gate*, I did not make any effort to make Californian life accessible to the Indian reader. So why should I do so for foreign readers? I can only hope that the characters and the story interest them sufficiently to make them want to read the book."

Apart from what Seth set out to do, what has been really done in *A Suitable Boy* is an outstanding achievement for any Indian English writer today. It is both comprehensive and compact—an able account of many forces that operated in the Indian society in the years immediately after Independence and a scintillating analysis of the dash of personalities, convictions and cultures. *A Suitable Boy* is both a reflection of the contemporary social nebulosity and a steady attempt to probe into that and determine how best that can be shaped and controlled.

The novel opens with a wedding ceremony that brings the said four families together and thereby allows Seth to place his main characters straight away on to his canvas. Mrs. Rupa Mehra's elder daughter Savita is getting married to Pran, a university lecturer in English and the son of the State Revenue Minister Mahesh Kapoor. Also present at the function are the anglicized Chatterji clan who reside at Calcutta, and the Khan family of the Nawab of Baitar, one of the largest land-owners of the State (The Nawab's twin sons, Firoz and Imtiaz are a lawyer and a doctor respectively. They do not fit into the popular mould of the idle sons of the feudal aristocracy). Apart from the Khans the other three families are interlocked through marriage. In addition to the network of relationships that emerge out of these family-webs, Seth has introduced a large cast of other characters drawn from across religions, languages, class and caste.

Right from the beginning, we find Mrs. Rupa Mehra informing Lata, her younger daughter, that like her elder sister Savita, she too will marry a boy of her (Mrs. Mehra's) choice. Lata's reaction to this "maternal imperative" (3) is typical of any other young Indian girl's reaction. Typical in the sense that there is no reaction, only indifference. Lata has no attraction towards arranged marriages, but she knows that she has to have one because she can never hurt the emotions of her family members by going against their decisions, especially her mother. "Because of my family," said Lata, "however much they irritate me and constrain me I cannot give them up. I know that now so much has happened I can't give up my mother."

Generally, Indian women, before marriage are brought up in such a protective and comfortable atmosphere that it requires immense courage and strength of mind to break away from that strong family bond. And there is always this risk that once you break free, it is almost next to impossible to get back into the fold. This holds true even now, even in the 21st century, while in the 1950s, the period when Seth's story is enacted, it was almost unthinkable. In this connection one may remember Anita Desai's views, who says that Seth's characters, "although in their rash youth, might be tempted by the possibilities of change, defiance, and the unknown, they learn their lessons and return chastened, to the safety and security of the familiar and the traditional represented here in the Indian fashion, by the great God, family" (1993).

In the first chapter itself Vikram Seth, amidst a cocktail of numerous ironical and humorous implications, and Mrs. Rupa Mehra "water works" (II), makes four clear-cut statements that ring true right through the book, till the end. All the statements are made by Mrs. Rupa Mehra, "the comic dupe par excellence" who tries to lay the foundation stone on which she expects all her children to build up their lives. The most fully realized and emotionally engaging character in *A Suitable Boy* is Mrs. Rupa Mehra who has only one mission left in life—to arrange a proper marriage for her youngest daughter, Lata. Mother and daughter are generation apart in their ideas, but not surprisingly they eventually do reach an agreement of sorts, as a result of which they find that they are closer than they had ever imagined. Mrs. Rupa Mehra however is a woman who is determined to take care of her family at any cost, in fact, to take care of them even if they do not wish to be taken care of. Seth sums her up as "Mrs. Rupa Mehra, torn between solicitude for Pran, concern for Savita who was due to deliver any day now, and desperate anxiety on behalf of Lata, would have liked nothing better than to have an emotional breakdown. But the press of events would not allow it at present, and she therefore abstained."

She is indeed a remarkable character, and not one that is soon forgotten. She is vividly drawn and seems to leap off the page with energy, vitality and wit. She is the typical Indian mother, always concerned about her children and always eager to see to it that they settle well in life. And yet, behind the apparent liveliness and positive tones to the whole mother and daughter drama, there are glimpses of resentment at the limitations of an economic and social world in which women had no future but what their husbands could provide—or their fathers, if they had been unlucky in the hunt. Intelligence and individuality were fatal defects in a woman whose value was being assessed in the marriage market. Here we can quote from Jane Austen who also wrote along similar lines. The tragedy to this is Austen was writing about an English society of the mid-19th century, while Seth is writing about a post-Independence India of the 1950s, which still has some echoes right now:

> Intelligence in women is a handicap to their social success where people wish to attach, they should always be ignorant. To come with a well-informed mind is to come with an inability of administering to the vanity of others, which a sensible person would always wish to avoid. A woman, especially if she has the misfortune of knowing anything, should conceal it as well as she can. I will only add, in justice to me, that though to the larger and more trifling part of the sex, imbecility in females is a great enhancement of their personal charms, there is a portion of them too reasonable, too well-informed themselves to derive anything more in women than ignorance. (qtd. in Neill, 1964:150)

The first statement of the novel itself "you too will marry a boy I choose" (3) becomes the harbinger of all the events that Lata, Seth's female protagonist, is made to experience throughout. Secondly, referring to Savita and Pran, the newly weds, Mrs. Rupa Mehra states with confidence that "they will be happy" (4) which in due course becomes a fact. Seth, right through the course of the novel, has always portrayed Pran and Savita as an ideal couple. Their love and affection blossom after their marriage. Their mutual understanding and trust towards each other help them in overcoming all the hurdles they face in their life. And Seth makes Lata review her actions regarding her matrimonial situation from the ideal level of Savita and Pran Kapoor's domestic life—"a gradual, stable attraction such as Savita's for Pran was this not the best thing for her, and for the family, and for any children that she might have?"

The third statement is again about Lata. Her mother, in a moment of annoyance and exasperation thinks "her younger daughter was going to prove more difficult than her elder" (4). At the moment she does not know how true her forecast is going to be. With Savita she does not have any difficulties, but her problems with Lata are going to be enough to last her a lifetime. Finally the fourth statement; which Mrs. Rupa Mehra also imparts upon Lata—"What is good enough for your sister is good enough for you" (5). This sage piece of advice only results in bringing forth a flippant and naughty comment from Lata—"We can't both marry Pran." But behind the apparent humorous rejoinder, we sense a bit of moralizing being done by Seth, almost in the Austen mould. If the beautiful and intelligent Savita is satisfied with the "lanky, dark, gangly and asthmatic" (4) Pran Kapoor, and their arranged marriage, then probably for Lata and for the likes of Lata, that is the ideal state of being, to remain happy and self-sufficient.

But the book, as has been mentioned earlier, is not about Lata only. Seth has provided his readers with a kaleidoscopic view of post-Independence India in the early years, which are in no way different from today's India. The scenes of political, social and individual turmoil are so much contemporaneous that they seem to be taking place in 1990s and not the 1950s. There is a certain Indianness to the lines, which makes it easier for us to identify with the characters:

> Now that the exchange of garlands was over, the crowd paid no great attention to the actual wedding rites. These would go on for the better part of an hour while the guests milled and chattered round the lawns of Prem Nivas. They laughed, they shook hands or folded them to their foreheads; they coalesced into little knots, the man here, the women there; they warmed themselves at the charcoal filled clay stoves placed strategically around the garden while their frosted, gossip laden breath rose into the air; they admired the multicoloured lights, they smiled for the photographer as he murmured "steady, please!" in English, they breathed deeply the scent of flowers and perfume and cooked spices; they exchanged births and deaths and politics and scandal

> under the brightly coloured cloth canopy at the back of the garden beneath which long tables of food had been laid out; they sat down exhaustedly on chair with their plates full and tucked in inexhaustibility, servants, some in white livery, some in khaki, brought around fruit juice and tea and coffee and snacks to those who were standing in the garden: samosas, kachauries, laddus, gulab-jammuns, barfis, and gajak and ice-cream were consumed and replenished along with puris and six kinds of vegetables. Friends who had not met each other for months fell upon each other with loud cries, relatives who met only at weddings and funerals embraced tearfully and exchanged the latest news of third cousins thrice removed, Lata's aunt from Kanpur horrified by the complexion of the groom was talking to an aunt from Lucknow about 'Rupa's black grand-children', as if they already existed. (13-14)

And it has a cast of characters so vast that one point or the other it gets confusing as to who is who in the scheme of things. But this is also typically Indian, as the large number brings to mind the facts that, India is really a very populous country and that the novel is not about a single individual or a single family or a single event, but of India itself, taken as a whole. But Vikram Seth's India is not the India of sex and passion, high fashion, fast car and slick life. It is an India of arranged marriages, self-made men, rationality and sanity, and tolerance and understanding. *A Suitable Boy* advocates calmness and humour as the two most dominant forces required to tide over successfully all the adversities of life.

A Suitable Boy is an all-encompassing, a "magnum opus" of social comedy in the great tradition of Jane Austen, Charles Dickens and R.K. Narayan interlaced with the political realism of Ghram Greene and Nayantara Sahgal. Sandwiched between the social comedy and the political realism is the murky and intriguing academic world of professor and Dr. Pran Kapoor, in the line of Srilal Shukla's *Raag Darbari.*

Just as the Industrial Revolution affected the England of Austen, Nehru's socialist and industrial revolution affected the India of the fifties. Nirad C. Choudhari, a sharp observer of the

Indian scene writes: "A far stronger force, in actual fact the only positive force, is the Hindu's insatiable greed for money.... It is this love of money which is the true motive behind the industrialization in England and India, the insatiable greed for money, led to the birth of a middle class. Mrs. Bennet and Mrs. Rupa Mehra, members of this class, find it increasingly difficult to search suitable boys for their daughters. In today's India, this social problem has assumed a monstrous form, where thousands of daughters are burnt for inadequate dowry. Very few writers have cared to probe the miseries and agonies of mothers of many daughters, with scant resources and who are caught in the vicious tentacles of caste, religion and conservative traditions. Vikram Seth, basically an English brown Sahib, sitting away from the growing and unfulfilling aspirations and consequent frustrations of this middle class, writes marvelously on this theme." And the best aspect of the whole narration is that it brings along with it a sense of humour, and sense of drama along with an easy, feel good factor in spite of all adversities.

After keeping as in suspense and wonder, almost in the fashion of an Agatha Christie who dun-it, as to whom will Lata marry, for one thousand, two hundred and ninety-six pages Vikram Seth makes his heroine deliver a passionate sermon against passion. Lata is trying to explain to her friend Malati as to why she has decided to renounce her love for Kabir Durrani, and instead marry Harish Khanna, the suitable boy:

> "...I am not myself when I am with him. I ask myself who is this—this jealous obsessed woman who can't get a man out of her head—why should I make myself suffer like this. I know that it'll always be like this if I am with him." "Oh, Lata—don't be blind" exclaimed Malati. "It shows how passionately you love him." "I don't want to" cried Lata, "I don't want to. If that's what passion means, I don't want it. Look at what passion has done to the family, Mann's broken, his mother's dead, his father's in despair. When I thought that Kabir was seeing someone else, what I remember feeling was enough to make me hate passion, passionately and forever." (1296)

This outburst by Lata is nothing new and has been reiterated countless times by literary characters throughout the ages, the most famous being the dramatic outburst by Catherine Earnshaw, to Nelly Dean, when she tries to explain her reasons for not marrying Heathcliff:

> I cannot express it; but surely you and everybody have a notion that there is or should everybody be an existence of yours beyond you. What was the use of my creation, if I were entirely contained here? My great miseries in this world have been Heathcliff's miseries, and I watched and felt each from the beginning; my great thought in living is himself. If all else perished, and he remained, I should still continue to be; and if all else remained, and he were annihilated, the universe would turn to a mighty stranger: I should seem a part of it. My love for Linton is like the foliage in the woods; time will change it, I'm well aware, as winter changes the trees. My love for Heathcliff resembles the eternal rocks beneath: a source of little visible delight, but necessary. Nelly, I am Heathcliff: He's always, always in my mind: not as pleasure, any more than I am always a pleasure to myself, but as my own being. So don't talk of our separation again: it is impracticable; and... (qtd. in Neill, 1964: 202).

Again on page 1333, Lata reiterates her disapproval of anything passionate and loud:

> I should run away, she thought, far from Harish, far from Arun and Varun and Ma, and the whole Chatterji clan, far from and Mann and Hindus and Muslims and passionate love and passionate hatred and all loud noises, just me and Malati and Savita and the baby. We'll sit on the sand and on the other side of the Ganga and go to sleep for a year or two.

But this time it is a toned down version of the aggression of the earlier lines. There is more escapism involved here than denunciation, as she is on the threshold of physical maturity, with two weeks remaining to her marriage. As any young girl, Lata is also scared of losing her virginity, and therefore is being reminded more of Kabir, and their love for each other. Lata knows very well that till she continues as unmarried, Kabir continues to be a reality for her, somebody she can extend her hand and touch anytime, but the day she marries, Kabir will lose his physical entity and become a part of her memory to be locked up forever. Since there is no escape from the complicacies that life poses before oneself, she becomes a bit fanciful (with an echo from Marvell's *To His Coy Mistress*) and thinks of running away from all her problems, with only those three persons by her side to whom she doesn't have to explain anything. She also betrays a bit of childishness within her as she imagines that she can sleep away all her troubles.

It is true Lata retains to the end an unexceptional, sketchily defined personality, but the characterization shows Seth's deep insight, honesty and truthfulness in portraying an ordinary Indian woman's gradual development towards maturity. At the beginning of the novel, Lata is nineteen year old and at the end, she is twenty. But the difference between the nineteen-year old Lata and the twenty-year old Lata is not just simply one year. Within this one year Lata grows from a moody and willful girl to a woman who realizes and understands her responsibilities and thereby acts accordingly. Lata's characterization also reveals to us a great deal of Vikram Seth's novel ideologies. Lata chooses Haresh not because of her mother's compulsions, but because of the simple reason that she wants to marry somebody like Haresh. At the time Lata accepts Haresh's proposal, her mother is having second thoughts about him because of some derogatory remarks made by her friends and relatives, concerning his involvement in the shoe business. Arun has also arrogantly rejected Haresh, on the plea that he is socially inferior to them, and therefore will be more of an embarrassment to their family rather than a useful addition:

> A second not unrelated point is that Haresh does not and can never aspire to, move in the same social circles as we do. A foreman is not a covenanted assistant, and Prana is simply not Bensten Pryce. The small of leather clings rather too closely to the name, the Czechs who are his bosses, are technicians, sometimes barely literate in English, not

> graduates from the best universities in England. In a certain sense by choosing a trade rather than a profession, after his graduation from St. Stephen's Haresh has downgraded himself. I hope you do not mind my speaking frankly on a matter of such importance to your future happiness. Society matters and society is exacting and cruel; you will find yourself excluded from certain circles simply by virtue of being Mrs. Khanna. (1293)

This negative and snobbish attitude of her brother propels Lata towards her fateful selection. She has not yet ceased to feel passionate attraction towards Kabir, yet she chooses Haresh, a decision that is both difficult and painful to her and her friend Malati. But she doesn't choose Haresh because he will give her riches, comfort or social recognition. Her unromantic and practical decision is a cry against stifling snobbery and blinding passion, and towards championing the cause of rationality, stability and economic productivity—"Haresh's feet touch the ground, and he has dust and sweat and a shadow. The other two are a bit too God-like and ethereal to be of any good for me" (1299). In *A Suitable Boy* Vikram Seth has allowed his heroine the opportunity of choosing between three men who are totally different from each other in their appearance as well as in their behaviour. And in keeping with this tradition, the courtship also takes place in three very different ways. Kabir Durani the handsome and dashing Muslim student is the first to enter Lata's life. Their love affair starts in typical storybook fashion, continues along the same lines, but sadly does not end with them living happily ever after:

> She smiled to herself now, not aware of her surrounding. Still holding the book, she looked up. And this was how a young man, who had been standing not far from her, was included, unintentionally, in her smile. He was pleasantly startled, and smiled back at her. Lata frowned at him and looked down at the page again. But she could not concentrate on it. (46)

In spite of Kabir's princely looks, and his capacity to sweep the heroine off her feet, Kabir is no knight in shinning armour. On the contrary, according to Mrs. Rupa Mehra, he is the most unsuitable of them all and whom Lata should avoid like plague. But Lata is unable to resist his charm and his oozing sexuality and falls desperately and passionately in love with him:

> ...She was drowsingly entranced by the sight of Kabir dressed completely in white, shirt unbuttoned at the collar, capless and with ruffled hair, running in to bowl or standing at the crease wielding his bat with what seemed like easy skill. Kabir was an inch or two under six feet, slim and athletic, with a fair to wheatish complexion, an aquiline nose, and black wavy hair. Lata did not know how long she sat there, but it must have been for more than half an hour. (147)

The romantic, impulsive Kabir kindles Lata's passion, without a single thought as to what he will do with her aroused sexuality, his lack of financial stability, and the impracticability of an inter-racial marriage in an India of 1950s. When faced with all these problems all of a sudden, he is unable to find any solution, which leaves Lata dejected, disgusted and feeling rejected, but still very much infatuated.

Savita Kapoor is one of the highly idealized characters in the novel. Seth seems to have more than a soft spot for her, than any of his other characters including his heroine. She is beautiful, intelligent, understanding and devoid of any sort of vanity. And she is the only one who understands Lata totally. Not even Lata's best friend Malati can compete with her in her acute perception of events and behaviours. She understands very well that what Kabir and Lata have for each other is an intense passion based mainly on physical attraction, which given enough time might "blow over" (180).

Lata was so relieved to talk to someone who loved her and understand her that she poured cut all her hopes and visions of bliss. Savita saw at once how impossible these were, but let her talk on. She felt increasingly sad as Lata grew more elated. "But what should I do?" said Lata. "Do?" repeated Savita. The answer that came to her mind was that Lata should give Kabir up immediately before their infatuation went any further, but she knew better than to say so to Lata, who could be very contrary (174).

Kabir and Lata's relationship is more in the mould of Arun and Meenakshi's love affair which fortunately could end in marriage. Arun and Meenakshi had met at a cocktail party, fallen in torrid, rapturous and elegant love, and got married within a month, to the shock of both families. But Seth the moralist tells us that it is far from being an ideal marriage, in spite of all that passionate attraction between the two. Lata however, renounces passion before she really gets the chance to taste its wild ecstasies. Excluding some very fleeting kisses, the closest she comes to the consummation of her passion is when as Olivia in *Twelfth Night* she tells Kabir who is playing Malvolio, "Wilt thou go to bed, Malvoio?" (781), a line which when she utters for the first time causes her great embarrassment. But Lata makes this rejection after a good deal of thinking and deliberating. Her relationship with Kabir has always been like she is being whirled around in a whirlpool. When she is with him she loses all her bearing and becomes an emotional wreck, which is too painful for her to bear and tolerate.

> ...When I am with Kabir, or even away from him but thinking about him, I became utterly useless for anything. I feel I am out of control like a boat leading for the rocks—and I don't want to become a wreck. (1298)

Her feelings for Kabir overwhelm her to such an extent that when she thinks about it in a calm and cool state of mind, a life without Kabir seems to be the sanest alternative possible. And Lata, unlike her mother or her brothers, is really a very sensible young lady.

The next man to enter Lata's life, though not in the strict sense of the term, is the gifted, intelligent, witty, but eccentric and materialistically spoilt poet, Amit Chatterji from Calcutta. Amit is Meenakshi's elder brother, and hence enters Lata's life more as a relative and a friend rather than as a suitor. To the broken hearted Lata, in dire need of a diversion, Amit's eccentricity serves as the best possible balm. His intelligence, wit and concern, all combine to bring out a cheerful and carefree Lata to the fore. Gradually Amit gets attracted by Lata's charm, innocence and simplicity. And Seth has made Amit's wooing of Lata at par with Kabir's wooing, though not as passionate, as

Amit is very far from being a passionate person. It is interesting to note that Amit's wooing comes in the form of a poem, the tone of which is controlled and careful, the overture touched with logic, and the title smacks of irony being directly borrowed from Swift—a composition that has a delightful play between passion on the one hand and witty scepticism on the other, a reminder of the metaphysical, particularly Marvell.

MODEST PROPOSAL

As you have asked for black and white,
May I send these lines to you
In the tacit hope you might
Take my type at least as true.
Let this distance disappear
And our hearts approach from far
Till we come to be as near
As acrostically we are. (1288)

In *A Suitable Boy* Seth mocks himself in the guise of Amit Chatterji; a loose self-portrait; for sitting about all day staring out of the window. Family friends remember Seth's parents tiptoeing around him and providing all his needs, but they also recall him working as if possessed. "He could not think about anything else, he couldn't do anything else," said one of his Delhi contemporaries, William Bissell. "Food, sleep nothing else mattered. We went to stay with the family in Shimla, where his mother was a judge, and he was closed all day in his room. He would only emerge in the evening in his dressing gown clutching a batch of new pages."

In *A Suitable Boy* Seth writes how his alter ego Amit rebuffs "all the efforts of his female admirers or their mothers to get know him better. He had remained faithful to Jane Austen. He appeared to be content to lead a life of contemplation". But in California Seth wrote a poem "Dubious", which he refers to whenever he is asked about his private life and even read out on the omnibus television profile of him a few years ago: "Some men like Jack and some like Jill / I'm glad I like them both." In *The Golden Gate,* too, there is a bisexual character that is generally believed to be another loose self-portrait.

But Amit's wit or passion does not move Lata and she rejects Amit on the ground that he is too much like her for them to have a smooth domestic life, and also more important is the fact that in his complete dedication to his Muse, she and subsequent marital responsibilities have no real value for him in the long run. He can always be a good friend but never a good husband:

> We are too alike. His moods veer and oscillate as wildly as mine. Can you imagine the life of our poor children? And if his mind's on a book I do not know if he'll have any time for me. Sensitive people are usually very sensitive—I should know. (1296)

Haresh resembling a cheerfully "Stakhonvite Hero of Labour" (1125) is the last to enter Lata's life. He enters her life as "the suitable boy", selected after a good deal of research work by Mrs. Rupa Mehra. But he is ironically portrayed by Seth as somebody who is socially awkward and unlettered in the sophistries of life. Nevertheless, he is acceptable to Lata because he is sincere, hard-working, honest, brave, outspoken, broad-minded, egalitarian, and last but not least, he is a staunch supporter of the family tradition.

She thought of Haresh, generous, robust, optimistic, impatient, and responsible. There he stood in Prahapore, as solid as a pair of Goodyear welted shoes twinkling his eyes affectionately at her from the pages of his letter and telling her as well as he could that he was lonely without her (1291).

All these positive qualities overrule the gaucheness and loudness in his personality. "Lata is not marrying Haresh: she is marrying a symbol of what Vikram Seth would like to proclaim as his hope for a new India—an ambitious, pragmatic, anti-snobbish, working-class, self-made Indian man", suggests David Myers (1994).

In addition to the above-mentioned reasons, Lata is also marrying Haresh because in her own way she is in love with him. Haresh's unaffected ways and sincere concern for everybody unconsciously endear him towards Lata, and to Lata this kind of steady affection looks far more enduring than the desperate emotions she feels for Kabir. She chooses the flickering but steady light of the star over the blinding but temporary brilliance of the lighting. Though Haresh is no handsome, mysterious stranger who sweeps Lata off her feet, yet there is sense of adventure and mystery in losing herself in his world, a world populated by people who are as unreal to her as Haresh is a reality. And the challenge of facing a totally different mode of life, with a man she likes and trusts, a man "as solid as a pair of Goodyear welted shoes" (1291) is an attraction by itself:

> But there was something adventurous in losing herself entirely in a world that she did not know with a man whom she trusted and had begun to admire and who cared for her so deeply and steadily. She thought of a paanless Haresh; smiling his open smile, she sat him down at a table so that she could not see his correspondent shoes; she ruffled his hair a bit, and well, he was quite attractive! She liked him. Perhaps, given time and luck, she could even learn to love him. (1292)

But this selection and the path through which it progresses might not be acceptable to everybody, particularly to the Western readers. Because more than anything else a sense of compromise seems to be the dominant trait responsible for the decision. Lata selects Haresh because she knows that under no circumstance can she have any future with Kabir. And the other topic for skepticism is that sexual fulfillment has no role to play in her scheme of things. This is the normal Indian attitude sanctioned by the sastras, that sex is a holy necessity towards the continuity of family in particular and life in general, and to that extent Lata's attitude is typically Indian, and for Seth that is a strong point. Thus for Lata sex is only a process for reproduction and something which she has to face as part of her marital duty. That is, Lata is talking about a lifetime of sexual union sans excitement and passion. On its face value it sounds too matter of fact and clinical, and hence disappointing:

> I won't feel I'll be making a fool of myself with him with regard to, well with regard to sex. (1298)

But before making any kind of specific interpretation, we have to keep in mind that Lata is just nineteen years old, a virgin, and is lacking in any kind of sexual knowledge until her mother presents her with the book dealing with sexual positions and habits, entitled "Ideal Marriage" (1331). Therefore there is no guarantee that this idea of passionless union will continue throughout her lifetime. There is every chance that Haresh, who is a man of the world in every sense, might rekindle all that sexual energy within Lata, which she says she can control where Haresh is concerned. Lata's innocence becomes very much evident when the narrator comments that, after she has read the Dutch author's sex manual she "was as much repelled as fascinated by what he had to offer" (1331). So there is no reason why Lata and Haresh's marriage won't turn out to be happy and wholesome in spite of Haresh being "the bronze casket" (1299), as Malati so candidly points out to Lata.

At the end of the novel, Lata is unable to see what happens to the "musammi" which she rolls along from the moving train towards the old monkey who was "contemplating her carefully and undemandingly" (1349), whether he gets hold of it or it is snatched away on the way:

> As the train began to move, Lata quickly reached down into the bag of fruit for another mussami, and threw it in his direction. He moved towards it, but the others, seeing it roll along, began running towards it too; and before she could see what had become of it, the train had steamed out of the station. (1349)

But all things considered, it won't be too much off the mark to say that life won't treat her in the same manner. Her future is almost clearly visible, unlike the future of her "musammi". Like Savita, she too will strive to be satisfied with whatever life will offer her and with somebody like Haresh beside her, who is as genuine a man as Pran is, it is therefore not too difficult to foresee her future which Seth has left unsaid and undiscussed.

Like Jane Austen who had talked about "marriages" in her books, Seth also talks about it in his book. He has distinguished it from "affairs", "romance", "encounters", "connections" etc.

But unlike Jane Austen's "marriages", which were final culminations of long relationships, Seth's "marriages" are mostly arranged ones, where the relationship flowers after the ceremony gets over. And where it is not an arranged one, it is only a mockery of all those values on which this lifelong bond is based upon. The narrator's evaluation of the situations is almost biased as evident from this, but very cleverly has argued it out through the length of the book as to why he is biased on this subject.

According to the narrator the basic emotion running through most love marriages is "passion", while for arranged marriages, it is affection. And usually, passion is something which can last for a few years, while affection can last through for a lifetime. The prime examples pertaining to this view are Savita and Pran Kapoor on one side, and Meenakshi a[illegible] Arun Mehra on the other. Savita and Pran's relationship has the solid foundation of such emotions as affection, trust, friendship and understanding, while all Meenaskshi and Arun have towards each other is an acute feeling of passion, and a reluctant tolerance of each other's idiosyncrasies. Also their acute passionate nature makes them vulnerable towards the sex appeal of other young men and women. When Pran and Savita's daughter Uma is born, she becomes the icing on their relationship, while Meenakshi aborts her second baby as she is not sure who the father of the baby is, because of her passionate involvement with Arun's friend Billy Irani.

Even Veena and Kedarnath Tandon have a smooth domestic life in spite of their painful memories, present financial constraints and future uncertainties. According to Seth an arranged marriage brings with it an inherent sense of understanding, adjustment and tolerance, the three prime characteristics required for any lifelong commitment. Being passionate about anything or over anything is worthy of momentary bliss.

This abhorrence for passion is something that Seth has probably imbibed from his admiration of the Victorian novels, particularly Jane Austen. Austen, by identifying love with marriage and ignoring passion, avoided the tragedies that blast convention and make a hell of heaven. "A Heathcliff in her world could have been exhibited only at a fair." It was a part of her philosophy that a happy marriage was the best thing for everybody. "It is a truth universally acknowledged that a single man in possession of a good fortune must be in want of a wife." One of her characters, a very young girl, remarks: "I would rather be a school teacher (and I can think of nothing worse) than marry a man I did not love." But her sister, who had known the worst, replies: "I should not like to marry disagreeable man any more than yourself, but I do not think there are very many disagreeable men. I think I could like any good-humoured man with a comfortable income" (qtd. in Neill, 1964: 149).

A good example of how passion can bring about one's downfall is shown in the story of Mann Kapoor. Mann Kapoor's uncontrollable passion for Saeeda Bai results in major crisis and suffering for all the characters involved. Mann, the happy-go-lucky man, "full of liveliness and charm and energy and affection" (1314), in a moment of unreasonable jealousy and fury stabs his best friend Firoz, the same person whom he had saved from murderous mobs during the Hindu-Muslim riots:

> He took the bottle of whisky out of his pocket and began to drink. He felt as if his heart had been crushed. Every night for a fortnight he had thought of her. Every morning when he had woken up, whether at the Fort or in Salimpur, he had lingered for a few minutes in bed, imagining that she was with him. No doubt his dreams too had been of her. And now, after these fifteen days away, she had granted him fifteen minutes of her time. And as good as given him to understand that someone else mattered far more to her than he ever could. (1188)

At the moment when he stabs Firoz, Mann is no different from those mobsters, whom he had viewed with such hatred and disgust when they had confronted him. While the mobsters were inflamed and blinded by false religious sentiments, Mann for his part is completely possessed by his infatuation for Saeeda Bai. So powerful is his passion and obsession that it is quite obvious that some great tragedy is essential for Mann to be able to renounce his obsession forever. The tragedy comes in the form of Firoz's stabbing; Mann being jailed for the crime, and as a result of these two devastating events, Mrs. Mahesh Kapoor is hastened towards her death.

Here, Seth's sense of the tragedy is almost Aristotelian. Some hidden weakness, some soft streak unseen by the outer world, unsuspected even by the possessor, undermines what is otherwise a good, perhaps potentially noble character. What seems a hostile destiny is in reality the failure of the individual to be true to the best that is within him, his surrender to the inherent weakness. Recognizing this truth, Seth has shown his skill in contriving situations that test his characters once the basic flaw, and its probable effect on the destiny, is discovered. The development of the character is lifelike and no melodramatic scenes or psychological miracles are necessary to explain surface changes, for these are seen to be related to the central core.

In Seth's theory romantic passion must necessarily end in some loss, since life is too frail to endure ecstasy. Lawlessness, discord and violence are the price we have to pay for failure to achieve self-knowledge and to live harmoniously. Passion and reason follow disastrously diverse laws.

Mrs. Mahesh Kapoor's death, at the personal level, is the most painful incident of the novel. Because of her selfless and self-sacrificing nature, this unassuming woman leaves behind a sense of colossal pain and loss, which finally forces Mahesh Kapoor to recognize and understand her true worth. The flippancy in the description can be noted, as also the seriousness, recognition that whatever may flower at the top, the foundation is a solid one:

> Fat, ligament, muscle, blood, hair, affection, pity, despair, anxiety, illness all were no more. She had dispersed. She was the garden of Prem Nivas.... She was Veena's love of music, Pran's astha, Mann's generosity, the survival of some refugees four years ago, the neem leaves that would preserve quilts stored in the great zinc trunks of Prem Nivas, the moulting feather of some pond heron, a small unrung brass bell, the memory of decency in an indecent time, the temperament of Bhaskar's great-grand children. Indeed, for

> all the Minister of Revenue's impatience with her, she was his regret. (1220)

Symbolically Mrs. Mahesh Kapoor is identified with the harsingar tree ("the tree flowered but kept nothing for itself") (1042). Her piety which was always mocked at by her husband and sons was never performed because she herself needed something from her gods:

> She prayed to them, and she asked for comfort from them: nothing for herself, but health for her family, a long life for her husband, blessings on her two grand children, and ease to the souls of those no longer there. (984)

"She is the moral centre of the novel and her husband's political ambitions, his impatience and his atheism are shown to be deeply flawed when contrasted with her lifestyle", suggests David Myers (1994).

Mahesh Kapoor, a freedom fighter and idealist, stands at the core of the political fable in *A Suitable Boy*. He is a fictionalized version of Damodar Swaroop Seth, a Nehruvian from Rohilkhand whose memory is preserved in Bareilly at a park consecrated in his name. He is, in essence, a symbolic figure representing those idealistic Congressmen who were hugely disillusioned by the decadence of the post-Independence Congress. "The tragic denouement of his political career is the culmination of a rapidly rotting political culture when real politic manipulation, nepotism, and communalism totally prevented the Indian political value system", says K.K. Kapoor.

As the first General Election of 1952 draws near, Mahesh Kapoor is on a dilemma. Should he compromise on his ideals to secure electoral success and remain loyal to the Congress or should he leave the parent organisation and join the Kisan Mazdur Praja Party (KMPP) floated by some idealistic leftist Congressmen? He confides to his wife. "Pran's mother, do you know what is happening in this country? The Congress is threatening to split down the middle. Everyone who is decent is leaving. P.C. Ghosh has gone; both Kripalani and his wife have gone.... Rafi Sahib with his circus skills is attending the meetings of both the parties...and Nehru himself is threatening to resign from the Congress... That is not why I spent years of my life in prison. I am sick of the Congress Party, and I too am thinking of leaving it" (753).

Mahesh Kapoor is committed to the goals of anti-feudalism, secularism and abolition of the Zamindari system. At the personal level he is also a determined fighter against feudal reaction, against the evil powers of communalism, against the opportunistic attitude of the politicians, and against the growing shadows of corruption and manipulation. In political terms he is revealed as a man of commitment and integrity, and a man capable of outweighing personal relationships for the betterment of larger, general objectives and his close friendship with the Nawab Sahib of Baitaar also helps him in this commitment, in the sense that Mahesh Kapoor's moral principles do not come in the way of their friendship. It remains as strong as ever.

"Who can protect us and our culture? Only people like you, who know us as we are, who do not prejudge us because you can judge from experience." Mahesh Kapoor did not say anything but he was moved by the trust reposed in him by the Nawab Sahib (1085).

But ironically, while this commitment of improving general human condition looks admirable from one angle, from the other angle it shows his ignorance and insensitivity towards the needs of his own family members. His preoccupation with politics results in his failure to understand that they need him as much as his politics needs him. Repeatedly he behaves high-handedly with his wife and son, as a result of which, when towards the end of the novel, tragedy engulfs him from all sides; the reader is left largely unconcerned and unaffected. The empathy is more with Mann and Firoz, rather than with their fathers. The fathers, in spite of possessing all the tragic potentials, remain minor figures when compared to the emotions that their sons evoke, when crisis strikes them. Like Mann, Firoz is made to suffer because of his sudden unwarranted passion for Saeeda Bai's daughter Tasneem, who in a typical Shakespearean tragic-comic twist, turns out to be his own half-sister. Firoz sees Tasneem for the first time at Saeeda Bai's place, when he had gone there to give the "monthly envelope" from the Nawab Sahib to Saeeda Bai. He is completely dazzled by Tasneem's beauty and feels a certain attraction towards her which leaves him with a "most profound and unsettling impression" (117).

> His mouth was dry. He felt strangely disturbed. Surely, he felt, even if we have not met on this mortal plane, we have met in some former life. The thought, counter to the religion he nominally adhered to, affected him the more powerfully for all that (117).

But unlike Mann, Firoz is neither impulsive nor hotheaded. Therefore, he does not pursue his attraction like Mann does by throwing all caution to the winds, but goes about it in a much more sensible and levelheaded manner. But, as mentioned earlier, in Vikram Seth's diary, passion is always synonymous with disaster. Therefore, both Mann's uncontrollable passion towards Saeeda Bai and Firoz's controllable passion for Tasneem suffer a similar kind of fate, though in different ways.

In Jane Austen's *Emma*, Mr. Knightley, while talking to Mrs. Weston, about Emma says, "it would not be a bad thing for her to be very much in love with a proper object". This term "proper object" is somewhat similar to Seth's term "suitable boy". But while Mr. Kinghtley wants Emma to fall in love with somebody who is thoroughly compatible with her, Mrs. Rupa Mehra, on the other hand, wants, her children to have arranged marriages with suitable boys or girls, of her own choice. She does not want them to fall in love at all and invite the risk of tying the knot with unsuitable partners. Her partiality for suitable persons and antagonism towards so-called unsuitable ones does not arise from the fact whether the two individuals are compatible enough or not, but to what extent the two persons are socially equal to each other, and how the connection can improve the family's social position.

In this respect Mrs. Rupa Mehra is no different from the hundreds and thousands of Indian parents who want a similar alliance for their children. On the face of it this type of arrangement looks satisfactory enough, as the man and woman can communicate on equal terms. But if we go deeper into the matter we realize that this type of outlook has resulted today in petty caste wars and minor and major religious squabbles. Lack of adequate number of inter-caste and inter-racial relationships has resulted in a total lack of understanding of the basic values of the other person's faith.

In *A Suitable Boy* Lata's family rejects Kabir for the simple reason that he is a Muslim. His good looks, his intelligence, his sincerity are all pushed aside as non-entities, and the only way he gets identified with, is by his religion. Similarly, towards the end of the book when we are informed that "the Banaras people had decided that Mann was no longer a suitable boy" (1341), it springs no surprise. We know that in spite of Mann being acquitted by the court, he is blacklisted for the rest of his life and any connection with him is a positive disgrace and strictly forbidden within the so-called social decorum. Only a family, which considers its daughters to be nothing but mere burdens or liabilities, will accept Mann as a prospective son-in-law. At another level, Kalpana Gaur in spite of being so highly compatible with Varun is not considered to be a suitable girl by Mrs. Rupa Mehra. In short, the title of the novel itself is a subtle irony on the whole gamut of Indian marriages, where the term suitability lacks depth and any definite direction. The meaning of the term varies from individual to individual, and it depends solely upon these individuals as how well they manage their affairs, their friendships, their marriages and their life.

As mentioned earlier, the book has a range of diverse themes running parallel to the main theme of the search for a suitable boy for Lata. The themes include politics, religion, customs, philosophy, art, culture, and academics. And the common connecting strand that runs through the centre of all the sub-plots as well as the main plot is an increasing revulsion against anything passionate or obsessive, which reaches its zenith with Mann stabbing Firoz in a moment of frenzied jealousy. But it is not only the sexual passion, also the passions for religion, politics, power, career, etc., which are given treatment in the book.

In a country as big and ethnically diverse as India, religion has always played a very important part in the life of an Indian.

Religious rituals pervade the lives of Indians more than they do the lives of most other people. Religious considerations are sometimes more vital than even economic factors. And for majority of Indians no other factor is more powerful and influential than their religious beliefs and faith. They are dogged followers of religion, firm believers in their respective gods and goddesses, sticklers for ritual and religious practices. In *A Suitable Boy*, the epitome of this kind of positive religious ideas and devotion is Mrs. Mahesh Kapoor, the least criticized character of the novel. Still, we do have communal riots; sometimes as the result of political manipulations and sometimes due to the despicable exploitation at the hands of some evil-minded persons who desire benefits at the cost of mass destruction. Always it is the common man who suffers, mainly because of a decided lack of that long forgotten virtue called tolerance. He is ruled exclusively by passion which blinds him towards anything rational and sensible.

In one revealing passage in *A Suitable Boy*, the narrator, while praising Pandit Nehru for his efforts at maintaining communal harmony also imparts upon the readers a subtle lesson as to how one can sustain that harmonious state:

> And thus his meetings ended, and on he went to the next one, always late, always late, always impatient, a man whose greatness of heart won the hearts of others, and whose meandering pleas for mutual tolerance kept a volatile country, not merely in those early and most dangerous years but throughout his own lifetime, safe at least from the systemic clutch of religious fanaticism. (1355)

Passion in religion is defined by Seth as fanaticism, bigotry and disgust towards other religions. The insanity and devastative power of such zealotry is in direct proportion to the blinding jealousy caused by lust and passion in sexual love.

"My sister! My sister!" Saeeda Bai laughed in Mann's face as if he had made some insane joke, "it is not my sister he is in love with". She tried to push Mann violently away. They fell onto the floor and Saeeda Bai screamed as Mann's hands went round her throat. The water in the bowl spilled over. The fruit bowl overturned. Mann noticed none of this. His mind was red with rage. The woman he loved had betrayed him with is friend, and now she was taking delight in mocking his love and his misery (1190).

Though this book was written before the *Ramjanamabhoomi-Babri Masjid* dispute took place (6th December 1992), yet the resemblance between that horrifying incident and one of the equally horrifying episodes in the book is chillingly uncanny. It not only shows Seth's acute power of perception and imagination, but also the temporal quality of such a volatile issue like religion.

The Raja of Marh has decided with passive support from some Hindu officials and politicians, to construct a Shiva temple on a piece of land contiguous to a mosque. The mosque is supposed to have been built on the ruins of an ancient, long-forgotten temple, and since he cannot destroy the mosque, the Raja of Marh decides to take the next best possible course to have a temple in the closest proximity. The Muslims of the area object to this abomination, a maulvi delivers an inflammatory sermon, "their religion was in danger. The barbarians were at the gates.... The land that the kafirs sought to build on–why sought? Were at this very moment building on–was disputed land–disputed in God's eyes, but not in the eyes of animals who spent their time blowing conches and worshiping parts of the body whose very names it was shameful to mention... and now the infidels who held power in the land wanted Muslims, when they turned their faces westward in prayer to the Kabba to face these same idols and these same obscene objects with their heads bowed" (233), Hindus refuse to back down, the government fails to install sufficient police protection, and communal riots break out in the evening.

It takes its usual course of killing, fighting, firing, bloodshed and then finally, a temporary abatement of weapons on both sides. Always it is a temporary abatement, never a permanent one, because the bitterness and the hostility never die, but lie dormant, awaiting resurfacing at the first possible opportunity.

The opportune moment arrives during the Dussehera festival which is also the period for Moharram celebrations. Passion, ego, and stupidity combine fatally resulting in a terrifying sequence of events. Blood flows freely and fire blazes all-consumingly. "Firoz closed his eyes, as if to shut out the terrible vision of the city in flames" (1063). In human terms, Seth's moral designs against religious fanaticism in *A Suitable Boy* reaches its climax in the horrifying scene when Firoz and Mann are attacked by a murderous Hindu mob:

> Mann and Firoz were sauntering along the dark lane of Katra Mast towards Misri Mandi when Mann stopped suddenly. The sounds he heard approaching them were not those he had expected. They were the sounds neither of a tazia procession—and surely it was too late for a tazia procession—nor the joyful sounds of Bharat Milap. The sound of drums had stopped on either side and neither "Hassan! Hussain!" nor "Jai Siyaram!" could be heard. Instead he made out the ominous, inchoate sounds of a mob, broken by screams of pain or passion–or shouts of "Har har Mahadeva". This aggressive invocation of Shiva would not have sounded out of place yesterday–but today it chilled his blood. He let go of Firoz's hand and turned him around by the shoulders. "Run" he said, his mouth dry with fear "Run". His heart was pounding. Firoz stared at him but did not move. The crowd was rushing down the lane now. The sounds grew closer. Mann looked around him in desperation. The shops were all closed, their shutters down. There were no side lanes within immediate reach. "Get back, Firoz," said Mann, trembling, "Get back-run! There's nowhere to hide here." "What's the matter—isn't it the procession?" Firoz's mouth opened as he registered the terror in Mann's eyes. "Just listen to me", Mann gasped—"Do as I say. Run back! Run back towards the Imambara. I'll delay them for a minute or two. That'll be enough. They'll stop me first." "I'm not leaving you," said Firoz. "Firoz, you fool, this is a Hindu mob." "I'm not in danger. But I won't be all right if I come with you. God knows what will be happening there by now. If there's rioting going on, they'll be killing Hindus there. "No". "Oh God". By now

> the crowd had almost reached them, and it was too late to flee. (1058-59)

The scenes depicted in the novel look as if straight out of the then released Hindi film *Bombay* which is broadly based on the devastating riots which took place in Bombay in the aftermath of Babri Masjid demolition, so routine-like, as if such scenes are not confined to any particular period or space, and they occur again and again, from time to time, as an inevitable part of the total Indian "adjustment", and hence such strange similarity. The counterbalance to this maniacal mob is the deep, enduring, inter-religious friendship between Mann and Firoz on the one hand, and between their fathers, Mahesh Kapoor and the Nawab Sahib on the other.

Symbolically, Seth's condemnation of any kind of fanaticism becomes clearly evident when the lunatic Raja of Marh's attempt to raise the "Shiva-linga" from the bottom of the Ganges and resurrect it to the great resentment among the Muslims of the area ends in abject failure. The gigantic phallus—an awesome symbol of both regeneration and destruction, of sexual and religious passions rolls back down the steps of the ghats crushing a priest on the way, and returns to rest in the holy waters:

> Down the rollers the great linga past the next step, and the next, and the next, gathering speed as it rolled. The tree-trunks cracked under the impact of its weight, it veered to left and right, but it kept rolling on down, down, swifter and swifter towards the Ganga, crushing the pujari who now stood in its downward path with his arms upraised, smashing into the burning pyres of the cremation ghat, and sinking into the water of the Ganga at last, down its submerged stone steps, and into its muddy bed. The Shiva-linga rested on the bed of the Ganga once more, the turbid waters passing over it, its bloodstains slowly washed away.

The tone of disrespect ("it veered to left and right, but kept rolling on down, down..."), of contempt ("sinking into the water of Ganga at last...and into its muddy bed..."), and projecting the "holy" phallus as an agent of destruction ("the tree trunks cracked under the impact of its weight...") and murder ("crushing the pujari who now stood in its downward path"), almost reminding the bloody communal riots ("its blood stains slowly washed way..."), are all integrated in an attitude that shows extremities of passion, to evolve towards a sane, rational outlook on life.

In a similar vein, in a different type of religious scenario, Seth's distaste and disgust towards power-hungry, fraud Swamijis and Sadhus, reaches its climax at the renowned Pul Mela festivals. This disgust is effectively portrayed through the eyes of the mild and peaceful, spiritual seeker Dipankar Chatterji. It progresses from an initial admiration to a final alienation and repulsion on Dipankar's side, when he realises that the abundant display of saintliness masks vanity and egoism to downright filthiness of mind ("It was all so unloving, possessive and defensive that Dipankar could hardly stand it.") (728). Like the earlier scenes of communal riots, again, the terrible scenes of stampede that take on the Pul Mela grounds is seen to be sickeningly parallel to the one that took place, inside the temple of Lord Jagannath at Puri, at the time of *Nagarjuna Vesa* (26th November 1993). The horror of the mass stampede, the crushing of the elderly and the frail to death, Bhaskar's miraculous escape from death, are all a further reinforcement made by Seth against involvement with religion and religious rituals in generals:

> Within fifteen minutes more than a thousand people were dead. Finally the police managed to communicate with the railway authorities and stop the trains. They set up barriers on the approach rout to the ramp. The loudspeakers started telling people to go back, not to enter the meal grounds, not to watch the processions. They announced that the remaining processions themselves had been cancelled. It was still not clear what had happened. Dipankar had been among the spectators on the other side of the main route. He watched with horror the carnage that was taking place less than fifty feet away—but with the Nagas between him and the ramp, there was nothing he could do. Anyway there was nothing he could have done except get killed or injured. He did not

> recognize anyone on the ramp, so tightly packed was the crowd. It was a hellish scene, like humanity gone mad, each element indistinguishable from the other, all bent on a kind of collective suicide. (734)

The tone of satire, a sharp disapproval ("there was nothing he could have done except get killed or injured..."), is evident as also man's debasement from an individual benign identity to a faceless murderous mass ("each element indistinguishable from the other all bent on a kind of collective suicide").

Dipankar returns to his home, and makes a final decision of taking up banking as a profession. His experiences at the Pul Mela moves him into a position of realization that philosophy, truth, spiritualism are all a "great big hoax", and ultimate peace lies in doing what one is most comfortable with. Dipankar gains this insight as a result of a very interesting discussion which he has with self-styled holy man Sanki Baba:

> Baba, how do you explain this? Dipankar pointed to the distant smoke from a huge funeral pyre, where hundreds of unidentified bodies were being burned. Is it all the lila of the universe, the play of God? Are they fortunate because they died on this auspicious spot at this auspicious festival?.... "I think there was a flaw in the administrative arrangements," replied the guru blandly. (749)

The implied irony is both pungent and horrifying – pungent in the question that Dipankar asked, "Are they fortunate because they died on this auspicious spot at this auspicious festival?" and horrifying in the answer of the guru, "I think there was a flaw in the administrative arrangement".

In the Indian subcontinent, politics, along with religion, is a way of life. Neither is allowed to exist without the other, but the coexistence is far from being a harmonious one. On the contrary the relationship is excessively volatile, with a majority of politicians perfect in the art of manipulation and exploitation.

In *A Suitable Boy* Pandit Nehru is praised in his brief appearance as the enemy of fanaticism, bigotry and racism and a champion of tolerance, unity and modernization. S.S. Sharma, the Chief Minister of Purva Pradesh, also received Seth's admiration due to similar kind of political sentiments. In a similar vein, though Mahesh Kapoor loses credibility on the family front, on the political front his is an ideal figure. Excessive involvement with political matters results in him behaving rudely and unreasonably with his wife and son. On the political front, however, he is a man of principle, and like his hero Pandit Nehru, champions the cause of unity, equality and tolerance.

A number of other people, some individually some in pairs, some in groups, and some in what could only be called throngs, spoke to Mahesh Kapoor during the morning and early afternoon. Cups of tea came from the kitchen and went back empty. Lunch time came and went, and the Minister Sahib remained energetic though unfed. Mrs. Mahesh Kapoor sent word to him through a servant, he waved him impatiently away. She would never have dreamed of eating before her husband did, but her main concern was not that she was hungry but that he needed food and did not know it. (325)

The subtle play of irony can be noted ("Cups of tea...Minister remained energetic though unfed"..."but her main concern was ....he needed food and did not know it"). But on the whole the portrait of the man is in total contrast to the anti-Muslim, Hindu right-wing ideas of Congress President Tandon at the central level and the Hindu baiting attitude of the "legislative vixen" (Contents) Begum Abida Khan at the state level. The contrast becomes more prominent when Mahesh Kapoor's rationality is equated with his "arch political rival" (15), L.N. Agarwal's authoritarianism and over-confidence. L.N. Agarwal, as the Home Minister of the state, is in charge of the humanitarian side of the state, but in his arrogance he overlooks the genuine problems of the people. Instead he only manages to aggravate the already volatile situation with his complete inability to perceive the scenario. Seth presents three different occasions to show how the man's insensitivity and high-handedness result in mass disaster, and at least on one occasion, his meanness and vengeful behaviour cause general embarrassment to the government.

The first occasion is his removing adequate police protection from the controversial construction site of the Siva temple, and relocating the force at the entrance of the Govind Shoe Mart as a possible precaution against picketing by the Jatav community. He also orders indiscriminate firing, if the necessity arose. Ultimately it results in killing and bloodshed. The second occasion is his underestimation of religious fanaticism and mass panic at the Pul Mela festivals on the banks of the holy Ganga. The third one is his lack of understanding the problems of the university students, and then a gradual alienation from them which incites him to order a vicious lathi charge which results in the death of a student leader. And his meanness as a politician becomes clear when on his orders, the police come to evacuate the Baitaar House, when not a single male member of the family is present to face them. But the final nail in the coffin is that, no occasion is he remorseful of his behaviour. On all these occasions, Agarwal is contrasted with the calmness, sensitivity and tolerant attitude of Mahesh Kapoor. His vociferous support for the Zamindari Abolition Bill and the Hindu code bill are perfect examples of this idealism.

Another minor but a very vital figure illustrating the deviousness involved in politics is Waris Mohammad Khan, the loyal servant of Nawab Sahib. Waris is transformed by greed and ambition from being a likeable young man into a treacherous and heinous man. He spreads false news among the voters informing them about Firoz's death in order to stir them up against Mann and Mahesh Kapoor, his nearest rival on the election platform. This exemplifies the level of baseness to which political ambitions can degrade a human being. Another minor figure demonstrating the ridiculousness of political ambitions is Netaji (the name itself is ironical), the petty village politician whose sole aim in life is to gain political mileage by latching on to figures with high connections in political and social circles.

Not only in politics, but also in administrative and academic circles, corruption is actively rampant. Merit takes a back seat and manipulation is the key method of getting things done. For effective counter-attack Seth's positive characters require a shrewdness of mind, and the hand of god on their side. Rasheed the socialist has high moral principles, and a sincere interest in upgrading the living standard of the poor people, but he totally lacks understanding, tolerance, cleverness and humour. And an excess of self-righteousness and a superiority complex flaws his high-standard principles. He fails to perceive the innate goodness of his own family members, and behaves hastily and immaturely in the affair of Kachheru and his right to a piece of land under the impending Zamindari Abolition Bill. As a result of which his family is forced to abandon Kachheru, their old servant, without any financial support, in his old age. In another incident, Sandeep Lahiri, IAS, is forced to bow, and then wait for his turn, when the corrupt Congress leader Jha banishes him to the department of Mines of Brahmpur because of his refusal to join on in their trade of general corruption and exploitation.

On the academic side, the most suitable candidate Pran Kapoor finally wins his much postponed promotion to Readership, but only after a brave fight against his diseased body, and against unsavoury politics in academia. Professor Mishra, the hypocritical villain, gives up his wily schemes not because he suddenly had a change of heart, but because fate intervenes in the form of a false news that Pran's father Mahesh Kapoor is about to win from his electoral seat and has all chances of again becoming an all-powerful Minister. Pran's promotion therefore is not so much the triumph of merit as "Karma", which, as Maggu Gopal says, is "actions according to the wishes of God" (798). All of Seth's characters at one point of time or the other are shown to be at the mercy of these unpredictable turns of fate and they provide an interesting variety to his plot, as well as a philosophical view that we are somehow ruled by our fates.

On the cultural front, the traditional Indian classical music gets priority in Seth's book. In India, Lucknow has always been considered to be the center of all arts and cultures, and a base from where musicians imbibe the essence of their music. Seth's Purva Pradesh cultural tradition is a reflection of this Lucknowvi tradition. But the portrayal is an ironic one, since, the advent of modernization also implies at one level, the deterioration of ancient heritage. This is best exemplified in the steady decaying of Nawab Sahib's country palace and his historic library and a gradual alienation of people from classical music and an increasing attraction towards light music and film songs, best exemplified by Varun, with his penchant for Hindi film songs. Seth has even given an ironic comment on the courtly style of living of the people of the state, which is made to look ridiculous and hilarious in the eyes of the modernized people of Calcutta:

> All that courtly culture with its Yes Huzoor and No Huzoor and nothing robust about it all, "How are you?" "Oh, well I'm alive."..."Yes I'll have two florets of rice, and one drop of dal...." All that subtlety, and etiquette and bowing and scraping and ghazals and Kathak. Kathak! When I saw those fat women twirling around like tops, I wanted to say to them, "Run! Run! Don't dance, run! (393)

It would the interesting to compare Seth's discussions on political debasement, social immorality, corruption and individual hypocrisy and dishonesty etc., to what we see around us now-a-days in India related to corruption, scams and political and individual hypocrisy etc., almost in a daily routine basis, as if the whole country has gone cancerous without any hope of remedy or salvation. To that effect *A Suitable Boy* is not only a comprehensive but also an extremely sensitive and intelligent creative document. It not only exposes, but also castigates, and also at the same time shows how best the human animal that has fallen to the lowest pitch of existence, willy nilly, due to himself, can also rise beyond, higher, to central place of sane, benign understanding and rationality. Seth's criticism, social, political, cultural and even familial, has a sharp edge which cuts, but which also cuts to form.

Commenting on the form of the novel, Seth explains that he had initially intended to write a short book of about two hundred and fifty pages concentrating mainly on Lata or Lata's mother's search for a suitable match for her. But he clarifies, "having begun it with a wedding and having lots of characters come to that wedding, I realised that I was quite interested I was writing a different kind of book" (Kohli, 1999: 12).

Seth uses a quasi-historical structure and focuses on the first few years after Indian Independence leading up to the first General Elections of 1952. The multi-linear narrative follows a chronological time pattern. This was a period of tumulus economic, political and communal upheavals. When Justice Chatterji compares the list of names of judges on the first page of the *All India Reporter* of 1948 with that of the previous year of 1947, he notices the absence of the names of large number of British and Muslim colleagues. The judge rules that "...in macrocosm these two pages reflect the passage of an empire and the birth of two countries from the idea tragic and ignorant that people of different religions cannot live together in one. Who'd have thought that things would have changed as much and swiftly as they had?" he asks (468-69).

The apparently uneventful narrative of social manners and lifestyles of the Indian middle class (Seth includes every minutiae including a visit to the zoo and animals seen therein) is offset with detailed accounts of social and political crises. "The nuts and bolts of political demographics" as Field puts it, "run through the novel set against the background of the partition" (1993: 46). Mrs. Mehra's search for a suitable son-in-law helps to make Seth's historical backdrop more intimate and human. The Indian nation-state is preparing for its first General Election under the Prime Ministership of Jawaharlal Nehru but there is a growing disillusionment with his leadership. This has led to a rift in the ruling Congress Party between the supporters of Nehru and Nehru's political rival, Purushottam Das Tandon. There are also parliamentary quarrels on the implementation of land reforms that require the appropriation of landed estates from Zamindars who had enjoyed large proprietary rights from the British Government. Memories of pain and feelings of insecurity are still fresh in the minds of those who had been uprooted from their homes during the partition of the Indian subcontinent, and violent communal clashes are not uncommon.

The political characters Vikram Seth uses fall into three categories. In the first group there are certain national figures like Jawaharlal Nehru, Rafi Ahmed Kidwai and Rajrishi Purushottam Das Tandon who appears in their real names. Seth minutely assesses their role in Indian politics and points out their feet of clay. In the second category are some leaders who appear with changed names but their characters are identifiable. There is the Purva Pradesh (Uttar Pradesh) Chief Minister called S.S. Sharma who seems to the spiting image of G.B. Pant. Then there are two state ministers, the secular Mahesh Kapoor who seems to be the dramatized version of Damodar Swaroop Seth, and L.N. Agarwal who echoes the personality of C.B. Gupta. In the last group are fictional characters that represent the emergent forces in the Indian polity. Between these two important figures are the "successful subaltern", Waris Khan, and "doomed idealist", Abdur Rasheed.

Anita Desai comments that 1951 was "not a year that is particularly memorable in modern Indian history, yielding up not even one momentous event to memory (and therefore) ...by choosing it rather than another, Seth displays his proclivity for the common place and quotidian" (1993: 23). On the other hand, Seth points out that he too had initially held the impression that the 1950s was a period of idealism of the freedom movement but extensive reading of newspapers of the era proved otherwise that this was neither "an innocent time" nor "a period of great public probity". Referring to the interviews that he conducted with people who had been young students at that time, Seth explains: "You'll realise what bitterness and cynicism had crept in already at that time" (Paranjape, 1993: 20-24). Seth points out to student riots and protests that were taking place in places like Lucknow to support this observation (*ibid*).

Seth is able to skillfully reproduce a society in transition largely due to his meticulous research evident in his through documentation of a number of historical events. It took Seth over eight years to complete the manuscript and he has acknowledged his debt to all those people who assisted him in the research and field work. These included meeting ex-freedom fighters; people who had visited courtesans at that time, and those affected by the abolition of Zamindari. Seth also spent time staying in different places like Banaras, Allahabad, in the countryside, or staying with a shoe-making family in Agra. He explains that intensive research was necessary "because how can you claim to write about something unless you know it, if not from the heart of it, then somewhere from the inside of it" (Paranjpe, 1993: 22). Also added are transcribed parliamentary debates on the Zamindari Abolition Bill, and arguments in the High Court in the language of the legislature. Also popular Hindi films of the time with social relevant themes are mentioned in the text.

The two epigrams from Voltaire pre-fixed to the text, "the superfluous, that very necessary thing" and "the secret of being a bore is to say everything" speaks of the author's intentions. *A Suitable Boy* has had its fair share of both detractors and supporters on account of Seth's tendency towards elaborate detailing. This in turn adds to the length of the novel and the "uneventfulness" of the narrative. "Were it 600 pages shorter," Jenkyns comments, "It would be obvious for what it is, a decent, unremarkable, second rate novel. As it is, after 1300 pages the feelings still persists that it is a little thin" (44). "The telling is smooth...reminding one of elaborate weaving," complains Srinath, "but where is the textile?" (1999: 38).

According to Srinath, getting past the myriad details of the novel is like dealing with "...onion peel that brings only tears to an impatient reader" (40). On the contrary Pico Iyer describes every page of the novel as "readable and true", and finds Seth's indebtness to India evident in respect of vocabulary and cultural matrix (1993: 20). As Buchan puts it, "...no stone of social India is left unturned", while writing a book "generally thought unwritable in the atomized and fluid societies of the late 20th century, except as historical pastiche or airport fiction" (1993: 31).

Anita Desai suggests that, "if Seth's novel is to have an artistic equivalent, then it is the folk painting on a village wall, a mural in a cave, or a stitched and embroidered quilt patiently patched together and embellished by that multiplicity of detail that gives it diversity and richness" (1993: 23). In terms of its "epic size", "spacious realism" and number of characters, the novel has been compared repeatedly with Tolstoy's *War and Peace* and George Eliot's *Middle March*. Pico Iyer proposes a third comparison when he considers *A Suitable Boy* as closest to

Tanizaki in his *Makioka Sisters*: "For it is, like the Japanese novel, at its heart on elegy as well as a comedy of manners, about a traditional society on a time of change, and about a leisurely world of graces giving way to a new, more democratic time." Iyer says that, "like Tanizaki, Seth locates these changes in the woman's curtained world of rituals, and uses a rich family's search for a husband as a way of making history intimate and human. And like Tanizaki, he has given us that unlikeliest of hybrids, a modest tour de force" (*ibid*).

Seth uses one of his own characters to highlight this process of writing fiction of such an epic scale. Amit Chatterji is writing a long first novel on the famine in Bengal. He compares his method of writing with the performance of a raag: "First you take one note and explore it for a while, then another to discover its possibilities, then perhaps you get to the dominant, and pause for a bit, and it's only gradually that the phrases begin to form and the table joins in with the beat...and then the more brilliant improvisations and diversions begin, with the main theme returning from time to time, and finally it all speeds up, and the excitement increases to a climax" (394).

The international success of Salman Rushdie's *Midnight's Children* in the 1980s made Rushdie's experiments with post-modernistic techniques of fiction a touchstone of comparison for other works of Indian fiction in English written in the late 1980s and the 1990s. Pico Iyer, for instance, makes a distinction between the "two strands of Indian fiction" that emerged in the 1980s as that of "compassionate realism" as in the novels of R.K. Narayan and Rohinton Mistry, and that of "pin-wheeling invention" as in the works of Salman Rushdie, Shashi Tharoor and Allan Sealy. Iyer reads *A Suitable Boy* as "a counter-Rushdie epic, relatively secluded and old-fashioned where Rushdie is determinedly topical and international, somewhat conservative in style and temper where Rushdie is willfully radical...Most of all, Seth is a peace-maker where Rushdie is belligerent" (1993: 20).

A Suitable Boy is often been evaluated on the basis of its "un-Rushdie like" techniques and Seth has faced severe criticism for his "rejection of multiple forms of post-modernism, and accompanying complexities of utterance, for a coherent, straightforward and linear narrative". In reply Seth reacts by expressing his desire to "strip fiction of ideas and style that only get in the way of a reader's enjoyment". In an interview with Peter Forbes and Allok Reich, Seth has said, "it doesn't matter what profusions in universities or critics in London or France or New York or Yale think about the current state of the novel. What will last as literature and what gives pleasure is clean, affecting, straightforward writing which appeals to the general intelligent reader" (1986, cited in Royan, 1994: 207). Seth explains that, "...books of that kind draw attention to themselves, act as sort of brilliant vehicles for the writers" own use of sentences and sub-conscious are books that I don't read". He continues: "I admire the Victorian and clear writes in general, those who try to portray the lives of other people rather than those who try to emphasis technique and their own particular finesse in the use of language. That seems to be like using a stained glass window to look out to see a particular view. I'd much rather have a clear window" (Paranjape, 1993: 23).

Krishna Rayan has categorized the two opposite poles of writing as statement and suggestion. The novel can be read as statement if its meaning is taken as a literal one. If it read as a suggestive text, then the personalities and situations presented can be claimed to be other than themselves, i.e. to have symbolic equivalents, and the whole text can be interpreted as having a wider significance from what is ostensibly told (1994: 207). According to Rayan what Seth practices with "conspicuous success" can be described as "the poetic statement" (207-8). Seth's style is direct and his vocabulary accessible. Rayan therefore describes *A Suitable Boy* as "a tour de force of neutral language" and "a triumph of sustained statement extending over 1,300 pages". In addition, Rayan says, "if Seth's specific achievement must be named, it can be said to consist in having rediscovered the full capabilities of statement as a, if not the, language of fiction" (208).

Rayan offers two other very significant observations in Seth's defence. First, he explains that if the characters and plot have their basis in historical records "which command the emphatic intellectual and emotional assent of a class of readers, then inevitably for those readers the literal or grammatical reference will be so powerful that the figurative or rhetorical significance, if any is intended, will be erased". Secondly, he argues that "whether a given work is a literary work is not decided by the author's classification, but by the readers' community consensus formulated and sustained over a substantial period of time. Therefore until the novel qualifies for membership of the canon, its suggested meaning cannot be accorded priority over its stated meaning" (206).

Viney Kripal in a detailed study in *The Third World Novel of Expatriation* says of the Third World writer (qtd. in Sastry, 1991: 142):

> His aspirations are shared by fellow natives both at home and in the new land. As an artist, he passes through various phases. He expresses his hope of assimilation to the white way of life through the marriage between coloured man and white woman; he conveys his disillusionment and sense of betrayal through their divorce or separation. His backward glance home conceals a yearning for the lost paradise; his criticism of the reality of home reaffirms the same longing, though in an inverted manner. As the distance in time from home increases (despite periodic visits) both the perspective of detachment as well as the realism of his art disappears; he grows allegorical, symbolic, cerebral, obscure, abstract, abstruse. His characters become typed and recondite, his situations abstract and contrived, his language convoluted, obscure and private. Above all, he continues to write about his experiences as a "coloured" expatriate and to awaken readers to the injustice of his situation.

Within the above description of the expatriate sensibility and its growth, one can see this pattern in the works of Rushdie, ranging from *Grimus (*1996) to *The Satanic Verses* (1988)—the expatriate writer's experimentation with language is also a consequence of his exile. Viney Kirpal in describing this language of extra-territoriality comments:

> The prolonged stay of the artist in exile begins to affect his language. Insubstantiality, abstractness, even strangeness begin to modify the language of the expatriate novelists. On the one hand, he essays to live within his experiences in the new land; on the other he continues to feed himself on a memory that devolves around experiences in the old. Nostalgia, allegory, self-consciousness, abstractness begin to imprint his literature, and also to affect the very foundation of literature—Language. His use of language exhibits a gradual movement away from rootedness towards unrootedness. Roughly distinguishing between his earlier and later fiction, there is a perceptible change from the language that captures and translates the active sensibility into the metropolitan language (English/French), to a language that displays the effects of deregionalisation, and exile. The language of the expatriates' earlier fiction is marked by realism, concreteness, materiality and the solidity of the earth—symbol of rootedness. The language of the later works is stumped by insubstantiality, absence, convolutedness and a shadowy, dream-like existence—symbol of a deconstructed existence. There is also, on the part of the novelist, a disinclination to draw the reader into the experience, which seems to grow increasingly inward and private.

With *The Satanic Verses*, Rushdie, the archetype immigrant reached the apogee of his development as on immigrant writer. Creating his own new technique of writing, he has established himself as a modernist beyond modernism, a teacher beyond tutoring, educating by allegory and parable, a writer with images that transcend the written word to successfully use surrealism to convey experience. But, contrary to this, Vikram Seth represents another aspect of the non-resident Indian finding his feet in an alien world.

For Seth writing is a simple business that has been slurred by academic critics and diverted from its original course by an obsession with style and modernist knowingness. "I don't read a lot of modern fiction, but it seems to me that too much of it is thesis fodder," he says, "since the rise of the academic critic, writing has had to have an increasing sophistication, as if subjects such as love, ambition and family are worthy only of the airport novels. Writers come out of university courses and carry into their writing academic concerns rather than the concerns of the general reader." Here, Seth's "reader friendly" approach can be compared to Dickens's about whom G.K. Chesterton has said with characteristic over-emphasis (qtd. in Neill, 1964: 161-162):

> Dickens stands first as a defiant monument to what happens when a great literary genius has a literary taste akin to that of the community. For this kinship was deep and spiritual. Dickens did not write what the people wanted. Dickens wanted what the people wanted. And with this was connected that other fact which must never be forgotten, and which I have more than once insisted on, that Dickens and his school had a hilarious faith in democracy and thought of the service of it as a sacred priesthood. Hence there was this vital point in his popularism, that there was no condescension in it. The belief that the rabble will only read rubbish can be read between the lines of all our contemporary writers, even of those writers whose rubbish the rabble reads....Dickens never talked down to the people. He talked up to the people. He approached the people like a deity and poured out his riches and his blood. This is what makes the immortal bond between him and the masses of man.... His power, then, lay in the fact that he expressed with an energy and brilliancy quite uncommon the things close to the common mind. But with the mere phrase the common mind, we collide with a current error. Commonness and the common mind are now generally spoken of as meaning in some manner inferiority and the inferior mind; the mind of the mere mob. But the common mind means the mind of all the artists and heroes; or else it would not be common. Plato had the common mind; Dante had the common mind; or that mind was not common. Commonness means the quality common to the saint and the sinner, to the philosopher and the fool; and it was this that Dickens grasped and developed.

If writers can be divided into those who are driven by the need to say something, and those who are motivated more by a desire to explore, then Seth is certainly the latter. As well as his poems, translations, travel book and novels, he has also written a libretto about dolphins and poems for children, and his last book, *An Equal Music*, is an ordinary sized novel about classical musicians set in London, Vienna and Venice.

The cruelty of fiction is that its organs may be in the right place, its complexion excellent, but if it has not breath, it will not move. *A Suitable Boy* did move. If one believes that works of art can embody the good, it was a virtuous book of enormous length but also of a blessed kind of quiet. It did not clamour, therefore one paid attention, enjoying the surcease of babble and garishness that had stirred much of the surface of sub-continental literature in English for sometime previously (McWilliam, 1999). "I have little doubt that ... Vikram Seth is already the best writer of his generation," and "three and a half pounds of perfection," Eugene Robinson and Jonathon Yardley said respectively. Both are literary critics for *The Washington Post*.

A Suitable Boy is written with a subtle, unobtrusive style that Seth attributes to his own taste and beliefs. "The kind of books I like reading are books where the authorial voice doesn't intrude too much—19th century novels and some 20th century novels as well," Seth said, "They don't try to pull up with the brilliance of their sentences as much as pull you into a world." On his style of writing this novel, Seth, remarked that, "With such a large cast of characters, a strong voice would have been too much. Easy writing makes down hard reading, and I think the opposite is true as well. The book is not more difficult to read than it has to be" (Robinson, 1993). True to his word, the novel begins with a statement from Voltaire, "the secret of being a bore is to say everything."

When the novel was published, Indian writing was still enamoured by Salman Rushdie but *A Suitable Boy* owed nothing to Rushdie's "manically inventive magic realism". It was written with the clarity and leisureliness, the almost Victorian confidence of a Victorian novel. It is a love story with little love and no sex. At two feet high in typescript, and 1,349 pages when published in hard back, it was the longest novel ever written in the English language. "A very large novel written by a very small Indian," as Seth puts it.

It is from his father, Prem Seth, who rose from comparatively humble beginning to a position of such respect in the Indian shoe business that he is known in Delhi as Mr. Shoe, that he appears to have inherited his conviction, his certainty in himself. Prem, Seth readily admits, is the inspiration for the shoe-making suitor Haresh in *A Suitable Boy* and there is a scene in the book that is drawn directly from Prem's life. Trying to force his way into the management of "Czech shoe company, Haresh is given the apparently impossible task of making a pair of shoes from start to finish in three days. "No poet has ever worked harder or more inspired to craft a poem than Haresh worked for the next three days on his pair of shoes." Haresh succeeds, of course, as did Prem.

The first Section of *A Suitable Boy* beginning with the wedding of the older sister of Lata, whose search for a husband is the heart of the book, was written quite quickly. But then Seth found himself blocked and realising he did not know enough about India in the 1950s, concentrated on research for a year. He buried himself in piles of old newspapers, records of legislative debates, gazetteers and memoirs, spent weeks in a village in rural Uttar Pradesh and with leather-workers in Agra, and talked to "musicians, judges, owners of parrots". "He didn't come out much," Bissell remembers. "But when he did he would corner the most obscure person, some old bureaucrat, and ask him hundred of questions, rapid fire. When I saw him he only wanted to talk about our dog Cuddles, who had a habit of biting people whose star was on the rise. Vikram wanted lists of all the people Cuddles had bitten. Cuddles appears in the book, Vikram didn't even change his name."

Though most England readers wouldn't notice, Khuswant Singh believes this concern for detail paid dividend, "I lived through that period and I couldn't find a flaw," he says, "it really is an authentic picture of Nehru's India." Nevertheless though India loves the success of its own in the wider world,

A Suitable Boy was not received with unequivocal praise here when it was published a few weeks ahead of its British release. *India Today* called it "bland" and "mundane" and the *Economic Times* complained it lacked "the sweep, the majesty, the range and the insights of the great books". But the reviews, with the odd exception, were extraordinary, not merely favourable, but adoring. Readers loved it too. That year, 1993, it outsold John Le Carre and Wibur Smith, and when it was left off the shortlist for the Booker Prize, all the broadsheet newspapers received letters of protest. The row, heated even by Booker standards, Anthony Cheetham, the boss of Orion, calling the judges a bunch of "cankers". It was also curiously revealing.

Most novels when they are published are praised or criticised, and that is that. But there was something about *A Suitable Boy* that demanded more. Its length, its scale, its ambition, its looking back in style to novels of the last century, not to mention the publisher's claims on the jacket, asked for it to be compared to *Middlemarch* and *War and Peace*, and although it had its critics—Margaret Foster called it "of entirely dubious literary merit"—when it was left off the Booker shortlist it seemed it had been rejected not on its own merits but because it had failed to come up to Tolstoy's mark. James Wood, the *Guardian's* former literary Editor says, "it is an extraordinary achievement and has permanently entered literature." And again, "but I still feel perhaps a little more strongly, and Seth has admitted this to me, that there's not so much darkness in him or his book, compared to say Tolstoy or George Eliot. The novel is very happy and consoling, but it is reluctant to commit itself, perhaps not to depth, but to exegesis. On the other hand, perhaps *A Suitable Boy* shows that what is seen as a prerequisite of this kind of literature, the particular quality of searching and intensity is possibly not so essential."

For Seth, such questions seem almost perplexing. He talks about the darkness in *The Golden Gate* and in his own life. "I have been close to suicide," he says. "There have been dark periods, when I've felt hopeless in love, when I haven't been able to see a way out of a situation. Metaphysical struggles if you like. At times I was acutely incapable of doing anything." In the end he comes back, with a shrug, to the fact that he writes what he writes, that *A Suitable Boy* was the story of Lata's search for a husband, that to put unnecessary darkness into it would have been a betrayal of its original purpose.

Seth's brother and sister both inspired characters in *A Suitable Boy,* as did his father, mother and grandmother and substantial part of the book read like extended family jokes. Family for Seth has always been an inspiration. As he told the *Post,* "my family downstairs and my brother and myself upstairs. For me, it provides stability." A sweeping panoramic portrait of a complex, multi-ethnic society in flux, *A Suitable Boy* remains the story of ordinary people caught up in a web of love and ambition, humour and sadness, prejudice and reconciliation, the most delicate social etiquette and the most appalling violence. The book includes everything from straight up action to long brooding descriptions, from fast paced dialogue to moody soliloquies from lovely portrayals of India and its landmarks to involving emotional moments.

In stylistic terms Seth has shifted from poetry in *The Golden Gate* to prose in *A Suitable Boy*. Seth has attempted in *A Suitable Boy* to pursue "a natural, reader friendly style devoid of literary acrobatics and experimentation, and a clear window approach, in contrast to the play of stained glass" (Basu, 67-69). Probably for such a mammoth book, where the story progress by demonstrating what the people do rather than what they think, any other style of writing would not have suited the narrative power of the fiction. The novel focusing on ordinary incidents required a very realistic one-to-one approach of narration so that the attention of the reader is not diverted from the scenes of action. And Seth, wisely, has taken recourse to two very important forms of presentation—irony and humour, and their concomitants, wit and urbanity. These are the two ingredients that transform an otherwise common fare into a real spicy dish.

"A Word of Thanks", with which the novel commences, sets the foundation on which Seth builds up his masterpiece. And his muse of directly addressing the reader in a self-depreciatory manner does serve his purpose of arousing the reader's interest:

> To these I owe a debt past telling:
> My several muses, harsh and kind;
> And (in the long run) did not mind;
> Dead legislators, whose orations
> I've filched to mix my own potations;
> Indeed, all those brains I've pressed,
> Unmerciful, because obsessed;
> My own dumb soul, which on a pittance
> Survived to weave this fictitive spell;
> And, gentle reader, you as well,
> The fountainhead of all remittance
> Buy me before good sense insists
> You'll strain your purse and sprain your wrists.

The element of humour is unmistakable ("Buy me before good sense insists /You'll strain your purse and sprain your wrists") as also the element of wit ("I've filched to mix my own potations". "Indeed, all those brains I've pressed / Unmerciful because obsessed"), and the whole tongue-in-cheek account is on the one hand suave and on the other has an implied gentle irony—an irony that encompasses the writer, the reader, and the whole project as such.

Also the contents in rhyme raise expectations due to its originality and attractive quality, which gradually proves to be an apt prelude to the whole. The contents-page itself is almost an abridged version of the whole story. Along with an idea of how the plot expands, this page also provides the reader with a picture of Vikram Seth's innate sense of humour and his interest for versification:

1. Browsing through books, two students meet one day.
   A mother mopes; a medal melts away.
2. A courtesan sings coolly through the heat.
3. A hopeful lover buys a parakeet.
4. A couple glides down-river in boat.
5. A mother hears that mischief is afloat.

While going through the contents-page the first impression that one gets is that the novel cannot be a total tragedy. Because in spite of the fact that a lot of bloodshed, fight, fury and death are cited as present in the plot, the contents somehow confer on the senses the joys of living rather than the despair arising out of loss. Akin to the rhyming-contents there are also present rhyming-couplets throughout the length of the book churned out with "appalling frequency" (485), by Amit, Meenakshi and Kakoli, which brings to mind the fact that Seth's earlier novel *The Golden Gate* (1986) was written completely in verse and that Seth is a splendid versifier:

> Kakoli felt that Lata and Amit were well matched but that each needed prodding. She rolled off a Kakoli couplet to consecrate their match: "Luscious Lata, born to be Lady Lata Chatterji." She was rewarded by the tinkle of Meenakshi's laughter, and the return of her service: "Luscious Lata, is it hard being wife of a famous bard?" Kakoli giggling, volleyed the ball across the net: "Oh, so hard it is in rhyme: Loving, doving, all the time." And Meenakshi continued the rally: "Kissing, missing, every day, Cuddling, muddling all the way." (881)

As mentioned earlier, humour and irony are the most effective weapons Seth has in his possession and he uses them judiciously to enhance the quality of his already rich and imaginative plot. Mrs. Rupa Mehra, arguably the most adorable character in the novel, gets to say and act the most humorous dialogues and scenes respectively. For example, the following scene (181-82), where she exhausts both the "embroidered handkerchief" and the "reserve handkerchief", the element of humour bursts on the reader through the "tonga-wallah":

> Mrs. Rupa Mehra came breathlessly through the door. She had been crying in the tonga. The tonga-wallah, concerned that such a decently dressed lady should be weeping so openly, had tried to keep up a monologue in order to pretend that he hadn't noticed, but she had now gone through not only her embroidered handkerchief but her reserve handkerchief as well. "Oh my daughter!" she said, "Oh, my daughter."... (180)

Or the following dialogues:

> "Who told you? Asked Lata. "Hema's Taiji ?" "Hema's Taiji? Is she in this too? Exclaimed Mrs. Rupa Mehra with new indignation. "She lets those girls run around all over the place with flowers in their hair in the evening"... "Malati! Malati! I'm talking about you, not about Malati. Studying medicine and cutting up frogs—" Mrs. Rupa Mehra's voice rose once more. (181)

Or as in the following, in both talk and action:

> ..."Still answering back?" Said Mrs. Rupa Mehra, infuriated by the mention of Daddy. "I will give you two tight slaps. She slapped her daughter hard, twice, and instantly burst into tears. (182)

She has been sometimes accused by Western critics as interfering and imposing, but seen in the Indian context she is nothing of the sort, instead she is the typical "Indian mother", always inquisitive and always concerned although her self-lamentations, her "water-works" and her "emotional-capital" (3) sometimes borders on the farcical level ("If he had been here, I could have worn the tissue-patola sari I wore for my own wedding", sighed Mrs. Rupa Mehra. "But it is too rich for a widow to wear" (3). Yet she retains to the end a personality which can only be viewed with indulgent affection. The dramatic irony of her situation lies in the fact that she considers herself to be a serious and sensible person who knows best for her children. The children in the meantime, while appearing obedient to all outward appearances, actually behave and take decisions independently. Towards the end of the novel Mrs. Rupa Mehra, taking full credit for what actually was Lata's independent decision, turns her match-making abilities to her younger son Varun. But not known to her, the "weak-willed" (1342) Varun has already been taken under the protective and passionate wings of the skillful and sensual Kalpana Gaur. Hence the implied irony in the following "decision":

> "You too will marry a girl I choose," said Mrs. Rupa Mehra firmly to her younger son. "But-but, Ma" Varun shifted from foot to foot. "A suitable girl, that is what I want for

> you," said Mrs. Rupa Mehra in an admonitory voice. "That is what your Daddy would have wanted. A suitable girl, and no expectations." (1343)

Frances Spalding, commenting on Seth's use of irony, says, "Seth uses the techniques of western novels, notably understatement and irony, but the end result is very different, more like the unravelling, continuous melodic line of Indian ragas than the contrapuntal, harmonic music of the English novel" (1993). Still, like the English novelists, to reveal human weakness, Seth's brand of humour also stretches from gentle irony to scathing satire:

> Soon Muslim mobs would be roaming around other parts of Brahmpur setting fire to Hindu shops and murdering any Hindu they could find. Meanwhile in Misri Mandi, three of the Muslim drummers who had been hired for the Bharat Milap, who were not even Shias and who did not care much more for the tazias than they did for the divinity of Rama, lay murdered by the wall of the temple, their drums smashed in, their heads half-hacked off, their bodies doused in kerosene and set alight—all, doubtless, to the greater glory of God. (1058)

These gory details of the horrifying scene ("their heads... and set alight") about people who are equally indifferent to "tazias" and "divinity of Rama", show how passion and lack of tolerance can transform ordinary, sane and mild human beings into something terrible and inhuman. Ordinary individuals, who at ordinary moments would probably faint at the sight of blood, do not hesitate to kill and murder, on the pretext that they are doing it to protect their religion. The situation, on the one hand, is extremely ironical ("all, doubtless, to the greater glory of God"), but at the same time also extremely unnerving, as, in the following passage, the narrator suddenly recognizes his one-time quiet, academic acquaintance as a member of the "gang":

> Mann was looking desperately around him. He knew there was no time to talk. Suddenly in the erratic, terrifying light of the blazing torches his eyes fell on someone he thought

> he recognized. "Nand Kishor!" He shouted. "What are you doing here in this gang? Aren't you ashamed of yourself? You're supposed to be a teacher?" Nand Kishor, middle-aged, bespectacled man, looked sullen. (1060)

In *A Suitable Boy,* all the Chatterji children including their dog Cuddles, are specially designed by Seth to impart a humorous touch to the lines. They are all intelligent, but very eccentric, and being witty comes to them naturally. In fact all the eccentric characters in the novel, such as Dr. Durrani, Ila Chattopadhy, Dr. Kishen Chand Seth, have all been given the status of great comic figures. Their eccentricity itself delivers the comic punch:

> Dr. Durrani was frowning in concentration, his eyebrows working up and down. "Curious, though, isn't it um, Patwardhan, that the number, er, beautiful er, shapes in all nature: I refer um, needless to say the er, benzene ring with its single and, er, double carbon bonds. But is it, er, truly symmetrical, Patwardhan or, um asymmetrical? Or super-operations of the, er, Pergolessi Lemma...not really like the er, rather unsatisfactory petals of an, um, iris. Curious, wouldn't you say...?" "Most curious," agreed Sunil. (1076)

The statements are broken and halting, and represent, apart from the comicality of the whole, a half-formed broken mind–a "curious" mind that lives in a world of its own. In this respect they are like the Shakespearean comic characters, who play the fool, while largely remaining unaware of their capacity for caricature. The seventy-year old Dr. Kishen Chand Seth, along with his thirty-five year old second wife Parvati is another one of Seth's "fools":

> Loudly sobbed Dr. Kishen Chand Seth. Astonished necks swivelled swiftly towards him—but to no effect.... By now Dr. Kishen Chand Seth was gasping almost asthmatically. He started pounding the floor with his stick to relieve his distress. Parvati took it from him and said, rather sharply: "Kishy! This isn't *Deedar* !"—and this brought him heavily back to earth. But not much later, the distress of Malvolio-cooped up in an inner chamber and driven from bewilderment almost to madness-evoked further heart-break. Several people around him stopped laughing and turned to look at him.

Seth's behaviour, quick change of mind, and the so-called "distress", conveyed to the reader in detached narration ("By now Dr Kishan Chand Seth...his distress." Or, "But not much later...his heart would break!"), show both feelings of sympathy, and a mix of irony and humour, sympathy apparently, but irony and humour implied ("Astonished necks ...swiftly towards him and several people around...look at him"). The reference to Malvolio, the joyless steward-cum-fool, clinches the issue, where on the one hand "distress" evoking further distress is comical, and on the other, the suggestion of ill will (Malvolio) has irionical overtones.

Conversation plays a major role in the novel, which reflects Seth's admiration particularly for the works of Austen, Dickens as well as other nineteenth century British writers. It also provides an insight into his inclination towards the "clear window" (Basu, 67-69) approach. His dialogues are tools for character exploration, and their gradual development. As in the following conversation between Lata and Kabir, where the narrator is absent and the scene has been taken over by the characters, where the pithy dialogues supported by brief reflections convey both the differences in attitudes as well as muted emotional clash:

> "Kabir, why didn't you tell me your last name?" "It's Durrani." "I know." Hearing him say it so casually brought all the cares of the world back on her head. "You know?" Kabir was surprised. "But I remember that at the concert you refused to exchange last names with me."...."You are Muslim," she said quietly. "Yes, yes, but why is all this so important to you? Is that why you've been so strange and distant sometimes?" There was a humorous light in his eyes. "Important?" It was Lata's turn to be amazed. "It's all-important. Don't you know what it means in my family?" Was he deliberately refusing to see difficulties, she wondered, or did he truly believe that it made no difference? Kabir held her hand and said, "You love me. And I love you. That's all that matters?" (171)

Furthermore, the dialogues, mostly humorous and ironic, are used effectively to advocate the writer's moral ideologies. For example, apparently funny, casual and nursery-rhyme like couplets of Kakoli Chatterji,

> Roly poly Mr. Kohli / Walking slowly up the stairs
> Holy souly Mrs. Kohli / Comes and takes him unawares.
> Mr. Kohli base and lowly, / Stares at choli, dreams of lust, / As
> the holy Mrs. Kohli / With her pallu hides her bust.

is actually a severe satire on sexual frenzy and lust of apparently mild looking men. Even the woman is not spared. Her apparent holiness is mocked at ("Holy souly Mrs. Kohli") and her apparent distaste for sex ("with her pallu hides her bust") is ironically viewed. The dialogues illuminate the vileness of not only the sexual passion, but also by implication, passion elsewhere, as in love, relationship, politics, religion, ambition, etc.

In a recent interview Seth has listed the different methods he adopted for securing accuracy and proper detailing of the past—"...reading just to get a spirit of those times.... Meeting people, ex-freedom fighters, people who'd visited courtesans at that time.... And then staying in different places like Banaras, Allahabad, or in the countryside, or staying with a shoe-making family in Agra. Just a few years doing this sort of thing because how can you claim to write about something unless you know it, if not from the heart of it, then somewhere from the inside of it." This provides a glimpse into the "detailed realism" of the mega novel. But the realism does not lie only in enlisting diverse groups of people, or a variety of scenes and situations, but also the account of a club's dining place suddenly assumes a realistic detail, and hence a vivacious identity:

> They entered the festooned hall, after the brightness outside, it was rather dark; there were a few groups here and there sitting down to lunch. Along the far wall was their own table for eight created by joining three small square tables together.... Mrs. Rupa Mehra was very impressed by all the arrangements. A thick white table cloth and napkins, several sets of knives and forks, good glasses and crockery, and three flower arrangements consisting of an assortment of sweet-peas...two waiters approached the table, and placed

> some bread on it, together with three dishes containing curlicues of Anchor butter. (1123-24)

That which could have been a routine place, to be seen immediately, to be forgotten afterwards, suddenly assumes a presence and a body, numerically and concretely identified, beginning with generalities ("the festooned hall", "rather dark", "few groups here and there"..."thick white table cloth"..."napkins"..."sets of knives and forks, good glasses and crockery"... "three flower arrangement"..."sweet-peas"..."two waiters"..."bread"..."three dishes" and finally "curlicues of Anchor butter").

The description of Mr. Justice Chatterjee's desk, in his study, is another instance of this type of commonplace account, which through a painstaking detailing is metamorphosed into a concreteness and body—a quick, sudden presence, almost like a blow:

> Mr. Justice Chatterjee was sitting in his study. In front of him lay a half-completed judgement. On his desk stood a black-and-white photograph of his parents, and another of himself, his wife, and their five children that had been taken many years ago by a fashionable Calcutta studio. Kakoli, wilful child, had insisted on including her teddy-bear; Tapan had been too small at the time to have had an articulate will at all. (465)

Invariably Seth's style reflects his relation to the subject matter, and is simultaneously direct, witty, ironic, critical and dramatic. The suspense and drama as to whom Lata will select as her husband at the end, gives the novel its gripping and absorbing power. The fortunes of her three suitors fluctuate dramatically, and at one point or the other, each one of them is shown as the most unpropitious one. It is to Seth's credit that he perfectly manages to maintain the suspense, and finally when the suspense thins, it springs a surprise on the reader. After so much of emotional turmoil, Lata coolly takes her decision, though it is true that will be quite sometime before she herself gets used to the idea:

> Her first instinct was to have a heart-to-heart talk with Savita or Malati, or her mother—or with each one of them. Then she decided that it would, if anything, only serve to confuse her. This decision was hers to make. She wrote to Haresh the same evening, accepting with gratitude and, indeed warmth—his often repeated offer of marriage. (1295)

The humour ("to have a heart talk with Savita or Malati, or her mother—or with each one....."), the rationality ("this decision was hers to make") and the sense of drama ("She wrote to Haresh the same evening...."), are all related to quick turns of mood and are integrated in the total structure. Even a bland statement like, "although Dipankar was utterly indecisive in his own life–or perhaps for that very reason—he was quite good at giving out useful suggestion into the lives of other", has its quota of wit and irony. Whatever the mood may be, whether comic, romantic or one of loss, the description is precise, persuasive and most potent. One of the high points of the novel, as far as Seth's evocative power is concerned, is the scene where Lata and Kabir go out for a boat-ride on the Ganga, at dawn. The joyous escapade, the youthful exuberance, the sparkling love, the shy intimacy, the comfortable camaraderie, all combine together, with the majestic Barsaat Mahal, standing as a mute witness to their romance:

> "Now sit and watch for five minutes," said the boatman. "This is a sight you will never forget in your lives". Indeed it was, and neither of them was to forget it. The Barsaat Mahal, site of statesmanship and intrigue, love and dissolute enjoyment, glory and slow decay, was transfigured into something of abstract and final beauty. Above its sheer river-wall it rose, its reflection in the Water almost perfect, almost unrippled. They were in a Stretch of river where even the sounds of the old town were dim. For a few minutes they said nothing at all. (167)

The points mentioned above are seen by implication, or may be called by an objective—co-relative, with the Barsaat Mahal standing as an image. It has two directions, one towards "love", "enjoyment", and "beauty", and the other towards "intrigue", "dissolute", and "decay". They contrast with each other. The final is "unrippled water", "dim sounds", and not the real thing but its shadow, "reflection" which ironically is "perfect"—not the action related to life, but non-action related to loss of it. The picture suggests both the exuberance of love along with its opposite, its loss, emptiness—in a way an intelligent exposition of the nature of relationship between Lata and Kabir.

Most of Seth's scenes are coated with humour, but there are also a few which reverberate with the horror of devastation and despair—Lata's last hopeless scenes with Kabir; the mistaken and murderous jealousy of Mann against Firoz; the funeral scenes of Mrs. Mahesh Kapoor; the suicide of the idealistic, but fanatic Rasheed; and Kabir, shattered and desolate walking on the banks of Ganga. Such scenes convey a deep sense of regret and tragic vision. Thus as with Kabir, at the end of his relationship with Lata:

> Kabir had been able to bring himself to come to the wedding. But though it was Thursday night, he had not gone to visit his mother either. Instead he took a walk by the Ganga; upriver, past the banyan tree, along the dhobi-ghat, past the Pul Mela sands underneath the Fort, along the waterfront of the old town, following the black water for miles until he came to the Barsaat Mahal. In the shadow of a wall, he sat down on the sand for an hour, his head in his hands. Then he got up to walk again, up the tall stairs, across the parapet and to the other side. After a short while he came to a factory, the walls of which came down to the Ganga and prevented him from going further. But he was too tired anyway. He pressed his head against the wall. The ceremonies will be over by now, he thought. He hailed a boatman, and took a boat down-river back to the university and his father's house. (1348)

The first thing that strikes the mind when one reads these lines is the tragic irony of Kabir's plight. This is the same place where his love had sparkled and climaxed. This is also the same place from where his love life had taken a turn towards the worse, as Lata had been sighted walking hand in hand with Kabir, which had brought on all those tumultuous events that took place in their lives. Now, sitting on the banks of Ganga, or walking on the sands, or taking a boat down-river, all he is left with is a colossal sense of emptiness and nothing—the quiet and silent monument is symptomatic of that. One may say, the style of *A Suitable Boy* is integrated with its quick changing situations, both physical and mental, and ranges from funny, ludicrous, to impeccable social manners, to such situations where sorrow, remorse, desolation are sublimated into tragic grandeur.

It is true that a majority of the novel's themes fall under the category of comedy of manners. Yet a heightened sense of tragedy which some of the scenes convey, makes us aware of the fact that this book, with a vast range of characters, some of them not unlike Shakespearean tragic heroes, is also about the tragic flaw of some very important characters. Mann, Mahesh Kapoor, Rasheed, and the Nawab Sahib are perfect examples of such tragic character sketches. But Seth's heroes, excepting Rasheed, do not renounce their lives; they renounce their tragic flaws and they are brave enough to look beyond their immediate tragedy. During Mrs. Mahesh Kapoor's cremation, Seth successfully weaves a scene of tragic suffering, where both Mann and Mahesh Kapoor's sense of guilt, despair and pain confer on them the awareness of their own selfishness and thoughtlessness. Their mutual suffering brings them together, and subsequent forgiveness on the part of Firoz renews their friendship with Firoz and his father—a friendship which is twice as strong as the previous one.

At the end of the story, the victory belongs to Haresh, and to rationality in general. Haresh gives up his ill-fated love for the Sikh girl and promises to devote himself whole-heartedly towards making his marriage with Lata successful. And Lata rejects passionate love and asserts steady affection as life's most enduring emotion:

> "There are two different kinds, I believe of human attraction. One that merely excites, unsettles, and makes you uneasy; the other that—Well, I can't remember exactly, but he talks about a calmer less frantic love, which helps you to from where you are already growing, 'to live wherever as yet I had

> languished'. I just read yesterday, it isn't in my head yet, but said everything that I couldn't express on my own." (1299)

But, these are not new themes with Vikram Seth. In his rhyming novel, *The Golden Gate,* his heroine Liz suffers grievously in her passionate affair with John. Instead, she receives a marriage proposal from her friend Phil, to which she initially responds:

> "To borrow wisdom from my mother,
> "It's love that makes the world go round!"
> "That's bullshit!" grunted Phil.
> "I have found that love's a pretty poor forecaster.
> I love a woman—and was dropped.
> I love a man—and that too flopped.
> Passion's a prelude to disaster.
> It's something else that makes us sure
> Our bond cans last five decades more." (11.20)

But by her wedding day two weeks later, Liz has accepted Phil's anti-passionate logic:

> Liz walks towards Phil. She's thinking, "Whether it's love
> Or not means nothing much.
> Love by itself a tightening tether,
> A habit-forming drug, a crutch." (11.23)

Thus Liz abstains from deceiving passion and marries Phil ["A good kind man who makes me laugh" (11.13)], saying, "And I'd far rather / Marry a man who's a good father" (11.22).

Yet every aspect of *A Suitable Boy* cannot be suitably accepted. The main plot is intertwined with a succession of sub-plots, which contribute little to the substance, or the imaginative power of the novel. In several instances scenes included to provide comic relief fail to impress. One such example is the humorous portrait of a Latin American diplomat with literary pretensions. Another instance is the apparently humorous conversation between Biswas Babu and his friend Burra Babu. At another level, for no apparent reason, Lata is made to come in contact with an incestuous uncle, while later, the birth of her sister's first child is narrated in the manner of a third rate Hindi soap scene. Also the author's detailed exploration into the inner turmoil of the Congress, including the Nehru-Tandon confrontation of 1951, can only interest somebody who is politically inclined, while for others, it is a tedious subject:

> S.S. Sharma made every possible effort to dissuade Nehru from what looked increasingly like a collision course between him and Tandon. In this, Sharma was one of many, for leaders like Pant of U.P. and B.C. Roy of Bengal had attempted to do the same. When they go to Delhi, however, they found Nehru as vaguely adamant ever. (990)
>
> ... ...
>
> With every passing day, however, it became increasingly clear that the month-long deadlock could not be resolved except by some desperate expedient. Tandon refused to reconstitute the Working Committee at Nehru's dictation and Nehru rejected anything less if he has to rejoin it. (991)

But these lapses are minor when compared with the excitement and interest that the book evokes as a whole, Seth's publishers have projected *A Suitable Boy* as a "landmark literary achievement". Nicholas Pearson, Seth's Phoenix House Editor, for example, has described the novel as "the most fantastic, magical book I had ever read on my desk."

The book, right from the time of its publication, has often been denounced as being a "populist work". But before doing that we must remember that its great bulk itself is a daunting task for readers who like instant entertainment. The book is meant for serious appreciation rather than to be read as a pulp fiction. But it is also a popular work in the sense that it has all those ingredients that one requires to hold the attention of both the Indian and foreign readers; with the Indians because they can identify themselves with the characters and the situations, and with the foreigners because it enables them to have a ringside view of India and the Indians, a subject which is fascinating for many. The popularity of the novel can be gauged from the fact that translation rights have already been bought in the French, German, Dutch and Swedish languages. Along with this, the Marathi rendering of Seth's opus as pointed out by *Asian Age* (16 June, 1995), has already hit the stalls. Also the novel's translations in Hindi and Bengali have met with great critical acclaim, "showing that it could be translated back into the languages which are represented in the novel" (Trivedi, 1998).

To conclude, if we can take one of Vikram Seth's character's words as his own, then, in short, Seth compares the process of his novel's development with that of a "banyan tree":

> ...it sprouts, and grows and spreads, and drops down branches that become trunks or intertwine with other branches. Sometimes branches die. Sometimes the main trunk dies, and the structure is held up by the supporting trunks. When you go to the Botanical Garden you'll see what I mean. It has its own life–but so do the snakes and birds and bees and lizards and termites that live in it and on it and off it." (483)

Like the big and legendary banyan tree at Shivpur in Calcutta that has innumerable props in addition to the main trunk, and has equally innumerable branches, and cloud-like leaves, the whole giving the picture of a gigantic creation, both massive and extremely impressive; *A Suitable Boy* with its main theme of a search for a suitable groom for Mrs. Rupa Mehra's daughter Lata, and innumerable other situations and projections involving four families, and the host of people inhabiting those families, along with multiple moods, motives and a whole range of complex emotions; is one of the most fascinating creations in words in contemporary Indian Literature as a whole.

WORKS CITED

Advani, Rukun. *India Today,* 11 March 1993: 12.

Basu, Sharbani. "Loser Takes All." *Sunday,* 17 Oct. 1993.

Bemrose, John. "Full-Lotus Fiction." *Maclean's 106: 22,* 1993: 46-48.

Buchan, James. "A Foreign Country is the Past." Review of *A Suitable Boy. The Spectator,* 27 March 1993: 32.

Desai, Anita. "Sitting Pretty." *The New York Review,* Vol. XLI, No. 10. 27 May 1993: 22-26.

Field, Michele. "Vikram Seth." *Publishers Weekly,* 10 May 1993: 46-47.

Goswami, Seema. "The Golden Boy." *Sunday,* 14 Feb. 1993.

Hansen, Thomas Blom. *The Saffron Wave: Democracy and Hindu Nationalism in Modern India.* Delhi: Oxford University Press, 2001.

Iyer, Pico. "India Day by Day." *Times Literary Supplement*, 19 March 1993: 20.

Kagal, Carmen. "The Great Indian Novel." Review. *Far Eastern Economic Review*, 13 May 1993: 50.

Kohli, Suresh. "Another Suitable Boy." *Hindu Literary Review*, Sunday, 16 May 1999: 33-34.

McWilliam, Candida. "Vikram Seth: Hearing the Key Theme." *The Financial Times*, 3 Apr. 1999: Online http://doononline.net/lightlights/seth/ft.htm

Mukherjee, Meenakshi. "Pantheon in Print." *Far Eastern Economic Review*, 9 December 1993: 36-37.

——. "The Anxiety of Indianess: Our Novels in English." Nilufer Bharucha and Vrinda Nabar, eds. *Mapping Cultural Spaces. Post-colonial Indian Literature in English*. New Delhi: Vision Books, 1998: 78-93.

Myers, David. "Vikram Seth's Epic Renunciation of the Passions: Deconstructing Moral Codes in *A Suitable Boy*." R.K. Dhawan, ed. *Indian Literature Today*. New Delhi: Prestige, 1994: 79-102.

Neill, Diana. *A Short History of the English Novel*. New York: Collier Books, 1964.

Paranjape, Makarand. "A Suitable Author." *The Week*, 9 May 1999: 32-33.

——. "A Conversation with Vikram Seth." *Indian Review of Books*, 16 Mar. 1993: 20-24.

Ram, Susan. "Disappointing Work." Review of *A Suitable Boy*, *Frontline*, 9 Apr. 1993: 110-12.

Rayan, Krishna. "Suggestion on Statement? Three Contemporary Cases." *New Quest*, 106, July-August, 1994: 203-8.

Robinson, Eugene. "A Tolstoy: On His First Try." *The Washington Post*, 1 May 1993.

Sastry, Chandrasekhar. *The Resident Indian: From Non-Being to Being*. Bangalore, India: Panther Publishers, 1991.

Seth, Vikram. *The Golden Gate*. New Delhi: Penguin Books in Association with Faber & Faber, 1986.

——. *A Suitable Boy*, New Delhi: Viking, 1993.

Singh, Khuswant. "The Genius of Vikram Seth." *The Hindustan Times*, 18 Apr. 1999: 13.

Spalding, Frances. "Fiction" Section. *The Times Educational Supplement*, 7 May 1993: 10.

Srinath, C.N. "Post-colonialism and Faction in Indian Fiction." *The Literary Criterion*, Vol. 34, 1999. 1: 33-40.

Trivedi, Harish. "Postcolonial Translation." Editorial. *IACLALS Bulletin*, August, 1998: 1.

Yardley, Jonathan. "A Dickens for the Sub-continent." *The Washington Post*, 25 Apr. 1993: 3.

6 An Equal Music

Vikram Seth's *An Equal Music* (1999), like *A Suitable Boy* (1993), is centered on an ill-fated love affair. "But if *A Suitable Boy* was a vast opera, *An Equal Music* is a sonata, sublime and melancholy" (Knorr, 1999). This is his music novel. "I have always loved music", said Seth, "but I've tried not to write about it because I loved it so much. I've always kept it as a kind of preserve. I was trained in Indian classical singing and I learned the tabla and a bit of Indian flute. But I turned to Western music somewhat late. I did a bit of piano and cello but it's pointless coming to it at the age I came to it. I have friends who are musicians. I probably have more friends who are musicians than literary people, especially in London." *An Equal Music* focuses on music and passion, draped in European settings. Much of the story takes place in London, though Vienna and Venice become central as well. Through the eyes of musicians, the reader sees these tours as holy pilgrimages. The novel resonates with Seth's precise details from the musical history of the cities to the large Campari sign on the isle of Lido, across Vienna from Venice to London.

Seth's novel examines the impact of Western classical music on the lives and hopes and fears and final, desperate choices of its European protagonists. "Seth's novel was stunning by many accounts, not the least of which was its grafting of the twin bulwark of the European tradition—its verbal and aural inscriptions onto the life of its thirty something protagonists," suggests Anjana Sharma. She continues, "Seth tells the story of a young man's growth and maturation—the loss and partial recovery, Pip-like, of his lost love, and the loss, and more certain recovery of his artistic self" (165).

The story is of Michael Holme, the self-tortured protagonist, butcher's son from the bleak north of England and the second violinist of the London-based Maggiore Quartet. Michael appears to be curiously and permanently in mourning for his life, for Julia, a woman he deserted in Vienna ten years ago on an impulse and could never track down again, for the destroyed movie houses and the sinister parking lots of Rochdale, for youth and the musical careers that might have been, for the teacher he turned against and who is dying, for the benefactor who may be dying, for the precious Italian violin he doesn't own and will never be able to buy. In his late 30s, Michael's life is all music and at the same time all "poetical tedium, gloomy walks through London, between rehearsals of the quartet, until he becomes a kind of high class stalker" (Knorr, 1999):

> I play the line of the song; I play the leaps and plunges of the right hand of the piano, I am the trout, the angler, the brook, the observer. I sing the words, bobbing my constricted chin. The Tononi does not object. I am not transposing his string quartets. Where a piano note is too low for the violin. It leaps into a higher octave. As it is, it is playing the songline an octave above its script. Now, if it were a viola...but it has been years since I played the viola.
>
> The last time was when I was a student in Vienna ten years ago. I return there again and again and think: was I in error? Was I unseeing? Where was the balance of pain between the two of us? What I lost there I have never come to retrieving.
>
> What happened to me so many years ago? Love or no love, I could not continue in that city. I stumbled, my mind jammed,
> I felt the pressure of every breath. I told her I was going, and went.
> For two months I could do nothing, not even write to her.
> I came to London. The smog dispersed but too late. Where are you now, Julia, and am I not forgiven? (5)

From the past that Michael is trying desperately to forget, surfaces Julia, the love of his life. Their relationship is rekindled by a chance sighting on a bus. Rather than a standard boy-meets-girl story, Seth expertly adds a few external themes to make it more interesting, and develops the characters well. "The novel sets the romance astride the tribulations of Michael's career as a classical musician," says Ashini Desai (Location: http://www.desijournal.com/book.asp?articled=57-14k). But *An Equal Music* is not a romantic saga like *A Suitable Boy*. This is a serious and poignant love story. This is the story of Michael for whom music and Julia are an essential and inseparable part of his life. It is also a story which reveals the "strange, precarious, obsessive, joyous and difficult life led by a professional musician; in this case, Michael, who plays second violin in the Maggiore Quartet," says Ann Skea (Location: www.eclectica.org/v3n3/skea_music.html-8k). The narrative deals with Michael's passionate relationship with his music, his deeply moving 12-year old attachment to his 270 year-old Carlo Tononi violin; and his intense love for a woman whom he loses twice over:

> As for the one I remember, I see her with her eyes closed,
> playing Bach to herself: an English suite. Gently her
> fingers travel among the keys. Perhaps I move too
> suddenly. The beloved eyes turn towards me. There
> are so many beings here, occupied, pre-occupied. Let me
> believe that she breathes, that she still exists, somewhere
> on this chance sphere. (7)

Seth explains that if the idea for *A Suitable Boy* germinated from a shred of conversation, it was more of a visual image in *An Equal Music*. Walking across a London Park on a very wet day, Seth and his companion Phillipe Honore (to whom he dedicates the book) see someone staring at his own image in the water of the Serpentine River in Hyde Park in Kensignton Garden. As they wonder about the man, Philippe Honore suggests that he might be a musician, and thereby the idea for the novel took root:

> Walking across a park in London on a very rainy day,
> I saw someone looking at his image on the southern lake.
> I had an inkling that this person would form an important
> part of my next book. But I did not know anything about
> his background. I was thinking about his background.

> A friend of mine, Phillipe Honore, was walking along with me and I kept wondering why he was staring at the water for. (That scene is how the novel begins) (Seth with N. Vidyasagar, 1999)

Nearly two decades ago, soon after he published his Tibet travelogue *From Heaven Lake* (1983), Vikram Seth was taken by his publisher to meet Nirad Chaudhari at Oxford. There was music playing when Seth entered Chaudhari's living room, and Chaudhari asked Seth if he could identify the composer. As Vikram Seth recounts it, "I said, it sounds like Mozart. Nirad Chaudhari's face lit up. Then added, or perhaps Haydn. His face fell. It was Haydn." "Music to me is deeper than speech," remarks Seth in the author's note at the end of the novel. He adds: "When I realised that I would be writing about it I was gripped with anxiety. Only slowly did I reconcile myself to the thought of it." Anjana Sharma in relation to this says that "gripped by anxiety" is a curiously apposite and unfortunately apt phrase since *An Equal Music* is at heart an anxious book, one where the nerve-wrecked world of the key players spills over to create uneasiness in the reader's own mind. An uneasiness generated in part only by the novel's plot line—a dense layering of losses with very few recoveries—because the narrative sweep and the subject choice leaves the reader more than slightly uneasy with exactly what Seth was trying to do when he wove this story, wrote this novel" (165).

Seth's passion for Western classical music—which dominates *An Equal Music*—is apparent in portions of his verse novel *The Golden Gate* (1986), just as sections of *A Suitable Boy* reveals his knowledge of Hindustani music. "I am an amateur," says Seth, "but I did once while fairly young, study a bit of tabla, a bit of flute. I studied Khayal for a short while under Pandit Amarnath at Shri Ram Bharati Kala Kendra. But the problem was I could only visit India for about three months at a time as I was studying in England and America." Western classical music came his way much later, while he was at university in England, "through musician friends who were very interested in composers like Bach and Beethoven." His brush with his favorite Composer Schubert came later while he was struggling with the 1,400 page magnum opus, *A Suitable Boy*.

In *An Equal Music*, with the magical world of Beethoven and Bach as a background, Seth weaves an impassioned tale of heartache, longing and the power of music. The lines have music in them. The author has succeeded in turning prose to poetry. The rhythm makes the novel very musical:

> What is the difference between my life and my love?
> One gets me low, the other lets me go.
> O Luke, O Luke, rack me no riddles more.

The book's style demonstrates the remarkable case of poetry masquerading as prose. Right from the first lines itself, as one begins reading the book, the way the lines are written, brings to the mind a very famous baritone voice, drenched in love and longing, reflecting back about his lost beloved. The voice belongs to the famous Hindi film star Amitabh Bachchan and the film, Yash Chopra's *Silsila*, (1981) in which music and lyrics played such an integral role.

One suspects that much of the novel might have been composed first as poetry and then rearranged as prose:

> These nights are cool, these days are bright with
> spring. The low green on the trees has spread right
> to their tops, and in the park the wide, clear sight
> that I so much loved of lake and low knoll through nets
> of bare twigs has been leafed out and curbed. The world
> is in bloom, and if I am irked or sad it is due to the
> sense, more strained with the drift of each day, that it is
> not mine to share. In a few days it will be May, and we
> will all be on that plane. (207)

The title of the book, feels Makrand Paranjape, "in that sense, might refer to the equal music of Vikram Seth's poetry and prose" (1999). The author, on queried about the title of the book, has answered, from referring to the epigraph from Donne at the beginning to suggesting that the book had as much to do with equable as with equal. An "equal music" therefore is music which has attained perfection; and since "music is the food of love", it plays a major role in a narrative of love lost and found and finally lost again. The book deals with perfect love, which is marked by balance, harmony, uniformity and tranquility. As Julia tells Michael, "making music and making love—it's a bit too easy an equation."

Seth's passion for music, his empathy with it and with the people who create and perform it, reflects through this book, making it totally different to anything else he has written. Michael is a complex, somewhat temperamental young man whose birthplace Rochdale, in the North of England, was once rich in orchestral and choral music. And, although music was never a part of his own parent's lives, at the age of nine, Michael was taken by Mrs. Fromby to a performance of Handel's *Messiah*. "More than anything else," he reflects, "I wanted to be a part of that noise." So, he immerses himself in music and with borrowed instruments he takes a scholarship to the Royal Northern College of Music in Manchester. Later he gets an invitation to join a master-class at the Musikhochschule in Vienna, and amidst great opposition from his parents, he becomes a professional violinist.

We learn Michael's story gradually as he goes about his daily routines of teaching, solitary practice and rehearsal, until he gets a fleeting glimpse of Julia—on a passing bus—whom he had once loved and left in Vienna and has been unable to find again since. The search for Julia, their meeting and its consequences, are woven into other larger themes. Music dominates both their lives, providing a counterpoint for every mood and action. And Seth keenly explores the strange dependence, and independence of the individuals involved in the Maggiore Quartet; the terrible dilemma of a musician who suffers almost total loss of hearing; and the plight of musicians whose precarious income prevents them from ever owning the finest and the most beautiful of instruments and who, like Michael, may lose their much loved but borrowed instruments at any time. The action moves between London, Vienna and Venice but the real life of the novel is the music—music equated with love and both seen as forming the totality of life's experience:

> Every rehearsal of the Maggiore Quartet begins with a very plain, very slow three-octave scale on all four instruments in

> unison: sometimes major, as in our name, sometimes minor, depending on the key of the first piece we are to play. No matter how fraught our lives have been over the last couple of days, no matter how abrasive our disputes about people or politics, or how visceral our differences about what we are to play and how we are to play it, it reminds us that we are, when it comes to it, one. We try not to look at each other when we play this scale; no one appears to lead. Even the first upbeat is merely breathed by Piers, not indicated by any movement of his head. When I play this I release myself into the spirit of the quartet. I become the music of the scale. I mute my will, I free my self. (10)

Seth's first real novel *A Suitable Boy* attracted a huge and enthusiastic public, most of whom had never set foot in India, but Seth writes first of all for the people who know the world he is talking about. "If musicians read *An Equal Music* and say, look, this isn't really true or something, or you glamorized our world, then I would think that, no matter what glowing reviews I get from the general reader, I would feel that to some extent it's failed artistically because it's falsified. Because I tend to write realistic novels, I really think the clearest judgement would be obtained from them. I do not try to make things deliberately referential or obfuscating so the general reader can't read it. It's just that the truest judges are those whom I'm describing."

Realism and reality played a curious part in the success of *A Suitable Boy*, as severe communal violence broke out in India around the time of its publication. When Seth was writing *A Suitable Boy*, the worst of it was yet to come, he said, "I was harking back to the 1950s, and then things had died down for about 20 years. I had no idea that what I was writing about—the attacks of temples and mosques—actually would take place two months before the book—while the book was actually being typeset. They said, how prescient you were, but I was not prescient at all. I never knew something like that was going to happen. Or else they said, you are piggybacking on what's already happened, but I couldn't have been blamed for that because it was already written."

The novel is in the first person narrative, and Seth explains why he chose to write in this mode. First, he understood that it was "notoriously difficult to write about an acceptable art form in an expository way and therefore the only means to get into music through words was to describe the thoughts of someone actually a musician himself. The use of the first person narrative becomes a device to get the point of view of music through the point of view of a musician. Secondly, the idea of telling an intense love story in the first person held a greater appeal to him (Kohli, 1999: 13-15). The first person here is not the author's first person. It is the protagonist's and provides both nearness and distance to the writer to whatever he is narrating.

Thirty-seven year old Michael Holden is a second violinist in an English quartet called the Maggiore. Besides playing in the quartet, Michael supplements his income by teaching the violin to a few music students, with one of whom he is having an affair. There is nothing in the relationship for Michael. It was more "through lust and loneliness...and laziness and lack of focus" (6). Michael is still intensely in love with Julia. And is still desperately obsessed with the one situation connected to this—his own terrible frustrated passion. His passionately imaginative mind moved along in a gloomy haze and only by surrounding himself to the emotional extravagances of sensation could he play at all.

An echo of this nature of almost aggressive awareness can be seen in the writing of Charlotte Bronte—"Imagination is a strong restless faculty which claims to be heard and expressed; are we to be deaf to her cry and insensate to her struggles?" Bronte's romantic nature conceived the creative impulse as a demonic force that sways and dominates its possessor—"When authors write best" (she argues in a letter to her publisher), "or, at least, when they write most fluently, an influence seems to weaken in them which becomes their master, which will have its way—putting out of view all behest but its own, dictating certain words and insisting on their being used whether vehement or measured in their nature, moulding characters, giving unthought-of turns to incident, rejecting carefully, elaborated old ideas and suddenly creating and adopting new ones" (qtd. in Neill, 198).

In Section 2.18 Michael relives the reasons for their break-up. While at the Musikhochschule in Vienna, he had an argument with his music professor over what he considered to be Carl Kall's inflexible attitude towards his own style of playing. Julia accuses Michael of being unable to stand authority—"And God save your heroes if they turn out to have feet of clay" (190). Michael considers Julia's defence of Kall as "an unbearable betrayal on her part" (82). He walks out on her, drops his studies and returns to England, where he almost becomes a fugitive. In retrospect, he realizes that there was some truth in Julia's accusation that he had been very "self-willed", and unable "to sift a musician's message from his playing, not his speech" (16). Michael later concedes that "it was as much my younger self, unyielding, unwilling to exchange a mentor for a dictator, or to sidle past a collision" (18). When he tries to renew contact with Julia, she refuses to call back or write, and he realises that he has lost her through his sudden departure and long silence. He has to live for the next ten years with the painful burden of his loss and foolishness. His life settles down to "a bearable aloneness" only because of his music (56).

In the opening section, Michael's French girlfriend Virgine asserts that Beethoven had arranged one of his trios (Opus 1, No. 3), which was Michael's favorite, into a clarinet string quintet in C. Minor. Michael becomes determined to track down opus 104. This quest leads him to the library in Manchester where he is able to locate a miniature score. He is also able to locate a recording of the opus issued in 1977, under a Czech label. It is on his way back after this successful mission, that he suddenly spots Julia for a few fleeting moments in a passing bus on the opposite side of the road, reminiscent of a typical Hindi film scene from Bollywood. Exactly like our filmy hero, he pursues her bus in a taxi, but she is gone by the time he catches up with the bus. His passionate love for Julia, which time has failed to subside, is reflected when he sits "under the arrows of Eros, and weeps" (43).

Julia re-enters Michael's life and the narrative only towards the end of part two, at a performance by the Maggiore at Wigmore Hall "the sacred shoe-box of chamber music" (p. 86). Michael learns that she has been married to an American banker from Boston called James Hansen since nine years. They have a seven-year-old son, Luke. Their love, which apparently never died, is rekindled. But, only with their love affair already underway does Michael discover that in the intervening decade she has fallen victim to a disease which has rendered her almost completely deaf. Despite her affliction, their romance and music-making both blossom. But, as expected, a time comes, when Julia's situation becomes unsustainable, and she has to choose between her family and her lover, between ensemble music and a solo career.

"As always with Seth's writing", comments William Sutcliffe, "the pleasure is in the detail. His description of the awkward four way marriage behind a string quartet is at once enlightening and touching, teasing out the minutiae of the frustrations, joys and bitterness in four musicians' entangled lives" (Michael's first suspicion that Julia has a hearing problem comes on page 142, yet, although this is the first dramatic pivot in the first half of the book, we only have to wait until page 149 before a full confirmation of this is given in a letter which gives an entire history of her medical condition) (1999).

A quartet is a good subject for a novel, providing sufficient personalities and a piquant mixture of grind and art. The other players are gay Piers, his disappointed sister Helen, and good-natured, latecomer Billy who likes chocolate biscuits and is in consequence, overweight:

> Finally, after an hour and a half we arrive at the second movement. It is dark outside, and we are exhausted, as much with one another's temperaments as with the music. But ours is an odd quadripartite marriage with six relationships, any of which, at given time, could be cordial or neutral or strained. The audiences who listen to us cannot imagine how earnest, how petulant, how accommodating, how wilful is our quest for something

> beyond ourselves that we imagine with our separate spirits but are compelled to embody together.
> Where is the harmony of spirit in all this, let alone sublimity?
> How are such mechanics, such stops and starts, such facile irreverence transmuted, in spite of our bickering selves, into musical gold? And yet often enough it is from such trivial beginnings that we arrive at an understanding of a work that seems to us both true and original, and an expression of it which displaces from our minds—and perhaps, at least for a while, from the minds of those who hear us—any versions, however true, however original, played by other hands. (14)

An Equal Music is smaller in size than Seth's *A Suitable Boy*, but is still quite extensive. In fewer than 400 pages, the author offers us "exquisite complexities, personal and lyrical, while deftly fielding any fears that he has composed a Harlequin for highbrows." During one emotional high, Michael tells Julia, "I don't know how I've lived without you all these years, only to realize, how feeble and trite my words sound to me, as if they have been plucked out of some housewife fantasy." In addition to the pitch of its love story, one of the book's joys lies in Seth's creation of musical extremes. As the Maggiore rehearses, moving from criticizing and impatience to music and perfection, the author expertly notes the joys of collaboration, trust, affinity and creation. "It's the weirdest thing, a quartet," one member remarks, "I don't know what to compare it to. A marriage? A firm? A platoon under fire? A self-regarding, self destructive priesthood? It has so many different tensions mixed in with its pleasures."

An Equal Music "is a novel in which the length of Schubert's Trout Quintet matters deeply, the discovery of a little-known Beethoven Opus is a miracle, and each instrument has its own being. Just as Michael can't hope to possess Julia, he cannot even dream of owning his beloved Tononi, the violin he has long had only on loan. And it goes without saying that Vikram Seth knows how to tell a tale, keeping us guessing about everything from what the Quartet's four-minute encore will be to what really occasioned Julia's departure from Michael's life, (or was it in fact Michael who abandoned Julia?). As this love story ranges from London to Michael's birthplace in the north of England to Vienna to Venice, few readers will remain deaf to its appeals", suggests Kerry Fried (Location: www.sholay.com/Books/seth.htm-22k).

Towards the end of part three, in a detailed letter to Michael, Julia explains that she is suffering from an auto-immune disease of the inner ear. This implies that the protective systems of her body are treating parts of the inner ear as hostile, and therefore destroying them. She is gradually going deaf with only lip-reading and hearing aids being her companions. But a time will come when the only music she will hear is the music in her mind. Julia has taught herself to watch the movements of other players and to play entirely from memory and imagination. She explains how her mental agony began three years ago and the tremendous support given to her by her husband James, who encouraged her to play again. "Music is the heart of my life. For me, of all people, to be betrayed by my ears was unbearable" (150). Julia admits to Michael that she had been "so hungry to speak of music—and to play it with someone who understands me as I was before all these changes in my life (137). Michael wonders; am I for her a static mark, a reversion to the days when music was for her an actual sense, not merely an imagined beauty" (156).

Michael gets a book on deafness to understand Julia's problem better. He makes his "first acquaintance with the elaborate chaos that lies behind the tiny drum-skins of my outer ears" (156). Michael becomes increasingly aware of "a world mad with sound: forms rip, trams rumble past vibrating under foot, coffee-cups clink and over the murmur from the busy bar I can hear the peristaltic cranking of—is it a fax machine or teleprinter? What does Schubert make of these noises?" (229). The pain and irony of a fine musician's encroaching deafness is skillfully presented by Seth:

> Voices in a score of languages surround us or, rather, me. At night, when sight diminishes, sound should take over. But of all this—the splashing of water against stone, the

> tweaking of a child's balloon, wheels bumping down the steps of a bridge, the flap of a pigeon's wing, high heels against the floor of the colonnade—what does she hear?
>
> Perhaps the deep thrum of the engine of a vaporetto; perhaps not even that. (263)

But Julia cannot reconcile to living in a "dual world which chafe each other" (168), and feels guilty about her acts of deception. She admits to her intense love for Michael but decides to forgo her love for her husband and son. Michael is her past, and she realizes that one cannot live in the past forever "I, of all people, who have a Before and an After, should have known that you can't relive your life" (325). She ends her relationship in part seven of the novel. "Her choice to opt for her dependable (though unmusical) businessman-husband James over the volatile and moody Michael, and her denunciation of passion for family and social order, is a thematic preoccupation once again repeated from *A Suitable Boy* and *The Golden Gate,*" says Mala Pandurang. (157). Julia's choice for stability as compared to passion reflects strains of Lata from Seth's earlier magnum opus *A Suitable Boy*. Lata in *A Suitable Boy* chose the stable and dependable Haresh rather than Kabir whom she truly loved because with Kabir she felt as if she was being whirled around in a whirlpool. Similarly Liz, in *The Golden Gate,* chose a pragmatic Phil over a romantic John because she understood that in the game of life what will last is steady affection rather than a passionate, romantic love relationship. For Julia, James had stood by her—"In the worst days when I could hardly recognize myself in the mirror, I saw in his eyes that I was myself" (327). But in Michael's presence, she becomes "restless and uncertain, afraid and guilty" (324).

Two types of stability one, social and familial, and the other, mental and internal, are depicted in the novel. Also stressed again and again is the fact that attachment to love and music also leads to a sense of order and stability though of a different type, and *An Equal Music*, in spite of the individual's sense of loneliness, suggests that.

In *An Equal Music*, Seth takes a conventional romantic plot and renders it new and compelling through the attractive clarity and precision of its prose. One of the most impressive aspects of this novel is the way in which it manages to convey music through Michael's daily drama and battles as a member of a quartet. The reader is thrown into the lives, whims and chemistries of classical musicians. One would believe Seth himself has toured in a quartet to Venice and bid at auctions for violins. An incredible level of research has been undertaken, and Seth duly acknowledges the contributors. But Seth himself is modest about his musical abilities, yet the fact that he was commissioned to write a libretto, later published as *Arion and the Dolphin* (1994), for the English National Opera in 1994, suggests he is no novice. However in the book, there are several moments when intense discussions on Schubert, Schumann, and Bach become too tedious for us commoners. The bits of German splattered throughout become rather difficult to understand, where no proper translation is given:

> A winter evening in the Wigmore Hall, the sacred shoe-box of chamber music. We have spent the last month practicing intensively for this night. The fare is simple—three classical quartets: Haydn's opus 20 no. 6 in A major, my most beloved quartet; then the first of the six quartets that Mozart himself dedicated to Haydn, in G major; and finally, after the interval, Beethoven's steeplechase-cum-marathon, the ethereal, joky, unpausing, miraculous, exhausting quartet in C sharp minor, which he composed a year before his death, and which, just as the score of the "Messiah" had consoled and delighted him on his deathbed, was to delight and console Schubert as he lay dying in the same city a year later.
>
> Dying, undying, a dying fall, a rise: the waves of sound well around us even as we generate them: Helen and I at the heart and, to either side, Piers and Billy. Our eyes are on our music; we hardly glance at each other, but we cue and are cued as if Hadyn himself were our conductor. A strange composite being we are, not ourselves any more but the bows, instruments, musicians—sitting, standing, shifting, sounding—all to produce these complex vibrations that jog

> the inner ear, and through them the grey mass that says: joy; love; sorrow; beauty.
>
> And above us here in the apse the strange figure of a naked man surrounded by thorns and aspiring towards a grail of light, in front of us 540 half-seen beings intent on 540 different webs of sensation and cerebration and emotion, and through us the spirit of someone scribbling away in 1722 with the sharpened feather of a bird.
>
> I love every part of the Haydn. It is a quartet that I can hear in any mood and can play in any mood. The headlong happiness of the allegro; the lovely adagio where my small figures are like a counter-lyric to Piers's song; the contrasting minuet and trio, each a mini cosmos, yet each contriving to sound unfinished; and the melodious, ungrandiose, various fugue—everything delights me. But the part I like best is where I do not play at all.
>
> The trio really is a trio. Piers, Helen and Billy slide and stop away on their lowest strings, while I rest—intensely, intently. My Tononi is stilled. My bow lies across my lap. My eyes close. I am here and not here. A waking nap? A flight to the end of the galaxy and perhaps a couple of billion light-years beyond? A vacation, however short, from the presence of my too-present colleagues? Soberly, deeply. The melody grinds away, and now the minuet begins again. But I should be playing this, I think anxiously. It is the minuet. I should have rejoined the others, I should be playing again. And, oddly enough, I can hear myself playing. And yes, the fiddle is under my chin, and the bow is in my hand, and I am. (86–87)

The title of the book is derived from one of John Donne's sermons describing life after death. "...where there shall be no cloud nor sun, no darkness, nor dazzling, but one equal light, no noise nor silence, but one equal music, no fears nor hope, but one equal possession, no foes nor friends, but one equal commission and identity, no ends nor beginnings, but one equal eternity" (epigraph to the text). John Carrey suggests that Donne's phase of leave taking "yields apt meanings" as it brings out the balance between the four instruments that the quartet aims at, and the unheard music in Julia's head matching the sound of her playing (1999: 13). Three stories are braided in *An Equal Music*: thirty-something Michael's music, his doomed romance and his violin. First story has Michael with his idiosyncrasies: wintry swims in the Serpentine, a frantic search for a long forgotten chamber work by Beethoven, ruminations on the Angel of Selfridges etc. The second story as mentioned earlier is the inevitability of separation from Julia that is quite evident to the reader right from the time the affair is resumed again.

But another separation that haunts Michael does not take place. He despairs of living a life without his violin, lent to him by the rich widow, Mrs. Fromby, but from the first mention, through all the worrying and visits to banks, the reader knows that Michael will not be separated from his dear Tononi. Mrs. Fromby who is a true lover of music will see to it that a valuable instrument is left in the right hands, rather than let it waste away by giving it to her nephew:

> Mrs. Fromby:
> I know you are dead and cannot read this. I wish
> I had known of your stroke.
> My life had shelved towards desolation. Thank you for not forgetting me and for assuming, though I did not visit, that I had not forgotten you.
> I will drive to Blackstone Edge at the right time each year.
> I will take your violin with me whenever I come up north.
> I never asked you where or from whom you bought it.
> That history has ended with you.
> What little I ever did for you is over, but what you have done for me will last till I too go.
> May something of your memory advise me, when I come to die, into whose hands I should deliver it.
> Both your friend and your fiddle thank you—from
> soul and soundpost respectively. (366-367)

The novel has a unique flavour—a strange pungent mingling of wild romance and domestic realism, of cosmic music and local details. Seth is a belated romantic who hails from no school, nor has any successive writer produced a work of similar tang. The two chief characters are drawn with an unforgettable poetic intensity. *An Equal Music* links an exciting and romantic story to a sober and honest realism—a tragic story that ends with an Aristotelian catharsis for all the players in the drama.

The book narrated in the urgent present, carefully constructed around dialogue and nuances, is not about sharply constructed characters. For 379 pages the readers experience Michael's panic attacks, his weeping fits, his ecstatic performances, his self-doubt, his occasional burst of wit—but the man as such is not really sketched in flesh and blood. The reader can only recall him in association to his quartet, his wandering around London, his relationships with women, his thoughts, his misgivings, etc. "*An Equal Music* is recounted at a different pitch than *The Golden Gate* and *A Suitable Boy*," says Mini Kapoor, "Missing is the warmth that permeated Seth's earlier books, the abundance and the breathlessness. His prose has been pared down for exactness of lives at a remove from fin de siecle hustle-bustle. Yet, something's familiar about this spare new cast: Seth continues to accord his characters a certain dignity that is virtually extinct in modern writing. That's what makes this world where a man worries he will be jailed for stepping on the grass so attractive, so unreal" (1999: 4).

Candida McWilliam, in a fine essay in *The Financial Times*, dated 3rd April 1999, says that "the cruelty of fiction is that its organs may be in the right place, its complexion excellent, but if it has not breath, it will not move. *A Suitable Boy* did move. If one believes that works of art can embody the good, it was a virtuous book, of enormous length but also of a blessed kind of quiet. It did not clamour, therefore one paid attention, enjoying the surcease of babble and garishness that had stirred much of the surface of sub-continental literatures in English for sometime previously." She continues, "*The Golden Gate*, Seth's accomplished homage to Charles Johnston's translation of *Eugene Onegin* (1977), was smug, but had every right to be. It caught California's freedom in its disciplined rhythms. Like its huge little brother, it withstands repeated readings." Seth's new novel addresses itself to what the author, in an after-note, says that he holds "dearer even than speech", that is music. "With his understanding of silence, periods, rhythm and tempo and his obvious attention to composition, he would seem a fine candidate for this challenge, to which Proust is one of the few to rise successfully."

Seth's instinct for the strange and unfamiliar is quite apparent from the way he has drawn Michael from the northern working class family. His father, a butcher, possesses a cat and a television. Michael returns to the small town of Rochdale on three occasions. His childhood experiences become important because his desire to escape his past is largely responsible for his present mental condition. His parents strive hard all day with the hope that their only child will escape life in Rochdale by opting for higher studies. But, when Michael is nine years old, Mrs. Fromby takes him to see a concert by "the small and ailing Barbiolli". Immensely impressed, Michael decides that "more than anything else I want to be part of such a noise" (67), and begs Mr. Fromby to teach him to play the violin. His refusal to go for higher studies leaves his parents "bewildered and betrayed" and "depraved of a happiness that they were due" (22). Instead, he goes to a music school in London and becomes a part of a small, enclosed rarefied world of classical music. Meanwhile, Rochdale becomes a victim to industrial planning, "it is a town with its heart torn out" (71). And Michael is determined to cut off links with the "distressed and constrained town" (22), now that he has moved into "an urbane world far outside his ken" (23). And yet he wonders why he mourns for it so angrily (72). "The warmth of the collective in *A Suitable Boy* has given way, to the solitariness of the individual," says Mala Panduarang (2001):

> It darkens above us during the quintet, as if the cells of life were dying. In the skylight above, the grey grows duller, darker. The last glimmer of the day is extinguished with the slow, grave trio. Noble, brooding, sorrowful, it helps one bear the world, and all fear of what may come in the sunless night.
>
> These hands move as those hands moved on paper. This heart beats and rests as that heart beat and rested. And these my ears. But did he never hear this played: not once, ever?

> Beloved Schubert, in your city I am adrift. I am consumed by past love; its germs long embedded, half-contained, have grown virulent again. There is no hope for me. I turned away four thousand nights ago, and the path was closed in by trees and brambles.
>
> I am eaten by futile pity. I make too much of much. From one city of shrunken power and lapsing music I travel now to another. Let there be some change in my state. Or let me live in a zone where hope is not a word.
>
> How can I long for what I do not gasp? (242-243)

An Equal Music has been hailed by some reviewers as "the finest novel about music ever written in English". Narrated in the present tense by Michael, the first half of the novel is almost magical, with its melancholic evocations of London's Hyde Park, and its descriptions of bracing Saturday-morning swims in the filthy, freezing water of the Serpentine. Swimming also leads to some of the odder scenes in *An Equal Music*, based on Seth's own experience as a member of the Serpentine swimming club: "You don't want to swallow too much of it, but if you did it wouldn't kill you. But now we have to sign all kinds of forms, how we won't sue anyone if we die," he said, laughing. "In the summer, it's a little-the-algae. It's actually nicer in the winter, cold though it is. The only slight danger is not the ice but when the ice is just forming, because then you get those little silvers and shards that you can't always see, and they can tear into you. I love swimming there, the back stroke."

As in his earlier novel, *The Golden Gate* in *An Equal Music* also, there is not an Indian in sight. But Seth does not see this as an issue. All his books are different, one-offs, he says, though there is a sense in which *An Equal Music* is more of a departure, a risk even. Most of his previous works has been characterized by a wry, humorous, ironic third-person narrative that observes the action from a distance. *An Equal Music* is told in the first person and the playfulness of the earlier works, the wit and comedy and gentle mocking of the characters, is missing. "It makes for a curiously un-Seth-like book, a book that might disappoint," says Brendan Bernherd (1999). It would be interesting to note here that, what Bernhard says to be "curiously un-Seth like" might just be another dimension in Seth's huge repertoire of writing.

But Seth is least bothered by anything. "I am ready for that." In another interview he said, "I do read my reviews. I know the review you are referring to. It was written by a novelist who, of all people, should know that a first person narrative incorporates the tastes and dislikes of the so-called narrator, not of the novelist. I mean, it is like saying if someone writes an autobiography of a cat, they must have a tail.... So I mean, here I am, I've written a libretto for a modern composer—not Michael, I, Vikram—written and composed for a modern composer (Alec Roth, wonderful composer) and I don't have any inbuilt prejudice" against modern music. It depends on what it is, really. I go by individual pieces and individual composers, and some I like and some I do not. As far as being a novella stretched out, you could say *A Suitable Boy* was a short story stretched out, or even a haiku. The only thing is, does it work? That's eventually how one judges a work of art. It's a very private communication between the writer and reader. If it does not work, the author can excuse himself as much as he likes, it's completely irrelevant. And if it does work, the critic can carp as much as he likes. It's equally irrelevant."

Shortly after Julia leaves him and goes back to her family, Michael gets news of Mrs. Formby's death and realizes that he is left with only a few months with his friend and companion of twelve years. "I've spent more time with it than with any living soul, but, well it's still not mine. And I'm not its" (127). The intensity with which he plays the violin in Vivaldi's Church, the Pieta, and also during practice, makes it an instrument with its own identity, almost giving it a flesh and blood feel. Seth evocatively describes the sensuous relationship between man and instrument "with the back of my hand I touch its back, its belly. How long we have lived together."

Michael is traumatized thinking about a life without his violin and cannot tolerate the thought of it lying "unplayed, unloved and unspeaking" (56). With the impending loss of the violin playing in his mind, Michael is almost on the verge of breaking down under the "ungiving pressure of thoughts". He is prone to "moments of dark panic" when things seem to be stressed out (such as the attack in Vienna at the Musikverein after the performance of the Trout, 5.11). But there is a reason for his claustrophobia. He explains these panic attacks are as a result of something that had happened when he was a kid. On his sixth birthday, while playing a game of hide-and-seek he had hid in a fridge. The door clicked shut behind him and he could not get out until someone happened to come into the room and heard his frantic screaming. He was rescued in a state of suffocated terror, and that is the reason why even now he is terrified of a closed atmosphere, be it mental or physical. And that is the sole reason why he lives where he does at Archangel Court, and pays a mortgage beyond his income, a place which is way above the ground level and which has nothing beyond it but the vast expanse of the sky and its mysterious ways.

When Michael gets into a state of absolute despair, Mrs. Formby's solicitor informs Michael that she has bequeathed the Carlo Tononi, circa 1727, to him. Michael can't believe his good fortune. "It was lost to me, now is found" (361). Filled with gratitude he asks the spirit of Mrs. Fromby, "What possessed you to repossess me of it, you who were close to death and lacked clear speech? Is it the violin alone you want to give me, or must learn some lesson from the world?" (361). It brings him back to life again. He resumes his routine life and starts playing in an orchestra; learning to live in a "sexless calm" (8.27). He stops behaving like "a self-centered bastard", and begins to hear the sound of music again "cracking, rippling, shifting, easing, cracking, sighing, this is not something I have heard before. It is a soft sound, easy, intimate" (376). A few months later Piers re-invites him back to the Maggiore. But the real freedom comes, when on a visit home, he places a white rose on his mother's grave and then as he plays the unfinished fugue from the *Art of Fugue* in memory of Mrs. Fromby, his soul is liberated from all bondage. "My hands are not cold, nor my mind agitated. I am in no dark tunnel but in the open moor" (379). Michael's relationship with his violin is ultimately the most satisfying and intimate one left for him.

A story of love lost, found, and then lost again, the novel ends with "an impassioned invocation of music—not time's—power to heal all wounds—or at least to make them bearable." Julia is playing the Art of Fugue to a packed hall, her husband and son are there in the audience, listening to her music: "It is a beauty beyond imagining—clear, lovely, inexorable, phrase echoing phrase, the incomplete, the unending *Art of Fugue*. It is an equal music" (380). Michael walks away grateful for having had the privilege of hearing such excellent music. He reflects: "Music, such music, is a sufficient gift. Why ask for happiness; why hope not to grieve? It is enough, it is to be blessed enough, to live from day to day and to hear such music—not too much, or the soul could not sustain it—from time to time" (381).

Once Vikram Seth, while giving a talk at Seymour Centre of Sydney University, Australia, was asked by a woman in the audience, whether music was a substitute for love or religion for Michael. In answer Seth said, "The remark that Michael makes about the controlling power of music is something that he needs as a philosophy, a refuge, relaxation and joy. He can't quite understand the other more formal religion, or religion as deeply felt by Julia." He again continued, "Music does take him out of himself, in an inexplicable way, and out of getting and spending (consumerism) and the selfishness that a spirit like him is prone to. I don't think it's meant as a high sounding sentence, I think basically he believes it. But is it true? That's difficult to say. Is it enough to hear such music from day to day? Should one not search for happiness? Should one hope not to grieve? These are things that are very natural to our human state."

L.K. Sharma suggests that the book will test the "English reader's response to an Indian locating a story in the Hyde Park and peopling it with non-Indians. Vikram Seth writing about Mrs. Rupa Mehra and the English literary society of Calcutta was one thing but capturing the emotions of Julia or the functioning of the Maggiore quartet is another" (1999: 10). In response to a question if it was hard to write of English characters as an Indian or to get under "the skin of a character with a different cultural, background," Seth replies that he couldn't have done it, if he had not lived in England. He explains: "When you write about someone, you get the information you need. But even then there are only a number of cultures I can enter. I could not write about an Italian fisherman from the inside. I have to know the culture intimately myself. I'd been in England as an undergraduate; I lived there for a number of years...altogether about seven years in a staggered way. And I love western music. So it was not a completely foreign world" (Mukherji, 1999: 35). What we see here is that the difference is only superficial. There are basic similarities—the functioning of the mind that is both balanced and yet unbalanced.

For Seth, writing about diverse themes and diverse places is a challenge and an attraction in itself. "I know from an editor's point of view or a publisher's point of view it's easier to slot me into a particular niche. But I know that I would be bored unless I wrote a book that in some sense was a challenge. And this might mean I vary the form by writing a poem or a play or a novel. Or set the stories in different countries or write in the first person as opposed to the third or in the present tense as opposed to the part or a very long novel as opposed to a short one."

But one form that Seth has used uniformly in all his three novels is the sonnet form. His affinity for this particular form is quite evident in all his works: "The particular sonnet form I used is a very interesting one. For a start, it's a tetrameter rather than pentameter form, the rhyme scheme is quite complex, and certain rhymes have feminine endings in fixed places. The result of all this is that it kept me pretty interested as a form. I didn't get bored with it. And since I owe that particular form to Pushkin, I thought I'd continue the homage in the next two novels I wrote, at least in the form of an acknowledgement or dedicatory poem at the beginning. Because other than those little poetic commonalties between three novels, there isn't very much that links them." The link is not through a particular form, it is in understanding, in approach and of attitude—exploring different dimensions of man's living through complexities of life.

"Seth's artistic goals seem to mirror those of the Maggoire quartet who spurn modern music in favour of the 'classic' repertoire against the grain of fashion—obsessed music critics who ignore and patronize their work," says William Sutcliffe. "Likewise", he continues, "Seth's approach to fiction is self consciously anti-modernist." Although his masterpiece, *A Suitable Boy* was widely acclaimed, much of the critical praise was dampened by a feeling that the book was not quite "serious" and was a little Soap Operatic in tone. Some of this criticism, which could just as easily be levelled at *An Equal Music*, seemed to "stem from the curious belief that clear, unfussy prose is somehow not "heavyweight". While the baroque, flashy contortions of Michael Ondaatje, Arundhati Roy, John Lanchester and the like are regularly slobbered over by literary prize juries, writers like Seth—whose poetry is in clarity—are inevitably passed over. The Arthur Rubinsteins, who make it look difficult, are held in higher esteem than the Alfred Brendels, who make it look effortless. *The New York Times* in one of its reviews greatly eulogizes Seth's clear style. "He was rightly praised for the fine detail, clear voice and witty style that marked *The Golden Gate*, and only wishes he had infused *An Equal Music* with more of those same qualities" (1999).

In the contemporary Indian English literary scenario, the author with whom Seth has always been compared with is Salman Rushdie. There are wannabes aplenty, but these two remain the two most suitable boys of Indian English Literature. The comparison and the competition, in the media, has been more intense, particularly after Rushdie's book, *The Ground Beneath Her Feet* (1999), got published, around the same time as *An Equal Music*. Since both books traverse the territory of music, the discordant notes played in the media have been quite jarring. Seth on being queried about this strange coincidence and whether he was worried by the whole thing said, "I didn't even know he was writing (*The Ground Beneath Her Feet*) until we were both in the course of publication. I cannot speak for him, but I wouldn't be surprised if he did not know either. So there was no way one could avoid it. Anyway, how could he write about classical music unless he was impelled to? And how could I write about rock unless it came from within me? ...The idea of our divvying up the field is pretty absurd. Love is a huge subject, music is a huge subject, and the fact that two writers from the same part of the world happen to be writing about it at the same time is not surprising. If we were both Icelandic poets writing verse sagas about the cravat, or the cummerbund, then one might suspect something was going on!"

In a brilliantly penned review, in *The Sunday Times of India*, April 11th, 1999, Jyotirmaya Sharma suggests that to argue that both *The Ground Beneath Her Feet* and *An Equal Music* are about music is to suggest that there is a direct link between Mick Jagger and Bach, or, that Baba Sehgal and K.L. Sehgal are one and the same thing. He opines that "Rushdie's novel has the dazzling exuberance, the verbose vanity, the inflated meanderings, and the cry of confessional anguish that characteristics much of his work. Rushdie inaugurated the arrival of a new form, an entirely different literary style which was welcomed by the literati like the appearance of a new comet. The triumph of the new genre lay in its ability to shock, question the sacred and re-evaluate values." In contrast, Vikram Seth's novel restores one's faith in the fictional form. It is a book written with "a bone-bleached economy of expression and emotion". As the novel progresses it implores the reader into a "lucid silence". There is a "sombre magic, a bracing, energizing after-glow that emanates from its pages."

An Equal Music places Seth in a tradition of modern fiction writers who have successfully combined a love story and the love of music as part of their narratives. "Seth's attempt goes beyond James Hamilton Paterson's brilliant but ultimately flawed *Gerontius* (1989), but compares extremely favourably with the novels of Thomas Bernhard," suggests Jyotirmaya Sharma. Seth's victory lies in his ability to create and sustain characters that have no direct relation to the author's cultural connections. Hopefully, it marks the beginning of the end of the expatriate Indian writer's continuous search for roots and infinite debates on the impossibility of home coming. This novel announces the ascent of the self-possessed Indian who rises above the narrow outlook generated by the modern nation state, yet is deeply immersed in a classical structure. "When this becomes possible, an appreciation of Bach's fugues and a Dhrupad aalap at the same time becomes a reality, without necessarily suggesting a cultural sell-out. It is a tantalizing thought whether Seth's achievement is in large measure due to the love story of Julia McNicholl and Michael Holme in the book. When all the narrow walls built by nations and territories collapse, all that will remain of us is love," continues Sharma.

Yet still, there are a few dissenting voices among Indians also, regarding this freedom from cultural influences: "Vikram Seth deserves the hype he has received. There is a compelling lucidity and simplicity in his writing, which is the hallmark of a greater writer. However, I am sometimes surprised at his ability to write books which have nothing to do with India. I am uncomfortable with this degree of cultural autonomy" (Pavan Kumar Varma, bureaucrat—writer in *The Sunday Times of India*, April 11th, 1999). But those types of comments have been very few and far between.

Seth, on being asked about his readers, has said: "It is certainly true that every book has certain ideal readers and certain less ideal readers. And then the general reader who may or may not take to a book" (Kohli, 1999). Seth accepts that the world of chamber music in *An Equal Music* is a world much different in degree than that of Ustaad Khan teaching Malati a raga in *A Suitable Boy*. "It is actually a situation where you gain and you lose certain readers. There were large chunks and sections in *A Suitable Boy,* which would have been totally incomprehensible to the Western reader. So there is nothing really that can be done about it" (*ibid*). Mann Kapoor in *A Suitable Boy* has heard western classical music, somewhere around three times in his life. He tells Sandeep Lahiri, the SDO of Rudhia, that most people he knew would not enjoy it. Lahiri disagrees: "I feel they would. Good music is good music. It is a question of exposure, I feel. Exposure and a little bit of guidance" (624). In any work of art it is the variety which matters. Variety and the capacity to sustain variety are both a virtue and power. Seth shows both.

Seth, on the issue of large readership, has said; "A large readership is important. I never expected to get it. I did not write any of the books with that in mind. I do not know what I attribute the popularity to. I suppose I'd have to say, going by the letters I get from readers; it's the characters in the story. I don't have a patron or independent means, so it does matter that the books sell. On the other hand, I wouldn't change a comma in order to get extra readership. The fact is, none of the books have been predictable sellers, and in addition to those books, I've written books of poetry and translation which certainly would not enable me to earn my keep."

"My programme now has a playback setting for piano called expressivo—a few controlled irregularities, and you can hardly tell it's a computer that's playing, not a human being. Soon they will perfect it, and you won't be able to tell. Performers will be redundant for all practical purposes," says Michael Holme's colleague on the Maggiore quartet as they go through their warm-up rituals at a practice session. "Nothing could be more out of beat with Vikram Seth's book than this horrifying vision," comments Mini Kapoor. "In our cyber age when computers already read out, in a range of accounts but without inflection, lengthy texts and millions of netizens type their way through a hectic social life, it details lives on the periphery, lives that beat to an older rhythm, lives that are calibrated on an alternative scale of human sensitivities and sensibilities."

Unlike *The Golden Gate,* which looked at a specific defining moment in contemporary American culture, there is no distancing of the writer from the host society in *An Equal Music*. Interestingly, *An Equal Music* has been received much more positively in India than did *A Suitable Boy*. Almost all the newspapers were vehement in their criticism of the Booker people when it was learnt that *An Equal Music* did not figure in the final list of shortlisted writers: "...where would Vikram Seth figure in this scheme of things. *An Equal Music* with its poignant love story between Michael and Julia set against London and Austria hardly throws open a colonial wonderland. So what if critics have hailed it as wonder work: irresistible, tense, deeply moving" (*The Times of India*, April, 1999). Seth received the Crosswords Prize for best fiction for 1999, and

Shobha De has even praised the novel as "a masterpiece" in *The Sunday Observer,* April 1999.

David Davidar claims that unlike most writers of Indian origin, Seth is very honest about his work. He writes only what he believes in, instead of relying on time-tested formulas. Seth has been lauded for "being honest enough to follow his inspiration and to opt for the universality and transcending power of the beauty of music". For example, Namita Gokhle argues that Vikram Seth "is international and should be appreciated as a writer about human beings, not as a peddler of Indian exotica.... Deeply rooted in his specific Indian identity, Vikram Seth is yet a citizen of the world in the best sense.... His genius should be evaluated in his control over his material, and in creating a credible world-in-itself which he can cohabit and explore" (1993: 4).

Several of the comments by the critics about the novel can be used on the jacket. "Seth gives the fullest portrait I have ever read in fiction of a musician's relationship to his music," says one. Another comment: "*An Equal Music* is that most delicate of creatures: a narrative with, at its core, the passion of an art form that lives outside language." And yet another finds that the book "pleases most in the ravishing refinement of its technique, its sure placing of scenes, and the unerring truth of its portrayal of a small, enclosed social world." Shyam Benegal, the film-maker, is enamoured by Seth's "great urbane quality and his incredibly wry sense of humour", while Mahesh Dattani, playwright, holds Seth in high esteem because he loves "the poetry inherent in his prose" (*The Sunday Times of India*, April 11th, 1999).

A tour de force of lyrical and emotive writing, *An Equal Music* is an unforgettable tale of love, lost and nearly regained, its events unfolding in the dramatic settings of contemporary London, Vienna, and Venice. Brilliantly interweaving themes of loss, longing, and power of music, Vikram Seth has created a deeply moving story about the strands of passion that run through all our lives. The novel, which portrays wrenching loss, also finds similar echoes in Michael Ondaatje's *The English Patient* (1992), and Graham Greene's *The End of the Affair*

(1999), stories where the lovers also find it impossible to be together. Yet, there is something ultimately satisfying in reading about such intense emotion, even if the story ends tragically. Arthur Golden, author of *Memories of Geisha* (1997), has this to say about *An Equal Music*: "Vikram Seth's accomplishment in bringing not only these characters so fully to life, but the rich ambience of the music as well—so difficult to render in world—is something of a miracle."

WORKS CITED

Bernherd, Brendan. Interview with Vikram Seth. *LA Weekly*, 6 Apr. 1999: Online. http://www.laweekly.com/ink/99/23/wls-bernherd.shtml.

Carey, John. "Music for the Mind." Review. *The Sunday Times*, 28 Mar. 1999.

Gokhale, Namita. "Vikram's Vocalist Strains on Literary Landscape." Delhi: *The Times of India*, 4 May 1999: 4.

Kapoor, Mini. "Seth sans Suspense." *The Express Magazine*, 25 Apr. 1999: 4.

Knorr, Katherine. "Vikram Plays to His 'Truest Judges.'" *International Herald Tribune* 23 Apr. 1999: Online. http://www.iht.com/IHT/KK/00/kk042399.html

Kohli, Suresh. "Another Suitable Boy." *Hindu Literary Review*, Sunday, 16 May 1999.

McWilliam, Candida. "Vikram Seth: Hearing the Key Theme." *The Financial Times*, 3 Apr. 1999: Online http://doononline.net/lightlights/seth/ft.htm

Mukherjee, Meenakshi. "Pantheon in Print." *Far Eastern Economic Review*, 9 December 1993: 36-37.

Neill, Diana. *A Short History of the English Novel*. New York: Collier Books, 1964.

Pandurang, Mala. *Vikram Seth: Multiple Locations, Multiple Affiliations*. Jaipur and New Delhi: Rawat Publications, 2001.

Paranjape, Makarand. "A Suitable Author." *The Week*, 9 May 1999: 32-33.

Seth, Vikram. *An Equal Music*. New Delhi: Viking, 1999.

Sharma, Anjana. "An Englishman's Novel? Vikram Seth's *An Equal Music*." G.J.V. Prasad, ed. *Vikram Seth: An Anthology of Recent Criticism*. Delhi: Pencraft International, 2004: 164-173.

Sharma, L.K. "*A Suitable Boy* unfolds *An Equal Music*". *The Sunday Times*, 11 April 1999: 10.

Sutcliffe, William. *The Independent,* 4 Apr. 1999: Online http://www.independent.co.uk/books/stories/BR002326.htm

Vidyasagar, N. "In the Business of Books." Interview with Vikram Seth. *The Times of India,* 11 April 1999.

7 Conclusion

Some few decades ago English-language writing in India was basically the province of a few writers who were more or less unknown to the Western and to the Indian public. One can call it a cruel irony of fate, but writers of the stature of Narayan, Anand and Rao etc., were read only by a miniscule percentage of people who were interested in English literature. Subsequently it took a couple of pioneers in the form of Salman Rushdie and Vikram Seth to open the floodgates to the Western reading public. In 1981, the publication and subsequent award of the Booker Prize to Rushdie's *Midnight's Children* brought about a notable change in the way Indian English fiction came to be read and written. In 1986, Seth published *The Golden Gate*, which showed the western as well as the eastern reading public that Indian writing in English could sell. More importantly, it gave confidence to the other Indian writers to be themselves, and not to follow any unwritten rule.

Vikram Seth is among the crop of these bold new writers. His impingement on the condition of Indian English Literature in the eighties was in consonance with the larger development of Indian English Literature at that time. First of all, Indian English Literature acquired much greater credibility on the one hand and much larger public reception. Secondly, it came to be reckoned as an important part of Indian Literature as a whole which was not the case before when Indian English Literature was largely viewed as somehow away from the mainstream of Indian Literature. Seth benefited from this change in perspective. His novels and poetry grew from a mind integral with Indian conditions of living. And yet it felt equally comfortable with conditions abroad. One remembers his admission that whenever he writes on anything, at whatever the place may be, he gets immersed in the place and situation, and remains completely confined to the conditions, both physical and mental, available there. This is particularly true to his novels.

The Golden Gate remains confined to the conditions and environment in California, *A Suitable Boy* to that of India, and *An Equal Music* to that of Europe. His movement in his poetry from America, to China, to India, is also indicative of that. It is not only the involvement with the lifestyle and the mindset available locally at the particular place and particular time. It is a continuous foray to the past, to the past conditions of living, to the past heritage, the way the structure of life has grown from the past to the present. What Seth exhibits is not so much a world-view, an awareness of what is happening in the world as a whole, while one remains stuck to his place or time, or trying to realize the universal conditions of living in one's specific areas of operation, what W.K. Wimsatt long ago termed as 'concrete universal'.

In Seth it is a self-contained and independent account and exposition in each case, and they join together in a complementary way, to communicate what he understands as the available life-conditions in the world as a whole. This is not the world-view as such, but differently can be termed as the view of the world as available in many forms, and Seth's credit lies in integrating in complementary relevance and signification. In this Seth's creative achievement is almost unique not only in Indian English Literature, but in Indian Literature as a whole. An outward movement, one can term it, but an outward movement where one gets naturalized wherever one goes. That is Seth's special achievement—an intellectual brilliance as well as perspective that is rare in Indian writing in English. Seth's writings have two directions, one towards India and related to India, where he got national recognition from Sahitya Akademi, India's National Akademi of Letters, along with such other distinguished writers as Amitav Ghosh, Shashi Deshpande and Upamanyu Chatterjie. Seth was the first person of his generation to receive such an honour. The other direction is towards the Indian diaspora where he merits comparison with such writers as Salman Rushdie, Amit Chaudhury and Jhumpa Lahiri etc. In both he shows a remarkable inwardness, and in both his achievement is extremely worthwhile.

Right from the time Seth started writing, he has defied categorization. That is the reason documentation of Seth's work does not easily give a structured picture, since he has radically changing genre and milieu with nearly every book he has written. And in addition to varying dramatically in form, all his books have been set not only in India, but in China, California, and in his latest book, London and Venice. Some critics have pointed out his uniqueness in this category on the basis that Seth does not show a strong sense of nationalism or angst towards imperialism, and that he is restrained and reticent in style and temper, unlike many of his contemporaries. On this issue Seth himself has said that, "my influences are very general. My reading is also very scattershot. I have been most inspired by someone whom I haven't read a single word of in the original —Pushkin—because he wrote in all sorts of different forms. He didn't succumb to the temptation to repeat himself simply to please public or a publisher, and at the same time he didn't mind repeating the same form if he was inspired to. He wrote so wonderfully that even in translation, or at least in certain translations, his vision comes across. I really admire him. And I suppose he gives me the courage to experiment with form. Of course other writers like Tagore, for instance, or Goethe—have written in very different forms. But Pushkin is very close to my heart because I like his mixture of levity and deep seriousness" (Kapur, 1999).

In a television interview with Akash Kapur, Seth has said that he was just a writer, not an Indian or a Commonwealth or any other writer. He says, "normal human interest makes people look for or explore worlds outside their own, whether in literature or in person." And although his books are set in different countries, it doesn't make him one of those stereotypical cosmopolitans who have a sort of mixed cultural experience in every book and feel they have to lay their ethnicity on thick. Seth further adds, "I think that the characters are so much more important than the writer. To be brought up short by the ethnicity of a particular writer throughout each book—that's not my style" (1999).

Yet, it is a fact and also a feature of his genius, that very often only the name of the author on the cover lets us know that we are reading a book by an Indian. 'He belongs to the world and the world belongs to him.' But at the same time it is also true that Seth's constant change in literary 'citizenship'—from the Californian poet of *The Golden Gate* to the Indian story-teller of *A Suitable Boy*, and finally to the European narrator of *An Equal Music*—has resulted in lack of adequate critical attention given to him. Bruce King in relation to this says, "Seth has been shamefully ignored by the academic critical elite, probably because he does not fit into current expectations of the post-colonial" (2001). But, in spite of everything, we can safely conclude that in world literature today Seth has a special place, and his books have the fullness of life and they portray an intellectual brilliance that is rare in Indian writing in English. Not only is he at home in the world, he has also placed Indian writing on the larger map where we don't have to go looking for translators. But these have been partly possible because people—those who would read these works, in Britain, America or Australia—now travel more, see Indian movies in London and Paris, frequent Indian restaurants and are familiar with the flavours. This cross-pollination has imparted character and substance to Indian writing which wasn't there before. And most certainly it speaks of the self-confidence of Seth and his contemporaries so far the language is concerned. Be it Seth, Rushdie or Arundhati Roy, they are all citizens of the world—and their writing shows it. And just like the writers, their dramatis personae too are citizens of the world, not specifically of India. And so far as Seth is concerned, his narrative has a stylistic flourish that we can relish even on repeat readings and that is what differentiates a great literary work from an average one.

Added to all that, his continuous emphasis on love and relationship, and his exploration of the complex and multiple layers of the same, from joy and excitement to distress, provide a strong perceptive and broad-based insight into the nature of things and conditions of living. It is both a critical and creative assessment. And again, Seth's control over linguistic structure and its concomitants, and the pleasure that a repeated reading of his books provide, make him one of the finest writers in the post-1980 Indian English Literature, and more importantly in the creative totality of Indian Literature as a whole.

WORKS CITED

Kapur, Akash. "The Seth Variations." Interview with Vikram Seth. *Atlantic Unbound,* 23 June 1999. Online. http:// www.theatlantic.com/ unbound/ interviews/ ba990623.htm.

King, Bruce. *Modern Indian Poetry in English.* Revised Edition. Delhi: Oxford University Press, 2001.

Select Bibliography

PRIMARY SOURCES

From Heaven Lake. New Delhi: Penguin Books India (P) Ltd., 1983.

The Golden Gate. New Delhi: Penguin Books India (P) Ltd., 1986.

A Suitable Boy. New Delhi: Penguin Books India (P) Ltd., 1993.

The Poems 1981-1994. New Delhi: Penguin Books India (P) Ltd., 1995.

- *Mappings,* 1981.
- *The Humble Administrator's Garden,* 1985.
- *All You Who Sleep Tonight,* 1990.
- *Beastly Tales from Here and There,* 1992.
- *Three Chinese Poets,* 1992.
- *Arion & The Dolphin,* 1994.

An Equal Music. New Delhi: Penguin Books India (P) Ltd. 1999.

SECONDARY SOURCES

Advani, Rukun. *India Today,* 11 March 1993: 12.

Agarwalla, Shyam S. *Vikram Seth's A Suitable Boy: Search for an Indian Identity*. New Delhi: Prestige, 1995.

Alexander, Meena. "Vikram Seth," Post-colonial Studies at Emory. Online. 9 Mar. 2003. http:// www.emory.edu/ ENGLISH/Bahri/Seth.html

"An Interview with Vikram Seth," Bold Type. 15 July 1999. Online. *http://www.boldtype.com/0599/seth/interview.html*

Ashcroft, Bill, Gareth Griffins and Helen Tiffin. *The Empire Writes Back: Theory and Practice in Post-colonial Literatures*. London: Routledge, 1989.

Basu, Sharbani. "Loser Takes All." *Sunday,* 17 Oct. 1993.

Bemrose, John. "Full-Lotus Fiction." *Maclean's,* 106: 22, 1993: 46-48.

Bernherd, Brendan. "Unequal Books". *LA Weekly,* 30 Apr. – 6 May, 1999: Online. http://www.laweekly.com/ink/99/23/wls-bernherd.shtml.

Bharucha, Nilufer E. and Vrinda Nabar, eds. *Post-colonial Indian Literature.* "Essays in Honour of Nissim Ezekiel." New Delhi: Vision Books, 1998.

Bharucha, Nilufer E. and Vilas Sarang, eds. *Indian English Fiction, 1980–1990: An Assessment.* New Delhi: B.K. Publishing Corporation, 1994.

Bhatti, P.S., ed. *Indian Publishing, Then and Now.* New Delhi: S. Chand & Company, 1987.

Bobb, Dilip and Vincent Digirolamo. "I am Looking Forward to Non-entityhood." Interview with Vikram Seth. *India Today,* 15 June 1986: 152-155.

Buchan, James. "A Foreign Country is the Past". Review of *A Suitable Boy, The Spectator, 27* March 1993: 32.

Carey, John. "Music for the Mind". Review. *The Sunday Times,* 28 Mar. 1999.

Chew, Shirley. "The Art of the Fugue." *The Times Literary Supplement,* 2 Apr. 1999: 22.

Currie, Jay and Michele Denis. Interview. "Hearing a Different Music." *January Magazine,* Online. 9 Mar. 2003. http://doonline.net/highlights/seth/speech.htm

Das, Bijoy Kumar. *Contemporary Indo-English Poetry*. Bareilly: Prakash Book Depot, 1986.

Das, Sahana. "The Reader and the Point of View: The Narrative Technique of *The Golden Gate*." Nilufer Bharucha and Vrinda Nabar, eds. *Mapping Cultural Spaces: Post-colonial Indian Literature in English*. New Delhi: Vision Books, 1998.

Desai, Anita. *Bye-Bye Blackbird*. Delhi: Vision Books, 1985.

——. "Sitting Pretty." *The New York Review*, Vol. XLI, No. 10. 27 May 1993: 22-26.

Derozio, Henry Louis Vivian. *Poems*. Calcutta: Oxford University Press, 1980.

Field, Michele. "Vikram Seth." *Publishers Weekly*, 10 May 1993: 46-47.

Ghose, Manmohan. *Selected Poems*. New Delhi: Sahitya Akademi, 1974.

Gokak, V.K. Selected and ed. *The Golden Treasury of Indo-Anglian Poetry*. New Delhi: Sahitya Akademi, 1989.

Gokhale, Namita. "Vikram's Vocalist Strains on Literary Landscape." Delhi: *The Times of India*, 4 May 1999: 4.

Goswami, Seema. "The Golden Boy." *Sunday*, 14 Feb. 1993.

Gupta, Santosh. "*The Golden Gate*: The First Indian Novel in Verse." Viney Kirpal, ed. *The New Indian Novel in English: A Study of the 1980s*. New Delhi: Allied Publishers, 1990: 91-100.

——, ed. *Contemporary Indian Literature: Position and Expositions*. Jaipur: Rawat Publications, 2000.

Hansen, Thomas Blom. *The Saffron Wave: Democracy and Hindu Nationalism in Modern India*. Delhi: Oxford University Press, 2001.

Hawkins-Dady, Mark, ed. *Readers Guide to Literature in English*. London: F.D. Publishers, 1996.

Hill, Rowena. "Vikram Seth's *The Golden Gate*: A Quick Look." *The Literary Criterion*, 21.4 1986: 87-90.

"Indian Writing in English." *Wikipedia, the Free Encyclopedia*. Online. http:// en.wikipedia.org/wiki/Indian writing in English.

Iyengar, K.R. Srinivasa. *Indian Writing in English*. Revised & Updated Edition. New Delhi: Sterling Publishers Private Ltd., 1990.

Iyer, N. Sharda. *Musings on Indian Writing in English (Fiction)*. New Delhi: Sarup & Sons, 1999.

Iyer, Pico. "India Day by Day." *Times Literary Supplement,* 19 March 1993: 20.

Jagadev, Prafulla Kumar. "Post-Independence Indo-Anglian Poetry: Themes and Structure." Diss. Utkal University, 1997.

Jain, Jasbir, ed. *Writers of the Indian Diaspora: Theory and Practice*. Jaipur: Rawat Publications, 1998.

Jenkyns, Richard. "As the Raj Turns: *A Suitable Boy* by Vikram Seth." *The New Republic,* 14 June 1993: 41–44.

Kagal, Carmen. "The Great Indian Novel." *Far Eastern Economic Review,* 13 May 1993: 50.

Katoky, P.C. "A Study of Sri Aurobindo and Four Others." *Indo-English Poetry*. Guwahati: Guwahati University, 1969.

Kapoor, Mini. "Seth sans Suspense." *The Express Magazine,* 25 Apr. 1999: 4.

Kapur, Akash. *Salon*, 13 May 1999: Online. http://www.salon.com/books/review/1999/05/13/seth/index.html

——. "The Seth Variations." Interview with Vikram Seth. *Atlantic Unbound,* 23 June 1999: Online. http://www.theatlantic.com/ unbound/ interviews/ba990623.htm.

Kesavan, B.S., ed. *India's National Library*. Calcutta: National Library, 1961.

Khair, Tabish. "No Golden Gate for Indian English Poetry? Reading Vikram Seth's Novel in Verse in the Context of Indian Poetry in English." In G.J.V. Prasad, ed. *Vikram Seth: An Anthology of Recent Criticism*. Delhi: Pencraft International, 2004: 49-59.

King, Bruce. *Modern Indian Poetry in English,* Revised Edition, Delhi: Oxford University Press, 2001.

Knorr, Katherine. "Vikram Seth Plays to His Truest Judges." *International Herald Tribune,* 23 Apr. 1999: Online. http://www.iht.com/IHT/KK/00/kk042399.html

Kohli, Suresh. "Another Suitable Boy." *Hindu Literary Review*, Sunday, 16 May 1999: 33-34.

Kripal, Viney. *The Third World Novel of Expatriation.* New Delhi: Sterling Pub., 1989.

——, ed. *The New Indian Novel in English: A Study of the 1980s.* New Delhi: Allied Publishers, 1990.

Kumar, Gajendra. *Indian English Novel: Text and Context.* New Delhi: Sarup & Sons, 2002.

Leslie, Jacques. "Rhyme and Reason." *Los Angeles Times Magazine,* 8 June 1986: 16.

Markandaya, Kamala. *A Handful of Rice.* Delhi: Hind Pocket Books (P) Ltd., 1966.

McWilliam, Candida. "Vikram Seth: Hearing the Key Theme." *The Financial Times,* 3 Apr. 1999: Online. http://doononline.net/lightlights/seth/ft.htm

Mehrotra, Arvind Krishna, ed. *An Illustrated History of Indian Literature in English.* New Delhi: Permanent Black, 2003.

Mohapatra, H.S. "A Burnt-Out Case: Vikram Seth's *A Suitable Boy and Realism.*" *New Quest,* 101, Sep.-Oct., 1993.

Mukerji, Debashish. Interview, *The Week,* 9 May 1999: Online http://www.the-week.com/99may09/life2.htm

Mukherjee, Bharati. *Wife.* New Delhi: Penguin, 1987.

Mukherjee, Meenakshi. "Pantheon in Print." *Far Eastern Economic Review*, 9 December 1993: 36-37.

——. *The Twice Born Fiction.* Delhi: Pencraft International, 2001.

——. "The Anxiety of Indianess: Our Novels in English." Nilufer Bharucha and Vrinda Nabar, eds. *Mappings Cultural Spaces: Post-colonial Indian Literature in English.* New Delhi: Vision Books, 1998: 78-93.

Multani, Angelie. "A Metrosexual Lovestory." G.J.V. Prasad, ed. *Vikram Seth: An Anthology of Recent Criticism*. Delhi: Pencraft International, 2004: 60-76.

Mund, Subhendu Kumar. *The Indian Novel in English: Its Birth and Development*, Delhi: Prachi Prakashan, 1997.

Myers, David. "Vikram Seth's Epic Renunciation of the Passions: Deconstructing Moral Codes in *A Suitable Boy*." R.K. Dhawan, ed. *Indian Literature Today*. New Delhi: Prestige, 1994: 79-102.

Naik, M.K. *A History of Indian English Literature*. New Delhi: Sahitya Akademi, 1982.

Naik, M.K. and Shayamala A. Narayan. *Indian English Literature, 1980–2000: A Critical Survey*. Delhi: Pencraft International, 2004.

Nair, Rukmani Bhaya. "Gender, Genre, and Generative Grammar, Deconstructing the Matrimonial Column." Michael J. Toolan, ed. *Text and Context: Essays in Stylistics*. London: Routledge, 1992: 227-254.

Narasimhaiah, C.D. "Introduction." *The Literary Criterion*, 26 (1), 1991: 1-11.

——. "Essays on Indian English Literature." *The Swan and the Eagle*. 3rd Edition, Revised & Enlarged. New Delhi: Vision Books, 1999.

Narayan, R.K. *The Guide*. Mysore: Indian Thought Publications, 1990.

Narayan, R.K. Interview with *India Today*, 5 Apr. 1999: Online. http:// www.rigzin.freeservers.com/ jhumpalahiri.htm# NARAYAN.

Narayen, Leela Lakshmi. "The Golden Bridge is Falling Down, Falling Down, Falling Down: A Study of Vikram Seth's *The Golden Gate*." *Critical Responses, Commonwealth Literature*. Department of English, Osmania University, Hyderabad. New Delhi: Sterling Publishers, 1993.

Neill, Diana. *A Short History of the English Novel*. New York: Collier Books, 1964.

Pandurang, Mala. *Vikram Seth: Multiple Locations, Multiple Affiliations*. Jaipur and New Delhi: Rawat Publications, 2001.

Paniker, K. Ayyappa. *Modern Indian Poetry in English*. New Delhi: Sahitya Akademi, 1991.

Paranjape, Makarand. "A Suitable Author." *The Week*, 9 May 1999: 32-33.

——. "A Conversation with Vikram Seth." *Indian Review of Books*, 16 Mar. 1993: 20-24.

——."*The Golden Gate* and the Quest for Self-Realization." John Thieme, ed. *ACLALS Bulletin. Eighth Series, No. 1. Contemporary Commonwealth Fiction*. Aarhus, 1989.

Parthsarathy, R. *Ten Twentieth Century Indian Poets*. Delhi: Oxford University Press, 1976.

Patel, Devesh. "Vikram Seth: A Poet in Exile." *Contemporary Poetry Review*, 25 Sep. 2000: Online. http://doononline.net/highlights/seth/contemporary.htm.

Pathak, R.S., ed. *Recent Indian Fiction*. New Delhi: Prestige Books, 1994.

Pearson, Nicholas. Review of *A Suitable Boy*. *Indian Express*, 21 Feb. 1993.

Perry, John Oliver. *World Literature Today*, 65 (Summer, 1991): 549-551.

Pollock, Sheldon, ed. *Literary Cultures in History: Reconstructions from South Asia*. New Delhi: Oxford University Press, 2004.

Prasad, G.J.V., ed. "Vikram Seth: An Anthology of Recent Criticism." Delhi: Pencraft International, 2004.

Rajan, P.K., K.M. George, A. Jameala Begum and K. Radha, eds. *Commonwealth Literature: Themes and Techniques: Essays in Honour of Prof. K. Ayyappa Paniker*. Delhi: Ajanta, 1993.

Ramachandra, Ragini. "Vikram Seth's *The Golden Gate: Some First Impressions*." V.N. Narendra Kumar, ed. *New Perspectives on Indian Writing*. New Delhi: Prestige Publications, 1997: 102-107.

Ram, Susan. "Disappointing Work." Review of *A Suitable Boy, Frontline,* 9 Apr. 1993: 110-12.

Rayan, Krishna. "Suggestion or Statement? Three Contemporary Cases." *New Quest,* 106, July-August 1994: 203-8.

Robinson, Eugene. "A Tolstoy: On His First Try." *The Washington Post,* 1 May 1993.

Rollason, Christopher. "On Some Aspects of Language in Vikram Seth's *A Suitable Boy.*" *Atlantic Literary Review* 3.3, July-Sep., 2002: 69–95. Online. http://www.geocities.com/atlanticliteraryreview

Sastry, Chandrasekhar. *The Resident Indian: From Non-Being to Being.* Bangalore, India: Panther Publishers, 1991.

Sengupta, Padmini. *Sarojini Naidu.* Abridged, edited and annotated by L. Radhakrishna Murli, Hyderabad: Commonwealth Publishing House, 1980.

"Seth Vikram." *Encyclopaedia Britannica, 2005,* Encyclopaedia Britannica Premium Service. Online. http://www.britannica.com/eb/article?tocld=9099522

Sharma, Anjana. "An Englishman's Novel? Vikram Seth's *An Equal Music.*" G.J.V. Prasad, ed. *Vikram Seth: An Anthology of Recent Criticism.* Delhi: Pencraft International, 2004: 164-173.

Sharma, L.K. "*A Suitable Boy* Unfolds *An Equal Music.*" *The Sunday Times of India,* 11 April 1999: 10.

——. "*Booker Shortlist Raises Hackles.*" *The Times of India* 27 Sep. 1993.

Sharrad, Paul. *Journal of the South Pacific Association for Commonwealth Literature and Language Studies.* No. 34–35, 1993.

Singh, Khuswant. "The Genius of Vikram Seth." *The Hindustan Times,* 18 Apr. 1993: 13.

Spalding, Frances. "Fiction" Section. *The Times Educational Supplement,* 7 May 1993: 10.

Sri Aurobindo. *Collected Poems.* Pondicherry: Sri Aurobindo Ashram, 1972.

Srinath, C.N. "Post-colonialism and Faction in Indian Fiction." *The Literary Criterion*, Vol. 34, 1999, 1: 33-40.

Sukla, Sheobhusan and Anu Sukla, eds. *Indian English Novel in the Nineties*. New Delhi: Sarup & Sons, 2000.

Sutcliffe, William. *The Independent*, 4 Apr. 1999: Online http://www.independent.co.uk/books/stories/BR002326.htm

Tapping, Craig. "South Asia writes North America: Prose Fiction and Autobiography from the Indian Diaspora." Shirley Geok-Lin and Amy Ling, eds. *Reading the Literatures of the Asian American*. Philadelphia: Temple University Press, 1992.

Theme, John, ed. *The Arnold Anthology of Post-colonial Literatures in English*, London: Arnold, 1996.

Trivedi, Harish. "Post-colonial Translation." Editorial, *IACLALS Bulletin*, August, 1998: 1.

Tejpal, Tarun J. "Epic Dimensions." Review of *A Suitable Boy*. *India Today*, 15 Mar. 1993.

Vidyasagar, N. "In the Business of Books." Interview with Vikram Seth. *The Times of India*, 11 April 1999.

Walsh, William. *Indian Literature in English*. London: Longman, 1990.

Yardley, Jonathan. "A Dickens for the Sub-continent." *The Washington Post*, 25 Apr. 1993: 3.

Index